BERLIN SPORTS

SPORT, CULTURE & SOCIETY

DAVID K. WIGGINS, SERIES EDITOR

Other Titles in This Series

Berlin Sports

Spectacle, Recreation, and Media in Germany's Metropolis

**Edited by Heather L. Dichter and
Molly Wilkinson Johnson**

The University of Arkansas Press
Fayetteville
2024

ISBN: 978-1-68226-256-6
eISBN: 978-1-61075-826-0

28 27 26 25 24 5 4 3 2 1

Manufactured in the United States of America

Designed by William Clift

♾ The paper used in this publication meets the minimum requirements of the American National Standard for Permanence of Paper for Printed Library Materials Z39.48–1984.

LIBRARY OF CONGRESS CATALOGING-IN-PUBLICATION DATA

Names: Dichter, Heather, editor. | Johnson, Molly Wilkinson, editor.
Title: Berlin sports : spectacle, recreation, and media in Germany's metropolis / edited by Heather L Dichter and Molly Wilkinson Johnson.
Description: Fayetteville : University of Arkansas Press, 2024. | Series: Sport, culture, and society series | Includes bibliographical references and index. | Summary: "Berlin Sports: Spectacle, Recreation, and Media in Germany's Metropolis presents a series of case studies that explore the history of sports in Berlin from the late nineteenth- to the early twenty-first century against the backdrop of the city's sharp political shifts, diverse populations, and status as a major metropolis with both regional and global resonance. Focal points include a long-distance equestrian race in the 1890s; the role of media in discourses around urban life, gender, and celebrity from the 1890s to the 1920s; the intersection of grassroots participation and spectatorship with international diplomacy at the elite level in the postwar and divided period; the relationship between recreational associations, immigration, and youth counterculture; and the use of the 2015 European Maccabi Games, an international Jewish sports festival, to grapple with the infamous 1936 Nazi Olympics and cast Berlin as a post-anti-Semitic city. Through these thematic lenses of spectacle, recreation, and media, these essays provide important insights about sport and urban space, Berlin sport as both unique and typical of Germany, and sport as a vehicle through which Germany has engaged with the wider world"— Provided by publisher.
Identifiers: LCCN 2024014825 (print) | LCCN 2024014826 (ebook)
ISBN 9781682262566 (paperback ; acid-free paper) | ISBN 9781610758260 (ebook)

Subjects: LCSH: Sports—Germany—Berlin—History. | Sports—Political aspects—Germany—History. | Sports—Social aspects—Germany—History. | Sports—Public relations—Germany. | Sports and state—Germany—History. | Antisemitism—Germany—History. | City and town life—Germany—Berlin—History. | Berlin (Germany)—History.
Classification: LCC GV612.5.B47 B47 2024 (print) | LCC GV612.5.B47 (ebook) | DDC 796.0943/155—dc23/eng/20240703
LC record available at https://lccn.loc.gov/2024014825
LC ebook record available at https://lccn.loc.gov/2024014826

Contents

Series Editors' Preface

There is no greater global phenomenon than that of sport. It permeates the lives of countless people, communities, and nations globally. Whether we recognize sport as competitive and bound by formalized rules or the movement cultures of diverse peoples engaged in distinct physical activities, sport abounds in all regions, cultures, and societies throughout the world. Sport is oftentimes celebrated because it has the power to bring people together from dissimilar backgrounds and because, through sport, individuals and groups may achieve extraordinary success, sometimes irrespective of race, gender, sex, sexuality, religion, class, (dis)ability, and identity. Conversely, sport may, too, be criticized due to persistent discrimination in its organizing structures and practices and threats it may pose to marginalized populations and vulnerable territories globally. For these reasons alone, sport is worthy of our scholarly attention and critique.

The Sport, Culture, and Society series aspires to promote a greater understanding of sport and disseminate scholarship and critical discourse related to the powerful influence of sport and its ability to change people's lives in significant ways. The topical, temporal, and regional focus of monographs and anthologies included in the series is extensive, ranging from ancient athletic traditions, colonial and postcolonial politics, apartheid policies, global sporting events, sport and the law, intercollegiate athletics, urbanization, and athlete biographies. Contributors to the series come from a vast array of disciplines and adopt different methodological approaches, some infusing multidisciplinary, interdisciplinary, and transdisciplinary styles and perspectives. Further, series contributors comprise a diverse group of scholars, including early career scholars and those with established reputations, whose contributions to the Sport, Culture, and Society series are characterized by exceptional and accessible scholarship.

Berlin Sports is an anthology that is both exceptional and accessible. In this collection, coeditors Heather L. Dichter and Molly Wilkinson Johnson underscore Berlin's important role as a sports metropolis, highlighting that the broader history of sport in Berlin far transcends the well-known and

well-studied 1936 Olympic Games. As such, Dichter and Johnson have
assembled a team of expert contributors from varying disciplines and career
stages to produce the first book-length study to explore the history of sport
in Berlin from the late nineteenth to the early twenty-first century. The
focus of *Berlin Sports* is indeed comprehensive. As such, the editors have
creatively organized the book. First, recognizing Berlin's complex political
and cultural history over the 130 years covered in the collection, the chapters
are presented chronologically, beginning in Imperial Germany, then moving
through the Weimar Republic, the Third Reich, Cold War division, and the
post-reunification era. Second, due to the wide range of sports disciplines
showcased throughout the collection, including football (soccer), equestrianism, basketball, tennis, boxing, skateboarding, and international sporting
contexts, the editors draw readers' attention to the three core themes that
emerge throughout the collection: sporting events as spectacle; recreational
sports, community, and identity; and media and celebrity. Further, individual authors creatively and adeptly weave together primary and secondary
source materials in each chapter to present Berlin's lesser-known sporting
histories. Importantly, all authors draw from the photographic archive to
construct new narratives to help shape understandings of past events, places,
and people. Although each chapter assumes a unique focus, surveying
distinct and important questions in Berlin's sporting history, collectively,
they work together to demonstrate that "the 1936 Olympic Games were by
no means the first nor the last time Berlin assumed such prominence in the
international world of sport."

David K. Wiggins and Christine O'Bonsawin

Acknowledgments

The University of Arkansas Press has for many years published within its Sport, Culture, and Society series a subseries of books on sport in an American city. We would like to express our gratitude to both David Wiggins and Christine O'Bonsawin, the series editors, and D. S. Cunningham, editor at the press, for their interest in expanding this subseries to a city outside of the United States. With that support, *Berlin Sports* was born.

The communication technology that became more widely adopted during the global pandemic allowed two scholars—who had been introduced via email as graduate students over twenty years ago but still have not met in person—to speak regularly to produce this book. An open call for papers provided a wealth of new and exciting scholarship on sport in Berlin, and it has been a pleasure to work with all of the authors who contributed chapters to this book: Barnet Hartston, Alec Hurley, Erik Jensen, Will Rall, Jeffrey Jurgens, and Kai Reinhart. We also thank Annemarie Sammartino who, as a scholar of urban history but not of sport, agreed to write the conclusion, which reflects on several themes within the volume as a whole.

We are grateful for the guidance of everyone at the University of Arkansas Press and especially of the anonymous reviewers, who provided valuable suggestions. We also thank all the contributors' institutions that provided funding to enable the inclusion of images.

Heather L. Dichter and Molly Wilkinson Johnson
August 2023

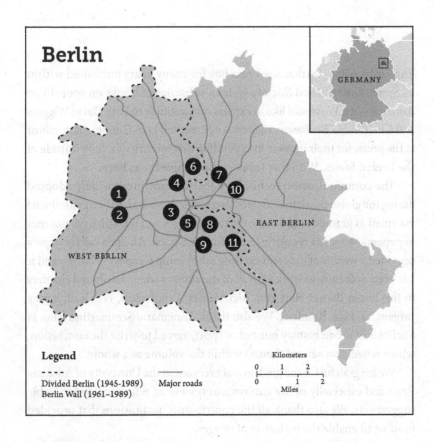

Berlin

GERMANY

EAST BERLIN

WEST BERLIN

Legend

---- Divided Berlin (1945-1989)
Berlin Wall (1961-1989)

—— Major roads

Kilometers
0   1   2

0   1   2
Miles

Berlin sports landmarks:
(1) Olympic Stadium
(2) Teufelsberg
(3) Breitscheidplatz
(4) Poststadion
(5) Sportpalast
(6) Herthaplatz
(7) Friedrich Ludwig Jahn Sportpark
(8) Gençlikspor Soccer Club
(9) Tempelhofer Feld
(10) Seelenbinder Hall
(11) Estrel Hotel

BERLIN SPORTS

Berlin as Germany's Sporting City

HEATHER L. DICHTER AND MOLLY WILKINSON JOHNSON

One of the most iconic stories of sport in Berlin, and of the Olympic movement more broadly, is that of African American athlete Jesse Owens winning four gold medals at the 1936 Olympics, colloquially known as the "Nazi Olympics" or "Hitler's Olympics." Aided by the overwhelming media presence in Berlin for the Olympic Games as well as by the stills and videos from Leni Riefenstahl's *Olympia*, the story of Jesse Owens—and the Berlin Games that formed its backdrop—has yielded documentaries, biographies, academic analyses, and children's books galore, both in the United States and internationally. The politicization of the Berlin Olympics, their racial politics, and the art and architecture of the Reichssportfeld (the elaborate sports complex and Greco-Roman stadium that stand as the largest intact architectural site from the Nazi era remaining in Germany) have been thoroughly explored. The association of Berlin with the 1936 Olympic Games is so strong that, to this day, any discussion of Berlin as an Olympic host city remains fraught with the heavy history of that event.[1] The enduring legacies of the Berlin Olympic Games even shaped the narrative framing of Germany's other Olympics, the 1972 Munich Games.[2] Yet, Berlin's role as sports metropolis far transcends the 1936 Olympic Games, and this collection brings the broader history of sport in Berlin to light.

While much of the city's sporting experience has mirrored developments in other major cities and across Germany, Berlin's unique political history has also contributed to striking differences. Since the advent of modern sport in the late nineteenth century, the city of Berlin has been central to five different political regimes identified with four different political ideologies: imperial, democratic, fascist, and communist. The creation in 1871 of a unified German Empire with Berlin as its capital coincided with the development of modern sport in the second half of the nineteenth century. Gymnastics and sport associations emerged as integral to the urban environment, with Berlin slated to host the (canceled) 1916 Olympic Games. With the end of World War I and the demise of the German Empire, Berlin became the capital of Germany's first democratic government, known as the Weimar Republic. The plethora of political parties that characterized the Weimar Republic was mirrored in the country's sport landscape, with people joining sport clubs based on similar political and religious divisions found in German society. With Adolf Hitler's rise to power and Berlin's transformation into the capital of the fascist Third Reich, both recreational and elite sports were centralized into Nazi organizational structures and subordinated to Nazi racial ideologies. With the defeat of the Third Reich in 1945, the four victorious Allied powers divided and occupied Germany, ultimately leading to the creation of two separate German states for half a century: the democratic and Western-aligned Federal Republic of Germany, created from the American, British, and French zones and including West Berlin, and the communist German Democratic Republic, created out of the Soviet occupation zone and with East Berlin as its capital. At the height of the Cold War, sport became a primary arena for the symbolic struggle between East and West Germany. West Berlin also absorbed many of the Turkish-born "guest workers" who migrated to Germany beginning in the 1960s. By the 1970s, Berlin was the world's second largest Turkish city after Istanbul, and by the early 1980s, non-Germans constituted 12 percent of Berlin's entire population.[3] In 1991, the reunified German government voted to move the national capital from Bonn to Berlin, unleashing a flurry of architectural and urban development projects for the capital city and even an unsuccessful bid to host the 2000 Olympic Games. Twenty-first century Berlin remains a locus of immigration, not only from Eastern Europe and Russia but also the Middle East and Africa, with an estimated one-third of all Berlin residents in 2022 coming from a migrant background.[4]

Berlin's status as a large, diverse metropolis and cultural center—an identity that coexists with its position as a capital city for much of the period from the late nineteenth century to the present—has fostered an urban identity that in many ways transcends its Germanness and presents particularly fruitful possibilities for the study of modern sport in the urban environment.

As David Clay Large argues, from the Wilhelmine era through the Cold War, many Berliners and other Germans have viewed Berlin, both affirmatively and with some degree of ambivalence, as a city that "belonged more to the world than to Germany."[5] Berlin has often drawn the attention of cultural critics and students of the city and of modernity itself. As Sabine Hake writes, Weimar culture displayed much "metonymic slippage" between "Weimar Berlin" and "modern metropolis."[6] Postwar divided Berlin continued to hold global significance, with the Berlin Wall functioning, according to Janet Ward, as a "synecdoche for the entire East–West line dividing Germany, Europe, and the world."[7] Since German reunification in 1990, Berlin has carefully cultivated its status as a global city. The 1990s featured many public debates and high profile architectural and urban planning engagements with Berlin's Nazi and communist pasts, and in the 2000s Berlin followed a successful urban marketing plan designed to draw creative and economic entrepreneurs, as well as tourists who wanted to visit historic sites such as the 1936 Olympic Stadium.[8]

Berlin Sports explores the history of sport in Berlin against this backdrop of the city's sharp political shifts, diverse population, and status as a major metropolis with both regional and global resonance. This volume is the first book-length study to explore the history of sport in the city of Berlin from the late nineteenth through the early twenty-first century. Scholarship has focused on sport more broadly in Germany or has been limited to a narrow time period or topic, including publications on the 1936 Olympic Games, the Cold War, the socialist World Youth Festival of 1951, and Berlin's bids to host the 1968 and 2000 Olympic Games.[9] With focal themes of spectacle, recreation, and media, this volume contributes to three areas of historiography: sport and urban space, Berlin sport as both unique and typical of Germany, and sport as a vehicle through which Germany has engaged with the wider world.

Similar to scholarship on the many US cities explored in the University of Arkansas's Sport, Culture, and Society series, this volume examines how sport—whether local sport clubs rooted in associational life, elite level sport, spectator sport, or international sporting events—both reflects and informs urban landscapes and civic identities in a dynamic city.[10] Indeed, European cities like Berlin share much in common with North American cities when it comes to sport as entertainment within the urban experience, such as the construction of large stadiums or the creation of ski jumps and hills in urban indoor arenas to provide lessons for people who living far from mountains.[11] In 2012, however, Thierry Terret and Sandra Heck lamented in a special issue of *The International Journal of the History of Sport* that minimal work had been done on sport and urban space in continental Europe, and in the decade following their special issue there has not been much further scholarship on this topic.[12] Considering multiple sports and time periods—through the challenges of playing football (soccer) among rubble and broken public transportation, the shifting ethnic composition of Berlin's neighborhoods, or the public spaces of the modern concrete jungle where young skateboarders could develop their skills and tricks—reveals the extent to which sport and the urban landscape shape one another in a single European city, just as they do in so many US cities.

Sport in Berlin, however, unfolded within a different context from sport in US cities in several striking ways. Berlin's political history makes the city's sporting developments unique relative to other cities in Germany and else-where around the world.[13] In many American cities, including those studied thus far in the University of Arkansas Press's series, individual athletes, professional teams, and university sports are integral to the cities' sporting identities.[14] In contrast, Berlin features no hallmark sport, team, or annual event, as five political regimes, wartime destruction, and four decades of division have fostered an ever-changing landscape of teams, allegiances, and venues, even as the desire to play and watch sport continued unabated across these political watersheds. The politics of memory have also shaped Berlin's sporting history, which is particularly evident in the site of Berlin's Olympic Stadium. The stadium complex remains a frequently visited sport heritage site in Berlin because of the 1936 Nazi Games.[15] Unlike in other European cities, where the professional football team's global prominence makes their modern stadium one of the city's top tourist destinations (such as Camp Nou in Barcelona or Allianz Arena in Munich), the Olympic Stadium complex's main draw for visitors remains its historic past and the fact that it is a large and intact example of Nazi architecture rather than its role as Hertha BSC's home ground or as the venue of any recent international sporting event.

Finally, this volume demonstrates that Berlin played an important role within Germany's sporting traditions with local, national, and global implications that extend far beyond the infamous 1936 Olympic Games. As the country's most prominent sports destination, with some of the best venues and home to numerous elite athletes and media outlets, Berlin provided many opportunities for Germany to engage with the wider world through sport. The city's sports writers, who were often athletes or sport officials themselves, contributed to and shaped both national and international discourses about gender, Orientalism, Taylorization, and modernity. Large sporting events that took place in Berlin contributed to international perceptions of the city, and the 1936 Olympic Games were by no means the first or last time that Berlin assumed such prominence in the international world of sport. Like other sport venues around the world, the Olympic Stadium and its larger complex has continued to host major international events, including numerous FIFA World Cups (1974 and 2006 men's, 2011 women's) and the 2009 track and field world championships. Coverage of international sporting events that have taken place in Berlin, along with attention to sport celebrities based in or visiting Berlin, shape the spectacle of sport within Berlin and influence how future athletes and fans—from anywhere in the world—engage with and perceive both the city of Berlin and country of Germany.

Through a series of case studies, *Berlin Sports* showcases the broad and diverse history of sport in Berlin from the late nineteenth century to the early twenty-first century. It begins with a long-distance equestrian race in the 1890s and continues with the role of media in spectacle, celebrity, urban life, and gender from the 1890s to the 1920s. It then turns to the postwar period and the years of German division, exploring both grassroots sports participation and spectatorship, as well as elite sports, as a medium of international diplomacy. Next, it analyzes recreational sport associations within the context of immigration and youth counterculture, before concluding with an examination of the 2015 European Maccabi Games, an international Jewish sports festival through which Berlin sought to grapple with the infamous 1936 Olympics and showcase contemporary Berlin as a cosmopolitan and multicultural city. Taken together, all of these sporting endeavors reveal the rich and varied sporting culture in Berlin.

Historical Overview of Sports in Berlin

Since the early nineteenth century, Berlin has played an integral role in physical culture and sport in the German lands. The German gymnastics movement (*Turnen*), led by Friedrich Ludwig *"Turnvater"* Jahn, began at the Hasenheide, to the south of Berlin, in 1811 during the Napoleonic Wars.

Gymnastics associations, known as *Turnvereine*, were strongly allied with burgeoning ideas of German nationalism and masculinity and spread across the country throughout the nineteenth century, and in 1861 Berlin hosted the second Deutsches Turnfest.[16] University fraternities in the nineteenth century adopted the military and aristocratic practice of fencing duels, which also reinforced German ideas of masculinity, honor, militarism, and nationalism.[17]

Following Germany's 1871 unification, gymnastics and later sports associations remained centers of civic life, recreation, and political and social identity in Berlin, the capital city of the new nation-state.[18] Accompanying Berlin's industrial growth, gymnastics and sports associations tied to working-class culture joined the city's recreational landscape by the 1890s. Reflecting the growing city's diversity, many gymnastics and sports associations of this era organized along confessional lines, including Catholic, Protestant, and Jewish clubs, such as Bar Kochba Berlin, Germany's first Jewish gymnastics club, founded in Berlin in 1898.[19] Newspapers, including sports pages, were integral to the booming metropolis, with *B.Z. am Mittag* unveiling its first sports supplement in 1905. Berlin's sports media covered recreational sports as well as the many sporting events that attracted spectators and fostered interest in sports celebrities.[20]

As British sports began to make inroads in Germany, the Berlin sport scene evolved.[21] The variety of sports played in Berlin, and Berlin's importance more broadly, led the International Olympic Committee (IOC) to select Berlin to host the VI Olympic Games in 1916, although World War I led to their cancelation.[22] Sport further exploded in Berlin during the Weimar years of the 1920s. The city hosted numerous sporting events and celebrated sports stars and their extraordinary feats from the German Grand Prix to world-champion boxer Max Schmeling.[23] Spectator sports were integral to Berlin life in the 1920s, inspiring not only the sports pages but also the creative and intellectual work of Berlin's intelligentsia. The fifth movement of Walter Ruttmann's famous film *Berlin: Symphony of a Big City* (1927) prominently featured spectator sports, including six-day cycling races.[24] Weimar feuilleton writers, such as cultural critic Siegfried Kracauer, engaged with mass sports and sports spectacle as a "magnifying lens" that helped them process modernity and the modern metropolis.[25] The interwar period was also a "golden age of women's sport" in Germany just as it was in the United States, Canada, and Great Britain. Women's sports teams and individual athletes drew large crowds and extensive media coverage.[26]

Sport during the Third Reich was entirely subsumed by Nazism. Sport clubs, like other associations in Germany, had to adapt to Nazi structures and racial policies as part of the process of *Gleichschaltung* (coordination). Socialist and communist sport clubs closed, and Jewish athletes could only participate in sport in the late 1930s via the few remaining Jewish sport clubs.[27] Sport and physical education played a key role in Nazi paramilitary efforts as Germany prepared for future war. Adults found recreational athletic activities through the Kraft durch Freude (Strength through Joy) organization.[28] Younger Germans participated in sport through the Hitler Jugend (Hitler Youth) and Bund deutscher Mädel (League of German Girls), which emphasized sporting activities with a martial aim, like boxing, or team sports to foster a sense of (Nazi) community for boys; sports for girls focused on their role as future child-bearers through activities such as rhythmic gymnastics.[29] During the Third Reich, physical education increased in importance within the school curriculum as well. Acknowledging the centrality of sport to the Nazi state, the Allies implemented a policy explicitly controlling sport during the first year of Germany's postwar occupation, thereby marking sport as an arena requiring denazification measures.[30]

After World War II, Berlin stood at the center of the Cold War, with political division shaping recreational sport and sport competitions. In some ways, the two Germanies' sport systems were interrelated, especially when athletes from both countries had to compete for a single German Olympic team before the IOC allowed both German states to have completely separate teams beginning in 1972. In 1963, there was even a short-lived proposal for West Berlin and East Berlin to host the 1968 Olympic Games.[31] For the most part, however, sport on both sides of the Berlin Wall followed different trajectories. Recreationally, West Berlin saw the revival of many prewar athletic clubs and the creation of new associations that encompassed established sports such as tennis and football as well as new sports such as skateboarding. As in the pre-Nazi years, West Berlin's sport clubs operated autonomously of the state as independent associations. In contrast, East Berlin's recreational sport landscape featured an array of centralized sport clubs tied to East Germany's industries or to national organizations such as the Free German Youth. The East German government carefully cultivated recreational athletics as a vehicle for creating new socialist citizens, "prepared," according to the slogan of the national sports program, "to work and to defend" their socialist state.[32]

Both Berlins also hosted international sport competitions. With excellent facilities remaining from the 1936 Olympics or built after 1945, West Berlin hosted international sporting events ranging from friendly competitions, such as a 1961 women's field hockey match between Scotland and the Federal Republic of Germany just one month after the construction of the Berlin Wall, to the 1974 FIFA World Cup, hosted by West Germany, which featured West Berlin's Olympic Stadium as a venue for several preliminary matches. West Berlin also hosted its first marathon in 1974, and the Berlin Marathon soon became renowned for the many world records set there.[33] East Berlin likewise hosted international sporting events, such as the 1966 Weightlifting World Championships, as well as socialist spectacles, such as the World Youth Festival in 1951 and the Friedensfahrt (Ride of Peace), which began in 1948 as a long-distance bicycle race between Warsaw and Prague and expanded in 1952 to include East Berlin.[34] As part of talent development to discover and cultivate future Olympians, East Berlin also began hosting the national Children's and Youth Spartakiade multi-sport competitions in 1966 at the Friedrich-Ludwig-Jahn Sportpark, which had been built in the 1950s as a major multi-sport complex.[35]

When Germany reunified in 1990, Berlin's sports culture began to grow back together, but this process was not without its challenges. The 1990 Berlin Marathon expanded to include parts of East Berlin, highlighted by the route through the Brandenburg Gate, which had been inaccessible for nearly thirty years due to the Berlin Wall.[36] Like the Federal Republic absorbing the East German *Länder* (states or provinces), the West German National Olympic Committee and national governing bodies incorporated East German sport at all levels. In terms of recreational sport, East Germany's centralized clubs devolved back into independent sport associations. On the level of elite sport, East Germany's national governing bodies ceased to exist. Elite teams either disbanded or became part of the Federal Republic's sport system, and East Germany's professional football clubs struggled to be part of the top German leagues due to their links with the East German secret police or military, as well as their struggles to navigate entirely new funding structures.[37] The East German state-sponsored doping project cast a shadow over many athletes, coaches, sport leaders, and sport scientists, affecting their careers after reunification.[38] Decades of division have left Berlin with less of an intertwined identity with a professional football club than many other cities in Germany and Europe, or with American football, basketball, baseball, or ice hockey teams in North American cities.

First German Children's and Youth Spartakiade on July 24, 1966, at the Friedrich-Ludwig-Jahn-Sportpark. *Photograph by Joachim Spremberg. Courtesy Bundesarchiv, Berlin.*

Just as sport played a key role in Cold War Berlin, they also constituted the centerpiece of Berlin's first major post-reunification initiative: an early 1990s bid to host the 2000 Olympic Games. Although not chosen by the IOC, Berlin was one of the five finalist cities, and Berlin's aspiration demonstrated the centrality of sport to Berlin's self-conception as a sports metropolis of global significance. The 1936 Olympic stadium complex continues to function as both a historical site for tourism and as a major events venue. The renovated stadium hosted the final of the 2006 FIFA World Cup, the first major sporting event held in reunified Germany, and over one hundred thousand fans overwhelmed Berlin's Straße des 17. Juni for the fanfest when Germany played in the semi-final. Berlin's Olympic Stadium was also the site of the 2009 world championships in track and field, and some Berliners continue to hope that the city will once again host the Olympic Games.

Structure and Themes

Set against the backdrop of Berlin's complex political and cultural history, the following chapters showcase a range of sports disciplines, including football, equestrianism, basketball, tennis, boxing, and skateboarding, as well as the city's role in hosting international sporting contests. The chapters included in this volume appear in chronological order, beginning in Imperial Germany then moving through the Weimar Republic, the Third Reich, Cold War division, and the post-reunification era. Although no chapter focuses solely on sport in East Berlin, two chapters address sport across divided Berlin in two different decades (the 1940s and 1960s). Collectively, the chapters work together to illuminate three core themes: sporting events as spectacle; recreational sport, community, and identity; and media and celebrity.

Sporting Events as Spectacle

Since antiquity, sports have been contested during major events or holidays and considered a spectacle. In Europe (as elsewhere in the world) this idea carried through the medieval and early modern periods.[39] As international sport expanded in the 1890s, Baron Pierre de Coubertin drew on these traditions to create the modern Olympic Games, making an international sporting event a spectacle itself. The second, third, and fourth Olympic Games all coincided with World's Fairs or other international expositions. Hollywood's involvement in organizing the 1932 Olympic Games in Los Angeles, along with the expansion of media (including print, newsreels, and radio) substantially expanded the spectacle of the Olympics and of sport in general.[40] Television and the technological expansion of live satellite transmission and color broadcasts further cemented sporting events as spectacles that could be experienced simultaneously across the globe, leading to the emergence of sports mega-events.[41] These developments affected more than just the biggest sporting events such as the Olympic Games and FIFA World Cup; other international events could expect similar global media coverage, albeit on a smaller scale, and cities vied for the opportunity to benefit from the spotlight as hosts.[42] This book offers fresh insights on events and spectacles within sport in Berlin by moving past the emphasis on the 1936 Olympics and demonstrating the city's enduring appeal as a site for large-scale sporting events with widespread spectatorship and significant media coverage.

Both singular events and routine sporting activities drew on the city's cosmopolitanism and served as spectacles. Barnet Hartston analyzes a long-distance equestrian event as a vehicle for nation-building, in part due to the elaborately organized ceremonies and extensive media coverage that accompanied it. This event drew on both burgeoning nationalism and a consequent desire to demonstrate a country's strength, just as the recent expansion of international sport did. The length of the ride allowed its extensive media coverage to emphasize several aspects of the event, including the athletes and their horses, contributing further to the event constituting an international spectacle even before the introduction of the modern Olympic Games. Alec Hurley explores Adolf von Guretzki's novelette "Raad" (Donner), which was serialized in the Illustrirte Deutsche Athleten-Zeitung, demonstrating that von Guretzki modeled competition venues and sporting activities set in Cairo after Berlin's entertainment halls of the 1890s, which frequently showcased gentlemen strength athletes from Europe as well Turkey and Egypt. Von Guretzki covered strength competitions and wrestling matches as a journalist in addition to serving as a referee and promoter for these sports, and his writing cultivated sport as urban spectacle, both within Berlin and as a broader urban phenomenon. Erik Jensen's analysis of the athlete-journalists who served as media correspondents in the Weimar Republic shows how the sport spectacles of that era, whether track and field, football, auto racing, tennis, boxing, or any number of others, reached audiences far beyond their immediate spectators, including the countless newspaper readers who eagerly consumed the sports press in order to participate in sports-obsessed public discourses.

Local sports likewise served as spectacles and drew significant crowds. Will Rall explores this phenomenon in the return of sport spectatorship to Berlin soon after the end of World War II through football matches and the 1946 city football championships. Over a period of six months, thirty-six teams divided into four groups contested the championship. The four groups did not match Berlin's occupation zones but rather the city's general geography. Against the backdrop of struggles to obtain food, clothing, and other material needs, as well as the challenges of unreliable public transportation, thousands of spectators traversed the war-damaged city weekly to watch the matches. Football spectatorship became a way for Berliners to embrace normalcy and learn to recognize and navigate postwar Berlin. In Kai Reinhart's examination of the development of skateboarding in West Berlin, public skateboarding shows on the Winterfeldtplatz drew a few hundred paying spectators in 1982. Even though skateboarding was first and foremost a recreational activity for its participants, it also drew spectators who wanted to watch these new feats. These public displays and, eventually, skateboarding championships helped cultivate West Berlin's encounters with *Funsports* imported from California and the lifestyles they encompassed.

When post-1945 Berlin served as the site for larger competitions, the organization of these sport spectacles had to contend with political actions and their legacies. Heather Dichter, through an examination of the complex negotiations to organize the Olympic trials for the all-German Olympic teams in 1964, explores the political and diplomatic challenges that underpinned many sporting events and spectacles. The Cold War division of Berlin meant that even basic levels of organizing turned these events into political spectacles well before the sporting action could take place. Because the IOC forced the two German states to compete in the Olympics as a single team in the 1950s and 1960s, the competitions between East and West German athletes for coveted places on the all-German Olympic team were of the utmost importance. Likewise, deciding where those athletes would compete for those spots—be it in West Berlin, East Berlin, or outside of the divided city—became a battle in itself. Berlin's postwar sport spectacles likewise had to contend with the Nazi era and its continued legacies. Molly Wilkinson Johnson's chapter revisits the 1936 Olympics through the lens of the 2015 European Maccabi Games, which were hosted in Berlin and brought over two thousand Jewish athletes to the capital of the former Third Reich. The 2015 European Maccabi Games show the continued power of the sport spectacle as a site for a range of political narratives, particularly regarding historical reconciliation. It also demonstrates the enduring hold of the Nazi period on popular imagination, as well Berlin's efforts to transcend that association and foreground a new Berlin defined by cosmopolitanism and open-mindedness.

As the country's capital and largest metropolis, Berlin has hosted many large-scale sporting events from the late nineteenth century to the present, and its local events have also had the ability to attract wide audiences. Regardless of the specific sport discipline, Berlin remains a desirable host city for sporting events, including the 2023 World Archery Championships and the final for the 2024 UEFA European Championships. Each new event provides an opportunity for Berlin to put itself on display for the world and project a new image of the city, its history, and its current politics.

Recreational Sport, Community, and Identity

The creation of sport clubs in Germany has, since the nineteenth century, formed a central part of associational and community life, and the importance of these clubs has continued through the twentieth century to the present. As new, broader political and social changes have appeared in German society, they have also arisen within Germany's sport clubs. As the most cosmopolitan city in Germany (and the world), Berlin provides a canvas on which Germans can negotiate and express a range of gendered identities. The diversity of Berlin's population in terms of ethnic and national background, political inclination, and religious identification and practice has made sport and recreation into sites for negotiations of multiculturalism and belonging. Closer examinations of sport clubs within Berlin demonstrate these ideas as they affect the city and its residents.

Jensen's exploration of the athlete-correspondents who wrote for Weimar Berlin's newspapers highlights the burst in athletic participation in Weimar Berlin, especially among women. The city's all-female tennis clubs, some of which were in Berlin's most fashionable neighborhoods, drew many members. During the Weimar years, recreational athletes existed along-side increasing numbers of individuals aspiring to compete at elite levels. Within tennis, ambition and competitiveness displaced the more leisurely aristocratic pursuit of the previous era, paralleling the broader Weimar ethos of meritocracy and upward mobility. In the world of track and field, scientific training methods began to prevail among serious athletes, yet some commentators expressed ambivalence about their implications for women, especially after two runners collapsed in the women's 800 meter race at the 1928 Olympics. Newspaper coverage, particularly essays written by athletes themselves, helped the public reflect on, and in some cases critique, these shifts in gender norms and social class as they played out within the world of sport.

Rall's examination of the rapid return of football to Berlin after World War II through the regeneration of old clubs and the formation of new ones, as well as the creation of leagues and tournaments, demonstrates the continued prominence of the club structure in Berlin life during what was an otherwise difficult time. Both clubs and individual athletes had to reckon with the denazification process. In many instances new clubs formed geographically across the city. These new football clubs, and the effort needed to participate in sport amid the devastation brought from the war, reveal the importance Berliners attributed to sport in general and football more specifically, as well as how they navigated and understood the city during its immediate postwar occupation.

Reinhart's examination of the introduction and development of skateboarding in West Berlin demonstrates that the strength of German associational life even pervaded the skateboarding counterculture. Long viewed as being outside mainstream sport (and not appearing on the Olympic program until 2020), skateboarding has typically been perceived as something that teenagers (mostly boys) pursued in opposition to convention, particularly within urban settings.[43] In that sense, Berlin was no different from California and other places where skateboarding grew popular. Yet, as Reinhart demonstrates, Berlin's skateboarders also created formal skateboarding clubs that followed the typical naming and structural trends of German sports clubs to ensure access to resources and safe public spaces to practice their sport. Thus, skateboarding in West Berlin became a hybrid phenomenon that blended elements of an international subculture with German institutional and organizational traditions. This informal sociability always existed alongside formal organization, and, especially after German reunification in 1990, skateboarding increasingly became associated with a broader lifestyle rather than with organized competitive sport.

Jeffrey Jurgens takes an ethnographic approach to understanding the role of football clubs within Berlin's Turkish community. Whether first generation immigrants or their children born in Germany, the people of Turkish backgrounds (primarily men and boys) who participated in Berlin football's associational structure did so as a way to reinforce their Turkish identity while also participating in "regular" German life. Through analyzing shifting names, identities, and membership rosters, Jurgens shows that Berlin's football landscape has in recent decades shifted away from ethnonational patterns to display considerable heterogeneity of membership and leadership, with many clubs often today identifying as diverse and multicultural.

Johnson's analysis of the 2015 European Maccabi Games reveals how the city of Berlin, as well as Jewish sport leaders, celebrated both the history of Jewish German sport in pre-Nazi Berlin and the revival of Jewish German sport, and Jewish German life more broadly, in the new Berlin. Indeed, many of the event's younger participants, interviewed by the media and profiled by Berlin's Jewish Museum, experienced the games first and foremost as a social and athletic opportunity rather than as a political spectacle. Parallel to this emphasis on thriving Jewish life was the broader multicultural context of Berlin. Clubs such as TuS Makkabi, with a Jewish name and loose connection to Berlin's very first Jewish sports club founded in 1898, had many Muslim and Christian members, displaying the same move away from ethnonationalism and toward heterogeneity that Jurgens emphasizes. Yet discourses about Berlin's Muslim population as potentially threatening to Jewish participants reveal the tensions that still exist underneath Berlin's self-proclaimed cosmopolitanism and diversity.

Sport clubs and events, as well as broader participation in and discussion of sport, allowed Berliners to engage with, define, and demonstrate their identities and communities. These representations were not static, as demonstrated by the shifting names and memberships of clubs or the ways in which Weimar Berlin's famous athletes-turned-sportswriters reflected on women's athleticism. Even when not explicitly addressed, the relationship between sport and masculinity is nonetheless apparent, be it when considering the appropriate behavior of imperial military officers when riding their horses; debating the propriety of women's middle-distance running in the 1920s; rushing to resume competitive men's football when it was women who dominated the immediate, rubble-filled, postwar landscape; or founding male-dominated Turkish football clubs. The act of participating in a sport or joining a club has often allowed Berliners to signal an affiliation with a specific community and to both reinforce and challenge existing social norms. Likewise, media coverage of recreational sport related to gender, ethnicity, generation, and social milieu has fostered broader public discussions and debates over society and social life.

Media and Celebrity

Sport and mass media have had a symbiotic relationship since at least the nineteenth century. As newspapers expanded their coverage of sport because of general interest in the subject, the widespread media coverage further expanded sport's popularity.[44] Each new media form—newsreels, radio, television, and social media—has repeated this pattern.[45] As the largest German city with the country's biggest media presence, Berlin attracted German and international athletes alike because of its venues, spectatorship, and exciting culture. Both media coverage of specific sporting events and commercial sponsorships contributed to athletes' heroic status and further solidified their position as celebrities.[46] In addition, the press has bolstered a range of governments and their goals through coverage of sporting events. The Third Reich and German Democratic Republic both had official state newspapers that clearly espoused the government's position, and while the imperial and democratic German states did not have official newspapers, sympathetic editors often promoted these governments' views. Traditional media coverage of sport in Berlin, regular columns by celebrity athletes, and fictionalized serials about sport all contributed to shaping the city's sporting landscape.

Both Hurley and Jensen explore the interaction between media, celebrity, and sport. Hurley's examination of the Berlin sportswriter Adolf von Guretzki's serialized novelette about a fictional celebrity strongman contrasts traditional and rural sport with sport in urbanized Berlin and its new sporting celebrities. As Hurley shows, von Guretzki employs several Orientalist tropes in his novelette, particularly in his descriptions of Bedouins as antagonists to the German strongman and his traveling companions in Egypt, while his depictions of Cairo paint urban Egypt in a highly flattering light. In the process, he reveals to his Berlin readers an urban-rural divide in the world of sport, both in the novelette and in Germany more broadly, and invites his readers to experience celebrity and spectacle, as well as sport, as integral features of the modern urban and cosmopolitan environment, with Berlin as its exemplar. During the Weimar period, Jensen shows how the commentary of athlete-correspondents in Berlin's leading newspapers engaged with the many transformations in German society, especially regarding scientific management, shifting gender roles, and urban modernity. In 1927, professional sportswriters even founded their own professional association and created an award for sports reporting. In addition to offering reporting and commentary, athlete-correspondents used the media to influence developments within and narratives about their own sports. Media, spectacle, and celebrity were thus mutually reinforcing in Weimar Berlin.

Throughout the twentieth and early twenty-first centuries, print media has continued to define sporting subcultures in Berlin. Even with the challenges of the immediate postwar period, Berlin's residents not only found ways to play football but also covered these matches and, ultimately, the city championship in the newly formed newspapers published across the four sectors of the city. In addition, as Rall notes, newspaper advertisements for football equipment and coverage of the deprivation of the occupation period demonstrates just how important the city's population believed football was. As Reinhart demonstrates, media helped the participants in the nascent skateboarding movement in the 1970s and 1980s both learn more about the sport from abroad as well as cultivate an identity as a subculture. German television coverage of skateboarding competitions in Berlin helped draw attention to the new sport. Skateboarders anxiously awaited copies of American magazines and VHS tapes, which helped with the Californization of this Berlin sporting subculture. Jurgens notes that German media often reinforced ethnoracial stereotypes through their coverage of football clubs and players of Turkish backgrounds by emphasizing their aggressiveness and that these clubs were more frequently on the receiving end of disciplinary punishments. Jurgens demonstrates that media portrayals, as well as the varied responses of football players of Turkish backgrounds, both reflected and shaped broader discussions about pluralism and national belonging.

Hartston, Dichter, and Johnson all look at how media has helped a range of figures, including political leaders and diplomats, to use sport in service of their broader goals. In the late nineteenth century, with the growth of competing ideas of internationalism and imperial tensions, the newspaper coverage of the Great Berlin-Vienna Distance Ride between German and Austrian riders allowed the German state—at least before the race finished—to ascribe national virtues to the German military competitors and their horses. Media coverage of the individual riders also emphasized their celebrity status. Although all of the riders in the Berlin-Vienna race were white European men, the event's media coverage nevertheless included tropes of Orientalism through their discussion of a small group of "Zulu" men that a young German officer brought from German East Africa to the race festivities, where they served as objects of spectacle and an advertisement for the further conquest of German East Africa. Thus the media and the race festivities themselves symbolically linked Germany's sporting and political stature with its colonizing project. As Hartston demonstrates, however, the outcome of the long-distance horse race also allowed German media to criticize the national narrative and express concerns about the state.

Berlin's later hosting of Olympic trials and other international sporting events also allowed the city and the governments in power over it to portray a specific image to both local and global audiences. In the 1960s, the two

German Olympic Committees took the positions of their governments with respect to the city of Berlin. Dichter traces how their negotiations over whether trials for the all-German Olympic team should take place in East and West Berlin and whether West Berlin even had the right to be considered part of the Federal Republic from a sporting standpoint—disputes which media in both German states actively reported—reveal how international sport served as a venue for diplomacy and attempts to achieve diplomatic aims. Johnson shows how, almost eighty years after the 1936 Olympics, Berlin's daily newspapers, as well as the weekly *Jüdische Allgemeine*, helped local and national political leaders as well as the organized Jewish German sports community present the 2015 European Maccabi Games as a symbolic reversal of the notorious "Nazi Olympics," and as proof not only of successful German-Jewish historical reconciliation efforts but also of Berlin's open-mindedness and multiculturalism. At the same time, however, some media coverage of security concerns at the games rhetorically marginalized Berlin's Muslim population, thereby exposing tensions in the city's vaunted cosmopolitanism. Each of these sporting events, from three different German states, shows how the media contributed to the promotion of diplomatic efforts and political narratives while simultaneously exposing the fractures within those narratives.

Media was thus an important part of the development and understanding of sport in Berlin. The Berlin media served both the local population and, through larger outlets, a wider German audience. When Berlin hosted international sporting events, the global media that descended upon the city also disseminated visions of Berlin to the world. Berlin's vast media landscape—from its numerous newspapers to television and the newer media forms of the twenty-first century—provides a wealth of material for further understanding of both the city and its sporting landscape.

Conclusion

The eight contributions in this volume and concluding chapter by Annemarie Sammartino reveal the vibrancy of sport in Berlin over the past 130 years. By moving beyond the most heavily researched aspects of German sport history, the following chapters incorporate new historical subdisciplines and trends to provide a deeper understanding of sport in Germany's most prominent city. The proliferation of media in the country's largest city allows the spectacle of sport, as well as sport's role in shaping and reinforcing identities, to reach an even wider audience than its immediate participants and spectators. Sport remained fundamental to Berlin's community and associational life in the postwar era even amidst the decline in religious and political organizational structures that dominated Imperial, Weimar, and Nazi Germany. Sport has continued to be a place where Berlin's multiculturalism and diversity have flourished at the local, national, and international levels for Berliners, Germans, and the world to see.

Notes

1. Richard Mandell, *The Nazi Olympics* (Urbana: University of Illinois Press, 1987); Reinhard Rürup, ed., *1936: Die Olympischen Spiele und der Nationalsozialismus*, trans. Pamela E. Selwyn (Berlin: Arlon Verlag, 1996); Thomas Alkemeyer, *Körperkultur, Kult und Politik: Von der "Muskelreligion" Pierre de Coubertins zur Inszenierung von Macht in den Olympischen Spielen von 1936* (Frankfurt am Main: Campus, 1996); Arnd Krüger and William Murray, eds., *The Nazi Olympics: Sport, Politics, and Appeasement in the 1930s* (Urbana: University of Illinois Press, 2003); Barbara J. Keys, *Globalizing Sport: National Rivalry and International Community in the 1930s* (Cambridge, MA: Harvard University Press, 2006), 115–57; Allen Guttmann, "Berlin 1936: The Most Controversial Olympics," in *National Identity and Global Sports Events: Culture, Politics, and Spectacle in the Olympics and the Football World Cup*, ed. Alan Tomlinson and Christopher Young (Albany: State University of New York Press, 2006), 65–81; David Clay Large, *Nazi Games: The Olympics of 1936* (New York: W. W. Norton, 2007); Christopher Hilton, *Hitler's Olympics: The 1936 Berlin Olympic Games* (Stroud: Sutton, 2008); Graham McFee and Alan Tomlinson, "Riefenstahl's *Olympia*: Ideology and Aesthetics in the Shaping of the Aryan Athletic Body," *The International Journal of the History of Sport* 16, no. 2 (1999): 86–106; Michael Mackenzie, "From Athens to Berlin: The 1936 Olympics and Leni Riefenstahl's *Olympia*," *Critical Inquiry* 20, no. 2 (Winter 2003): 302–36.

2. Kay Schiller and Christopher Young, *The 1972 Munich Olympics and the Making of Modern Germany* (Berkeley: University of California Press, 2010), 56–86.

3. David Clay Large, *Berlin* (New York: Basic Books, 2000), 466–67.

4. "Mehr Menschen mit Migrationshintergrund in Berlin," Rundfunk Berlin-Brandenburg, February 4, 2022, accessed January 11, 2023, https://www.rbb24.de/panorama/beitrag/2022/02/berlin-migration-anstieg-bezirk-mitte-wachstum-international.html.

5. Large, *Berlin*, xxii.

6. Sabine Hake, *Topographies of Class: Modern Architecture and Mass Society in Weimar Berlin* (Ann Arbor: University of Michigan, 2008), 7.

7. Janet Ward, *Post-Wall Berlin: Borders, Space and Identity* (New York: Palgrave Macmillan, 2011), 26.

8. Brian Ladd, *The Ghosts of Berlin: Confronting German History in the Urban Landscape* (Chicago: University of Chicago Press, 1997); Andreas Huyssen, *Present Pasts: Urban Palimpsests and the Politics of Memory* (Stanford: Stanford University Press, 2003); Karen E. Till, *The New Berlin: Memory, Politics, Place* (Minneapolis: University of Minnesota Press, 2005); Claire Colomb, *Staging the New Berlin: Place Marketing and*

the Politics of Urban Reinvention Post 1989 (Abingdon: Routledge, 2012); Clare Copley, *Nazi Buildings, Cold War Traces and Governmentality in Post-Unification Berlin* (London: Bloomsbury Academic, 2020).

9. For sport in Germany, see Alan Tomlinson and Christopher Young, eds., *German Football: History, Culture, Society* (Abingdon: Routledge: 2006). While this volume focuses on a single sport (football) across the entire country, no chapters are about Berlin specifically. See also Alan McDougall, *The People's Game: Football, State and Society in East Germany* (Cambridge: Cambridge University Press, 2014), which provides a comprehensive look at football in East Germany, including several Berlin clubs, but without a specific focus on Berlin.

For sport within a specific context, see Jutta Braun and Hans Joachim Teichler, eds., *Sportstadt Berlin im Kalten Krieg: Prestigekämpfe und Systemwettstreit* (Berlin: Christoph Links Verlag, 2006); Christopher Young, "'Nicht mehr die herrlichste Nebensache der Welt': Sport, West Berlin and the Four Powers Agreement 1971," *German Politics and Society* 25, no. 1 (2007): 28–45; Kay Schiller, "Communism, Youth and Sport: The 1973 World Youth Festival in East Berlin," in *Sport and the Transformation of Modern Europe: States, Media and Markets 1950–2010*, ed. Alan Tomlinson, Christopher Young, and Richard Holt (Abingdon: Routledge, 2011), 50–66; Molly Wilkinson Johnson, "Mega-Events, Urban Space, and Social Protest: The Olympia 2000 Bid in Reunified Berlin, 1990–1993," *Central European History* 52, no. 4 (2019): 689–712; Heather L. Dichter, "The Diplomatic Maneuvering Against the Short-Lived 1968 Berlin Olympic Bid," *Contemporary European History* 33, no. 2 (2024): 514–28. Claire Colomb touches on Berlin's 2000 Olympic bid within the context of urban marketing strategies in Claire Colomb, *Staging the New Berlin*, 89–105. Elizabeth Strom explores Berlin's 2000 Olympic bid in "In Search of the Growth Coalition: American Urban Theories and the Redevelopment of Berlin," *Urban Affairs Review* 31, no. 4 (1996): 468–70. Mathew Rose investigates the corruption in Berlin's city politics that influenced Berlin's 2000 Olympic bid in *Berlin: Hauptstadt von Filz und Korruption* (Munich: Knaur, 1997).

10. Steven A. Riess, *City Games: The Evolution of American Urban Society and the Rise of Sports* (Urbana: University of Illinois Press, 1991); John Bale, *Sport, Space and the City* (London: Routledge, 1993).

11. Nadine Rossol, *Performing the Nation in Interwar Germany: Sport, Spectacle and Political Symbolism, 1926–36* (Basingstoke: Palgrave Macmillan, 2010); Robert A. Lewis, *The Stadium Century: Sport, Spectatorship and Mass Society in Modern France* (Manchester: Manchester University Press, 2016); Ronald A. Smith, "Far More Than Commercialism: Stadium Building from Harvard's Innovations to Stanford's 'Dirt Bowl,'" *The International Journal of the History of Sport* 25, no. 11 (2008): 1453–74; Annette R. Hofmann, "'Bringing the Alps to the City': Early Indoor Winter Sports Events in the Modern City of the Twentieth Century," *The International Journal of the History of Sport* 29, no. 14 (2012): 2050–66.

12. Thierry Terret and Sandra Heck, "Prologue: Sport and Urban Space in Europe: Facilities, Industries, Identities," *The International Journal of the History of Sport* 29, no. 14 (2012): 1940.

13. Michael Krüger, "Sports in the German University from about 1900 until the Early Years of the Federal Republic of Germany: The Example of Muenster and the 'Westfaelische Wilhelms-University,'" *The International Journal of the History of Sport* 29, no. 14 (2012): 1981–97; Sandra Heck, Paul Nierhaus, and Andreas Luh, "Myth or Reality of the Revier Derby? Schalke 04 versus Borussia Dortmund (1947–2007)," *The International Journal of the History of Sport* 29, no. 14 (2012): 2030–49.

14. Chris Elzey and David K. Wiggins, eds., *DC Sports: The Nation's Capital at Play* (Fayetteville: University of Arkansas Press, 2015); Stephen H. Norwood, ed., *New York Sports: Glamour and Grit in the Empire City* (Fayetteville: University of Arkansas Press, 2018).

15. Molly Wilkinson Johnson, "The Legacies of 1936: Hitler's Olympic Grounds and Berlin's Bid to Host the 2000 Olympic Games," *German History* 40, no. 2 (June 2022): 258–77; Monika Meyer, "Berlin 1936," in *Olympic Cities: City Agendas, Planning, and the World's Games, 1896–2016*, 2nd ed., ed. John R. Gold and Margaret M. Gold (London: Routledge, 2011), 215–32; Miranda Kiuri and Jacques Teller, "Olympic Stadiums and Cultural Heritage: On the Nature and Status of Heritage Values in Large Sport Facilities," *The International Journal of the History of Sport* 32, no. 5 (2015): 684–707.

16. Horst Ueberhorst, *Friedrich Ludwig Jahn and His Time, 1778–1852*, trans. Timothy Nevill (Munich: Heinz Moos Verlag, 1978); Christiane Eisenberg, "Charismatic National Leader: Turnvater Jahn," *The International Journal of the History of Sport* 13, no. 1 (1996): 14–27; Annette R. Hoffman and Gertrud Pfister, "Turnen—A Forgotten Movement Culture: Its Beginnings in Germany and Diffusion in the United States," in *Turnen and Sport: Transatlantic Transfers*, ed. Annette R. Hoffman (Münster: Waxmann, 2004), 11–24; Heikki Lempa, *Beyond the Gymnasium: Educating the Middle-Class Bodies in Classical Germany* (Washington, DC: Lexington Books, 2007).

17. Kevin McAleer, *Dueling: The Cult of Honor in Fin-de-Siècle Germany* (Princeton: Princeton University Press, 1994); Ute Frevert, *Men of Honour: A Social and Cultural History of the Duel* (Cambridge: Polity Press, 1995), 72, 84; Karin H. Breuer, "Constructing Germanness: The Student Movement from the *Burschenschaft* to the *Progressbewegung*, 1814–49," (PhD diss., University of North Carolina, 2002).

18. Arnd Krüger, "Deutschland, Deutschland über alles? National Integration through Turnen and Sport in Germany 1870–1914," *Stadion* 25 (1999): 109–29.

19. On working-class sports, see Arnd Krüger, "The German Way of Worker Sport," in *The Story of Worker Sport*, ed. Arnd Krüger and James Riordan (Champaign, IL: Human Kinetics Press, 1996), 1–26, and the many essays collected in Hans Joachim Teichler and Gerhard Hauk, eds., *Illustrierte Geschichte des Arbeitersports* (Berlin: Dietz, 1987). For sports and religious identity, see Swantje Scharenberg, "Religion and sport," in *The International Politics of Sport in the Twentieth Century*, ed. James Riordan and Arnd Krüger (London: Routledge, 2007), 90–104; Michael Krüger, "Gymnastics, Physical Education, Sport, and Christianity in Germany," *The International Journal of the History of Sport* 35, no. 1 (2018): 9–26; Daniel Wildman, "Jewish Gymnastics and Their Corporeal Utopias in Imperial Germany," in *Emancipation through Muscles: Jews and Sports in Europe*, ed. Michael Brenner and Gideon Reuveni (Lincoln: University of Nebraska Press, 2006), 27–43.

20. Peter Fritzsche, *Reading Berlin 1900* (Cambridge, MA: Harvard University Press, 1996), 79–81.

21. Christiane Eisenberg, "The Middle Class and Competition: Some Considerations of the Beginnings of Modern Sport in England and Germany," *The International Journal of the History of Sport* 7, no. 2 (1990): 265–82; Christiane Eisenberg, *"English Sports" und deutsche Bürger: Eine Gesellschaftsgeschichte 1800–1939* (Paderborn: Ferdinand Schöningh, 1999); Christiane Eisenberg, "Football in Germany: Beginnings, 1890–1914," *The International Journal of the History of Sport* 8, no. 2 (1991): 205–20.

22. William Durick, "Berlin 1916," in *Encyclopedia of the Modern Olympic Movement*, ed. John E. Findling and Kimberly D. Pelle (Westport, CT: Greenwood Press, 2004), 63–69; Karl Lennartz, "Die VI. Olympischen Spiele Berlin 1916," *Stadion* 6 (1980): 229–50.

23. Sigfried Gehrmann, "Symbol of National Resurrection: Max Schmeling, German Sports Idol," *The International Journal of the History of Sport* 13, no. 1 (1996): 101–13; Erik Jensen, "Crowd Control: Boxing Spectatorship and Social Order in Weimar Germany," in *Histories of Leisure*, ed. Rudy Koshar (Oxford: Berg, 2002), 79–101; Andrew Ritchie, *Quest For Speed: A History of Early Bicycle Racing 1868–1903*, 2nd ed. (Jefferson, NC: McFarland, 2018); Christiane Eisenberg, "Massensport in der Weimarer Republik: Ein statistischer Überblick," *Archiv für Sozialgeschichte* 33 (1933): 137–77; Frank Becker, "Sportsmen in the Machine World: Models for Modernization in Weimar Germany," *The International Journal of the History of Sport* 12, no. 1 (April 1995): 153–68.

24. Hake, *Topographies of Class*, 250.

25. Theodore F. Rippey, "Athletics, Aesthetics, and Politics in the Weimar Press," *German Studies Review* 28, no. 1 (2005): 101.

26. On Weimar Germany, see Erik Jensen, *Body by Weimar: Athletes, Gender, and German Modernity* (Oxford: Oxford University Press, 2013); Katie Sutton, "The Masculinized Female Athlete in Weimar Germany," *German Politics and Society* 27, no. 3 (2009): 28–49. On women's broader sports participation in the interwar period, see Bruce Kidd, *The Struggle for Canadian Sport* (Toronto: University of Toronto Press, 1996), 94–145; Gerald R. Gems, Linda J. Borish, and Gertrud Pfister, *Sports in American History: From Colonization to Globalization* (Champaign, IL: Human Kinetics, 2008), 248–55; Jennifer Hargreaves, *Sporting Females: Critical Issues in the History and Sociology of Women's Sport* (London: Routledge, 1994), 112–44.

27. G. A. Carr, "The Synchronization of Sport and Physical Education Under National Socialism," *Canadian Journal of History of Sport and Physical Education* 10, no. 2 (1979): 15–35; Hajo Bernett, *Sport und Schulsport in der NS-Diktatur* (Leiden: Brill, 2017); David Imhoof, "Sharpshooting in Gottingen: A Case Study of Cultural Integration in Weimar and Nazi Germany," *German History* 23, no. 4 (2005): 460–93.

28. Shelley Baranowski, *Strength through Joy: Consumerism and Mass Tourism in the Third Reich* (Cambridge: Cambridge University Press, 2007).

29. Michael H. Kater, *Hitler Youth* (Cambridge, MA: Harvard University Press, 2004), 30, 82.

30. Heather Dichter, "'Strict Measures Must Be Taken': Wartime Planning and the Allied Control of Sport in Occupied Germany," *Stadion* 34, no. 2 (2008): 193–217.

31. Noel D. Cary, "Olympics in Divided Berlin? Popular Culture and Political Imagination at the Cold War Frontier," *Cold War History* 11, no. 3 (2011): 291–316; Dichter, "Diplomatic Maneuvering"; Schiller and Young, *The 1972 Munich Olympics*.

32. Molly Wilkinson Johnson, *Training Socialist Citizens: Sports and the State in East Germany* (Leiden: Brill Academic Publishers, 2008), 69–85.

33. Roger Robinson, "The Record-Breaking History of the Berlin Marathon," *Runners World*, September 20, 2022, accessed July 6, 2023, https://www.runnersworld.com/races-places/a23085728/berlin-marathon-history/; Marlen Reusser, et al., "Increased Participation and Decreased Performance in Recreational Master Athletes in 'Berlin Marathon' 1974–2019," *Frontiers in Physiology* 12 (2021): 1–10.

34. Johnson, *Training Socialist Citizens*, 165.

35. Johnson, *Training Socialist Citizens*, 204.

36. Andreas Conrad, "Berlin-Marathon 1990: Zum Start ein Sprint durchs Brandenburger Tor," *Der Tagesspiegel*, September 25, 2015, accessed July 6, 2023, https://www.tagesspiegel.de/berlin/zum-start-ein-sprint-durchs-brandenburger-tor-4404067.html.

37. Jutta Braun, "Auf Jahre unschlagbar? Die deutsche Vereinigung als Sportereignis," in *1989–Eine Epochenzäsur?*, ed. Martin Sabrow, Tilmann Siebeneichner, and Peter Ulrich Weiss (Göttingen: Wallstein Verlag, 2021), 120–43; McDougall, *The People's Game*, 313–38.

38. Karen A. Volkwein and Herbert R. Haag, "Sport in Unified Germany: The Merging of Two Different Sport Systems," *Journal of Sport and Social Issues* 18, no. 2 (1994): 183–93.

39. Wray Vamplew, John McClelland, and Mark Dyreson, eds., *A Cultural History of Sport*, 6 vols. (London: Bloomsbury Academic, 2021).

40. Mark Dyreson and Matthew Llewellyn, "Los Angeles is the Olympic City: Legacies of the 1932 and 1984 Olympic Games," *The International Journal of the History of Sport* 25, no. 14 (2008): 1991–2018.

41. Maurice Roche, *Mega-Events and Modernity: Olympics and Expos in the Growth of Global Culture* (London: Routledge, 2000); Maurice Roche, *Mega-Events and Social Change: Spectacle, Legacy and Public Culture* (Manchester: Manchester University Press, 2017).

42. David Black, "Dreaming Big: The Pursuit of 'Second Order' Games as a Strategic Response to Globalization," *Sport in Society* 11, no. 4 (2008): 467–80.

43. Iain Borden, *Skateboarding, Space and the City: Architecture and the Body* (Berg: New York, 2001).

44. Steve Tate, "Edward Hulton and Sports Journalism in Late-Victorian Manchester," *Manchester Region History Review* 20 (2009): 46–67.

45. Dave Berkman, "Long Before Arledge . . . Sport & TV: The Earliest Years: 1933–1947—as Seen by the Contemporary Press," *Journal of Popular Culture* 22, no. 2 (1988): 49–62; Garry Whannel, "Television and the Transformation of Sport," *Annals of the American Academy of Political and Social Science* 625 (September 2009): 205–18; Brett Hutchins and David Rowe, *Sport Beyond Television: The Internet, Digital Media and the Rise of Networked Media Sport* (New York: Routledge, 2012).

46. Benjamin G. Rader, *American Sports: From the Age of Folk Games to the Age of Televised Sports*, 4th ed. (Saddle River, NJ: Prentice Hall, 1999), 134–43.

CHAPTER ONE

A Failed Showcase

The Great Berlin-Vienna Distance Ride of 1892

BARNET HARTSTON

Long before dawn on an unseasonably warm Saturday morning in October 1892, people began to stream into the area near the Tempelhofer Feld, a military parade ground to the south of Berlin. They arrived by the thousands on city trains, carriages, and hired horse-cabs, and some even walked great distances to reach what was then the very southern edge of the city. At the exact same time, large crowds also started to gather in an open area outside the town of Floridsdorf, a small suburb to the north of Vienna and almost six hundred kilometers from Berlin. In both locations, people milled about excitedly amid flowers, flags, and patriotic bunting, under the glow of electric lights powerful enough that they could be seen for miles around. These German and Austrian spectators had gathered to witness a unique spectacle: the start of a long-distance horse race where German military officers rode southward toward Vienna while their Austro-Hungarian rivals simultaneously raced northward toward Berlin. In total, almost two hundred men on horseback raced against time after being released from the capital cities in small groups over the course of three days. Long-distance horse races were not uncommon during this era, but contemporary observers agreed that a race of this size and length, organized as a competition between nations, had never occurred before.

The race served five key practical and symbolic functions in German society. First, it was a carefully orchestrated diplomatic spectacle meant both to demonstrate the strength of the German-Austrian alliance and to act as a kind of internal diplomacy, reinforcing bonds between individual realms of the German Empire. Second, the race was explicitly framed as a practical military exercise, where rider endurance and tactics—as well as equine suitability—could be tested. Third, the race was an international sporting event that centered on both individual glory and national honor. Like the first modern Olympics, which would be held just a few years later in 1896, the Berlin-Vienna Distance Ride was a sporting competition where participants represented not only themselves but also their nation of origin. Fourth, the race was designed as a showcase for the host cities that served as its start and endpoints: Berlin and Vienna. Elaborate post-race festivities were planned in these cities, including tours, performances, ceremonies, and parades that were explicitly designed to show visiting riders and dignitaries the best of what each city had to offer.[1] Finally, the fifth function of the Great Berlin-Vienna Distance Ride was perhaps its most central. Beyond its purposes as sporting diplomacy, practical military training, international competition, and urban showcase, the race was also a staged cultural event designed to glorify and reinforce the broader populace's respect for the aristocratic elite and the values of martial masculinity. In other words, this event was conceived as a nationalist spectacle in which ordinary people were intended to not only cheer for their countrymen but also observe elite cavalrymen with admiration.

While grand international sporting spectacles such as the Great Berlin-Vienna Distance Ride can have the power to unite national communities, reinforce traditional values, and support existing hierarchies, their reception by ordinary people is often quite complicated and nuanced. Occasionally, large-scale sporting spectacles can even exacerbate existing political divisions, challenge shared values, and undermine social hierarchies—especially if something within the sporting event goes terribly wrong. In the case of the Great Berlin-Vienna Distance Ride, four factors served to challenge and even undermine the original purposes of the event: unruly crowds at the Tempelhofer Feld who approached the event on their own terms, a persistent sense of the inferiority of Berlin as a city of culture, startlingly poor results by German riders in comparison to their Austrian counterparts, and most importantly, the death of more than twenty horses and the gruesome maiming of dozens more—an occurrence that shocked spectators gathered in Berlin, unleashed a torrent of public criticism in the Berlin press, and threatened the sacred image of the masculine military elite.[2]

The Intended Functions of the Berlin-Vienna Distance Ride

The Great Berlin-Vienna Distance Ride of 1892 was first and foremost a well-orchestrated act of diplomacy through sport. Strengthening German-Austrian relations had become especially important as the fragile alliance of the Three Emperors' League that had linked Russia, Austria, and Germany began to collapse, in part over conflicting priorities in the Balkans. The alliance had formally ended in 1887, but ties between Germany and Russia had been maintained through the secret Reinsurance Treaty organized by Chancellor Otto von Bismarck. Once Bismarck resigned in 1890, however, his successors dropped the Reinsurance Treaty and relations with Russia quickly grew more distant.[3] In this context, strong reciprocal bonds between Germany and Austria were essential to building a united front against their potential foes. Although the two Central European empires had been allies for more than two decades, their priorities were not always identical—and memories of the Prussian-Austrian War of 1866 had not completely faded on either side. Certainly, any public event that could draw the military forces (and general populations) of the two empires closer together was welcome, both to cement diplomatic ties and to demonstrate the strength of this alliance to rivals such as France and Russia. In fact, one could argue that the race itself was only a pretext for the fraternization and formal diplomatic exchanges that came afterward.[4]

Celebratory post-race events in Berlin and Vienna provided numerous opportunities for cavalry officers to dine with their counterparts in large communal banquets called *Liebesmahle* (love-feasts) that featured reciprocal toasts to the two kaisers, mutual praise for past deeds, and plenty of informal drinking and socializing. A full ten days after the competition began, the post-race festivities climaxed with German kaiser Wilhelm II's three-day formal visit to Vienna. If this was not enough, after the German kaiser's visit ended, all of the riders, officials, diplomats, and royal entourages boarded trains for Dresden, where they started the cycle of pageantry all over again for the benefit of King Albert of Saxony. The riders had not passed through the Saxon capital of Dresden during the race, but they had passed through the Saxon town of Bautzen just over fifty kilometers away. Thus—in a still-federalized German Empire that preserved internal hereditary dynasties, noble titles, and privileges—a formal ceremony to pay respect to King Albert was obligatory.

As the ceremonial events in Dresden demonstrate, in addition to functioning as an international diplomatic initiative, the Berlin-Vienna Distance Ride also furthered the project of building internal unity within the relatively young German Empire. The empire had been founded just twenty years earlier, and in many ways its governmental and military structure still reflected a federation of states rather than a fully centralized power structure. While there was only one German emperor, the states of Bavaria, Saxony, and Württemberg all retained their own monarchs, diplomatic corps, and military units—although the latter were supposed to function under unified command during a war. This meant that even two decades after formal unification, true integration within the German Empire was still an ongoing, and sometimes very sensitive, process. Of the 154 German riders who initially reserved a spot in the race, ten were from the Royal Saxon Cavalry, four from Württemberg, and seven from Bavaria. Even Prussian riders were rarely from Berlin and its environs but were instead from estates scattered across the Prussian realm. While each of these cavalrymen rode for the glory of their military unit and their own local or regional *Heimat* (homeland), the fact that they all set off from Berlin signified that they rode for the glory of the German Empire as well.[5]

While international and internal German diplomacy were the primary key functions of the Great Berlin-Vienna Distance Ride, the organizers also placed enormous significance on a second important function of the race: the event as a practical military exercise. Riders were asked to submit post-race reports that discussed their choice of horse breed, methods of training, habits of feeding and watering before and during the race, particulars of the riding equipment used (including bits, harnesses, and shoes), how they treated wounds to the horse and repaired worn equipment, as well as their overall race strategy and execution. These reports were seen as vital for ascertaining the limits of rider and horse for extreme wartime situations.

Of course, the use of equestrian competitions as training for war was not a new phenomenon. Traditional equestrian endurance events such as fox and boar hunting had become vital training for cavalrymen over the course of the nineteenth century, especially as the role of cavalry shifted primarily to patrolling and passing messages across long distances in unfamiliar landscapes.[6] General Heinrich von Rosenberg, a key figure in the development of first the Hanoverian and then the German cavalry, argued that in the crucible of war most patrols would not typically make use of main roads when seeking to flank the enemy since doing so exposed them to attack. He suggested, therefore, that hunts and formal steeplechase racing provided the best practical experience for cavalrymen and would test the mettle of both men and horses.[7] To this end, both the German and Austrian emperors sponsored regular army steeplechases (*Armee Jagdrennen*, literally "army hunt races") where cavalrymen competed for monetary prizes and honors bestowed directly by royal hands.[8]

In addition to its role as a diplomatic mission and military exercise, the Berlin-Vienna Distance Ride had a third function as a competitive international sporting event. Organizers and riders sought to distinguish it from sporting events that were merely competitions for pleasure, money, or public show—a distinction represented by its labeling as a distance ride (*Distanzritt*) rather than a horse race (*Pferderennen*). The line between sporting events and military training had long been blurred. Although fox and boar hunts were often exclusive private affairs, steeplechase races featuring military officers were usually public occasions. This was especially true for the annual Große Armee Jagdrennen (Great Army Steeplechase), one of Berlin's most popular racing events. Attendees for these races often included members of the royal family, visiting foreign dignitaries, and military officers in full dress (alongside their luxuriously dressed companions). In addition, attendance by the general public was encouraged by the offering of reduced admission, the scheduling of special trains from different areas of the city, and the publishing of guides and maps of the race course in various sporting newspapers to help novice spectators follow the action.[9] As the Große Armee Jagdrennen and the Great Berlin-Vienna Distance Ride featured some of the best horse racers in Germany, these events also inspired intense wagering, both locally and internationally.

Journalistic coverage of races such as the Große Armee Jagdrennen was common in both the sport sections of popular Berlin newspapers as well as in a few newspapers exclusively dedicated to sports. In fact, the original idea to organize a long-distance race between German and Austrian cavalrymen came not from the two governments nor from elite riders themselves, but from a public relations stunt advanced by a fledgling sports media outlet. In October 1891, the racing newsletter *Turf*, a new Berlin publication struggling to gain an audience, sent a challenge to cavalry officers in Austria-Hungary to join their German counterparts in a distance race from Berlin to Frankfurt and back, which it tentatively planned for March of 1892. Unfortunately the *Turf* newsletter folded before the proposed date of the race, but it was only thereafter that the idea caught on in high military circles. According to the journalist Gerd von Ende, the number of sporting newspapers in Berlin increased dramatically during the late 1880s and early 1890s, and smaller newsletters like *Turf* competed with more established, aristocratic-oriented sporting papers such as *Der Sporn*. This trend reflected both the increased public interest in sports such as horse racing and the overall growth of Berlin newspapers into a truly mass media during this era.[10]

While the sporting world was fascinated by the Berlin-Vienna Distance Ride as a gentlemanly competition, the organizers of the event also put substantial effort into planning post-race activities that would showcase the two host cities. For example, in addition to multiple formal dinners and welcoming ceremonies, German riders arriving in Vienna were treated to special events including a play at the Burgtheater, a performance at the Vienna State Opera, a formal military review at the imperial stables (*Stallburg*), and a performance at the Spanish Riding School.[11] This was a difficult lineup for organizers in Berlin to match. The weeklong festivities for Austro-Hungarian riders in Berlin focused on similar kinds of activities, including a presentation of Austrian horses and riders at the new Tattersall hippodrome, horse races at both the Charlottenburg and Westend racetracks, a steamboat trip up the Havel River to Potsdam, a tour of the Sans Souci Palace, and a boar hunt with hounds in the Grünewald Forest.[12] Major Berlin newspapers such as the *Berliner Tageblatt* paid special attention to the public ceremonies at the Charlottenburg and Westend racetracks and depicted them as watershed moments for the city:

> To make it clear, there has never been a sporting festival like there was in Berlin yesterday. Modern Berliners cannot remember anything like this, and certainly neither can the "old folks." The crush of the crowd may have been as great—or even greater—at the Union Club Jubilee at the Hoppegarten racetrack on June 13, but one thing was lacking there that completes the perfect image of such festivities: a grand entrance. And Berlin has never before seen a kind of entrance such as the one we witnessed yesterday.[13]

Such descriptions of glitz and glamour were likely exactly what the German government and military had hoped for. The race was a dazzling spectacle that captivated the German public and depicted Berlin as a thriving political, cultural, and sporting center.

Finally, and most importantly, the Great Berlin-Vienna Distance Ride was intended to serve as a public celebration of elite martial masculinity as represented by the German cavalry. Although one might expect such a sporting event to be a showcase for masculine values and attributes, the centrality of martial masculinity to this race was made explicit not only in the pre- and post-race speeches by military leaders and participants but also in the press coverage of the race itself. For example, the general inspector of the Austrian cavalry, Otto Freiherr von Gagern, gave a rousing speech the day before the race to the assembled Austrian riders in which he emphasized four characteristics that were required of elite cavalrymen: self-mastery, energy, love of riding (*Reiterfrohsinn*), and riding spirit (*Reitergeist*).[14] Gagern was appealing to part of a military code of honor that was shared with the Germans and emphasized physical courage, loyalty, boldness, self-assurance, obedience, self-sacrifice, and comradeship.[15] Later, in a post-race speech about his own experiences as a rider, the Prussian baron Clemens von Reitzenstein echoed these sentiments and suggested that the race had been essential in building riders' morale and strength of will (*Willenskraft*) through hardship and suffering. "A firm will," he argued, "is the foundation for a good soldier. . . . The will allows the accomplishment of anything."[16] Just as the legendary King Arthur might have sent his brave knights out on a quest to test their mettle, here the two kaisers sent cavalrymen on a quest that would test their quality as riders and trainers and their tenacity as military men.

Unlike an Arthurian quest, however, this event was clearly a performance of masculinity meant for public consumption. Journalistic accounts of the race from across Germany often breathlessly laud the values of elite martial masculinity, celebrating the riders as epic heroes whose display of willpower, vigor, and bodily endurance was unparalleled in history. An explicit link between the race participants and military heroes of past generations was aided by the fact that the two top finishers were both from noble families tied to famous military victories. The victor, Austrian count Wilhelm von Starhemberg, was descended from Count Ernst Rüdiger von Starhemberg, a military governor of Vienna who was credited with saving the city from an Ottoman siege in 1683. The Prussian rider Baron Clemens von Reitzenstein, who finished second, was descended from generals who fought important

A sketch of Berlin crowds greeting Austro-Hungarian riders at the Tempelhofer Feld based on a woodcut by the painter Georg Karl Koch (1857–1931), who specialized in animal paintings and sporting scenes. Georg Karl Koch, *Ankunft und Empfang des ersten österreichischen Reiters am Ziel auf dem Tempelhofer Felde bei Berlin am Morgen des 4. Oktober*, published in *Illustrirte Zeitung* 99, no. 2572 (October 15, 1892). *Courtesy of the Bayerische Staatsbibliothek München, 2 Per. 26–99, S. 418.*

battles in the Seven Years' War and the Napoleonic Wars. Together, the racing exploits of these two men served as proof of the continued health and vigor of the hereditary nobility. As one popular book on the race written by the Dresden schoolteacher Andreas Hugo Elm suggested:

> The outcome [of the race] was astonishing: it was almost unthinkable what Count Starhemberg and Baron von Reitzenstein had accomplished! And it was all completely true. These youngest offshoots of great old noble families may have had ancestors who sat bravely in their saddles, charging with lances during festivals and formal jousts; but what were those acts compared to the accomplishments of their descendants?[17]

Both Starhemberg and Reitzenstein had already achieved a degree of notoriety for their racing prowess in previous events across Europe.[18] Their success in the Berlin-Vienna Distance Ride, however, cemented their statuses as both scions of ancient hereditary nobility and as modern sporting celebrities.

The Berlin-Vienna Distance Ride as a Failed Showcase

Although the Berlin-Vienna Distance Ride attracted widespread interest and enthusiasm, its public reception was far more ambivalent than organizers had hoped. Four things contributed to the failure of this event as a ritual of unity and as a showcase for elite values: unruly crowds that treated the event as public entertainment, the relatively poor performance of German cavalrymen, the continued perception of Berlin as an inferior center of culture, and, most importantly, public anger at the systematic mistreatment of horses in the race.

Although the Great Berlin-Vienna Distance Ride was staged as a nationalist ritual, popular attendance and enthusiasm for the race should not necessarily be equated to proof of the crowd's successful indoctrination. As the historian Jakob Vogel has argued, members of the German bourgeoisie and working classes often enthusiastically attended nationalist events such as parades and memorial celebrations but imbued them with their own meaning and their own distinctive forms of sociability. This is what Vogel has labeled "folkloric militarism": an acceptance of militaristic imagery and rituals as part of everyday life *without* a necessarily deep internalization of nationalism and militarism. Vogel argues that most working-class men who attended nationalist celebrations with their families were still likely to join unions, maintain skepticism of the ruling elite, and vote for the Socialist Party.[19]

Certainly, various sources depict wild jubilation within the crowd gathered at the Berlin Tempelhofer Feld when news came of German successes— as well as sincere enthusiasm when the first Austrian riders approached the finish line. However, as one might expect, crowd behavior was not always purely honorable or patriotic. For example, the liberal *Berliner Tageblatt* described how members of the public engaged in all kinds of mischief during the long pauses between such events. Pranksters, for example, rushed in to "congratulate" passengers on any ordinary carriages that happened to accidentally pass under the finish line arch, which extended over the main road southward toward the village of Tempelhof. Other young men dared to harass mounted police if they thought they could blend into the crowd and get away with it.[20] Elm's otherwise generally positive account of the race disparaged the gathered Berlin crowd for being dominated by enterprising women who sat for hours at tables and chairs they rented so that they could both see the action and be seen by members of high society—including prospective matches.[21] The tone of this journalistic coverage of the crowds was often sarcastic and reflects common bourgeois stereotypes of political and social outsiders, such as women and the working classes, as inherently irrational or disorderly; however, such coverage also reveals that the crowds were engaged in their own meaning-making and were far from passive receptacles for nationalistic propaganda.

The popular daily *Berliner Tageblatt* also described additional sideshows that took place near the starting line that served as popular entertainment. For example, on the first day of the race, Alfred Flasch, the owner of a leather factory in the Moravian town of Brünn (modern Brno), appeared before the crowd and announced his intention to set off on a fifteen-year-old decommissioned cavalry horse alongside the official racers. He apparently made it all the way to Vienna but arrived days after the leading official competitors.[22] The *Berliner Tageblatt* also described Gustav Wedell von Wedellsborg, a fifty-year-old Danish cavalryman who appeared at the Tempelhofer Feld with his nephew and two bicycles to announce they would ride all the way to Vienna on their "steel horses." The pair made it to Vienna and then promptly announced to Viennese reporters their intention to continue their cycling tour to Paris and Brussels.[23] Finally, a man named Morello from the small Silesian town of Leobschütz (modern Głubczyce) appeared at the starting line wearing a black-and-white checkered footracing costume and declared that he intended to make it to Vienna faster than any of the horses. Unlike the "amateur" elite cavalrymen, Morello was a "professional" athlete who competed primarily for monetary gain, and his associates eagerly took bets from the local crowd. According to the *Berliner Tageblatt*, Morello made it just more than 120 kilometers before retiring with an injury.[24] Since the starting line at Tempelhofer Feld was at the very southern edge of urban Berlin, these barnstorming athletes could announce their quests in front of the gathered spectators and then set off directly into the countryside. It is not clear how many of these alternative racers succeeded in making a profit; at the very least, however, many of them got their names mentioned in newspaper accounts of the great race.

The *Berliner Tageblatt* also reported on another "sideshow" with a passing mention of a young colonial officer named Moritz Merker, who had caused a sensation by bringing a small group of richly clad young "Zulu" men with him to the Tempelhofer Feld.[25] At the time, Merker was a twenty-five-year-old lieutenant who had recently returned from a stint in German East

Africa. It is unclear under what aegis he had brought the young African men with him or what other destinations they had on their itinerary. However, it is likely that such public interactions were intended to pique popular interest in and to win public support for the German colonization of East Africa—a violent conquest that was still underway. Ethnographic displays of indigenous people often drew large crowds at Berlin panopticons, zoos, and other arenas of popular amusement where, as the historian Angela Zimmerman argues, they presented what were purported to be authentic displays of indigenous culture and dress.[26] These ethnological expositions (*Völkerschauen*) were intended for popular entertainment and edification about the colonial mission; however, the transport and display of indigenous people was frequently coordinated with the Berlin Anthropological Society, an organization which both verified the seeming authenticity of the participants and used them for study.[27] Although the people brought to Germany for such displays were treated as curiosities by gawking audiences, scholars such as Zimmerman have demonstrated that the performers themselves often resisted instructions and sometimes openly challenged their portrayal as "primitives."[28] Overall, these depictions of crowd behavior at the Berlin-Vienna Distance Ride demonstrate that the event was an opportunity for ordinary Berliners to gather socially, just as they would at a county fair or concert. Spectators at the Tempelhofer Feld cheered enthusiastically for German riders and celebrated elite sportsmen on both sides; however, the crowds were far from passive observers or gullible consumers of nationalist propaganda.

The usefulness of the Berlin-Vienna Distance Ride as a rallying point for German nationalism was also tempered by an important second factor: the disastrous performance of most German riders. By the end of the first day of the race, it was abundantly clear that German riders were progressing remarkably poorly compared to their Austrian rivals. Several of the most highly regarded German riders either fell or had their horses falter early in the race. Worse yet, reports streamed in of Austrian riders making astonishing progress and appearing at checkpoints long before they were expected. In the end, only two of the top twenty race finishers and fourteen of the top forty-two overall finishers were German. In fact, only the very late heroics of the German rider Clemens von Reitzenstein salvaged an otherwise catastrophic overall performance. Reitzenstein's mad dash for victory at the finish line in Vienna on the final race day was only derailed by a last-minute, accidental detour in the fog. He thus ended up in second place behind the Austrian rider Wilhelm von Starhemberg. After Reitzenstein's bold finish, the Germans at least had a hero to publicly venerate. Nevertheless, such a poor overall performance inevitably led to recriminations about the quality of German horses and horsemen.[29]

Third, although the race was designed in part as a showcase for Berlin, there were some significant discordant notes in the press coverage of the city during the post-race celebrations. Popular newspapers such as the *Berliner Tageblatt* generally covered the post-race festivities in positive, if not reverent tones, yet alongside these breathless descriptions of pomp and circumstance there was a pervasive sense that Berlin as a whole had failed to measure up to her sisterly rival. Ironically, while this feeling likely reflected the fact that Berlin lacked equivalents to Vienna's illustrious Spanish Riding School, State Opera, and Burgtheater, the journalists of the *Berliner Tageblatt* most vigorously projected this sense of inferiority onto the allegedly deficient beauty and couture of the Berlin women who attended public celebrations. For example, the newspaper voiced this backhanded praise for Berlin women gathered for the public reception for Austrian riders at the Westend racetrack:

> The most beautiful women of Berlin had made themselves up to try to erase the old stereotype in the hearts of the Austrian visitors that Viennese women are more beautiful than those in Berlin. . . . And what an amazing sight for a picture! Such a colorful and animated scene with so many beautiful women and maidens! Certainly, when the Viennese make comparisons with their local racetrack, they will necessarily come to the conclusion that the sumptuous costumes [*Toilettenluxus*] featured here are very different than their own. And that, despite this fact, some of the women who appeared yesterday accomplished something quite extraordinary! But for us it was and will always be a few individuals—the great majority of the female visitors to the racetrack are really still thoroughly not "chic"![30]

The *Berliner Tageblatt* concluded that the most alluring women in the crowd were all "Danube women," including the famous actress Jenny Gross, who was a fixture in Berlin theaters.[31] At least for writers and readers of this prominent newspaper, German cavalrymen were not the only ones whose performance fell short in this public event; German women had proven themselves to be second-rate performers as well. Thus, a spectacle originally intended to demonstrate the glory of the German capital by celebrating its masculine heroes and feminine charm ended up only reinforcing a sense of Berlin's cultural inferiority.

In the end, any concerns about unruly crowds, German sporting performance, or the inferiority of Berlin's culture and couture paled in comparison to public outrage generated by the cruel fate of dozens of horses used in the race. To the shock of spectators at the Tempelhofer Feld, the first Austrian rider to reach Berlin, Aladar von Miklós, arrived on Marcsa, a twelve-year-old brown mare who was fully covered in blood from a shoulder wound and had both flanks ripped open by her rider's spurs.[32] Over the next few days, several other Austrian riders also arrived with seriously injured animals. The stories of suffering were even worse for German riders and their horses. Take, for example, the German hero Reitzenstein, who rode frantically to Vienna on the last day of the race to salvage German military honor. Before Reitzenstein could even sign his official time card, his mare, Lippspringe, whom he had driven forward with spurs over the last few kilometers of the race, collapsed in a heap at the finish line. She remained there for several hours before finally being carted away. Despite veterinary treatment, Lippspringe died of a lung infection a few days later.[33] These two examples were far from isolated incidents. A number of riders reportedly beat, kicked, spurred, and dragged their horses forward in desperate attempts to finish the race—many long after any hope for victory had been lost. Although accounts vary, it is likely that somewhere between twenty and thirty horses died during or soon after the race and dozens more were seriously—perhaps permanently—injured.

In response to this horror, Berlin journalists and critics from across the political spectrum began to level charges of animal abuse against the German military. One of the first political critics in Berlin to take aim at the race was the notorious Maximilian Harden, whose pugnacious nature and fearlessness made him a bête noire for German elites in the decades before World War I.[34] Harden commented on the race with his trademark bitter sarcasm: "20,000 Marks to the winner! Prizes and laurel wreaths in the Hofburg in Vienna! A spirited ride through the countryside and then golden festivities in the days afterward! Certainly all that more than compensates for a few poor dead nags."[35] Other satirical journals were equally merciless, including Berlin's infamous *Kladderadatsch*.[36]

Even nominally apolitical journals and magazines reacted with indignation at the race's equine toll. Perhaps the most damaging critique was a short

A sketch titled *Schwache Aussichten* (Poor prospects), based on a watercolor by the military painter Carl Becker (1862–1935), who was a regular contributor to the popular journal *Illustrirte Zeitung*. The sketch was published in *Illustrirte Zeitung* 99 no. 2572 (October 15, 1892). *Image courtesy of Bayerische Staatsbibliothek München, 2 Per. 26–99, S. 416.*

article in the family-oriented *Die Gartenlaube*, a journal from Leipzig that had a middle-class readership across Germany numbering in the millions.[37] In an article entitled "The Distance Ride and Humanity," the magazine did not pull its punches, vividly contrasting the lavish feasts awaiting the victorious riders in Berlin and Vienna with the bleak and senseless suffering of their animal cocompetitors. If German elites committed such unspeakable acts against animals, the *Gartenlaube* asked, then how could they condemn the old and barbaric Spanish practice of bullfighting? If they committed such acts purely out of blind ambition, then how could they condemn a poor carriage driver for beating his emaciated horse, when his offenses were somewhat mitigated by ignorance or extreme poverty?[38] These largely middle-class journals were consistent in their criticism: elite cavalrymen who mistreated their horses for sport were even more vile and detestable than lower-class horse-cabbies or bull-baiters who abused animals out of sheer ignorance or uncultivated savagery. Here then, in the Berlin-Vienna Distance Ride, elite martial masculinity had revealed its true decadence.

The controversy eventually spurred the directors of the Association of Animal Protection Organizations in the German Empire, a coalition of sixty-four local and animal protection organizations with almost fifty thousand members, to send a formal petition to the German Reichstag that demanded measures to guarantee such episodes of "animal mistreatment, which shock the public conscience, would never again occur."[39] For many prominent German journals, including Leipzig's *Die Grenzboten*, this kind of petition was a half-measure at best. *Die Grenzboten* insisted that animal protection societies, especially those in Berlin and Vienna, should not waste their time with polite protests but instead demand the prosecution of riders on charges of animal cruelty.[40]

Ironically, at the same time the middle-class *Grenzboten* insisted that military elites be subject to animal cruelty laws, the Socialist leader August Bebel referenced the Berlin-Vienna Distance Ride in a Reichstag debate over the infamous Lex Heinze, a series of laws pushed by Kaiser Wilhelm II that promised harsh punishment for the most immoral of criminals— especially pimps, prostitutes, and pornographers. In his parliamentary speech, Bebel explicitly compared the barbarism of some participants in the Great Berlin-Vienna Distance Ride, who whipped and spurred their exhausted horses to death, to a maniac who smears petroleum on a cat and then sets it alight. Bebel's point was that acts of "barbarity" existed across all classes; the Lex Heinze, however, would never be utilized to prosecute members of the upper classes.[41] Bebel's angry tirade was answered by other Reichstag deputies who sought to defend the riders from such slander.

Meanwhile, the formal petition sent by the Association of Animal Protection Organizations finally received consideration in Berlin by the Reichstag Commission on Petitions in May 1893. There, a representative of the Prussian Ministry of War suggested that the death and injury of horses in the event was regrettable; however, he insisted that the purposes and benefits of the Berlin-Vienna Distance Ride had been clear and that the military administration was unaware of any behavior that could remotely be classified as animal abuse.[42] Thereafter, the commission voted (with only one dissent) that the Reichstag had no jurisdiction to act on such a petition. No further action was taken.

Despite the strong official government defense of the riders, substantial criticism had already begun to emerge from within the military itself. Perhaps the most important was from General Heinrich von Rosenberg, who was a key figure in the development of the German cavalry, one of the founders of the Hanoverian Riding Club, and widely seen as a master of cavalry tactics and training. In the *Militär-Wochenblatt*, a weekly Berlin newspaper written by and for members of the German military, Rosenberg praised the participants in the Berlin-Vienna Distance Ride for their incredible performance. However, he also regretted the sacrifice of so many noble horses for what he saw as rather negligible military usefulness. In the crucible of war, he suggested, most patrols would never be required to travel such distances. Extreme distance rides, therefore, were much less useful as either training exercises or measures of military effectiveness than shorter rides over the open countryside—such as traditional hunting rides.[43] Rosenberg certainly did not mean his comments as a challenge to the integrity of the individual riders. Nevertheless, his printed remarks reverberated through the upper levels of the military. If this was not enough, even former chancellor Otto von Bismarck criticized the event in an interview with the journalist Hans Blum. According to Bismarck, "Such a performance would never be required of horse and rider during wartime, and it was thus a true shame that noble horses were sacrificed in this foolishness."[44]

Interestingly, in the midst of this public firestorm, several of the riders, including three of the four top finishers, chose to defend themselves in public with speeches and published accounts of their experiences, which often included detailed descriptions of their relationship with their own horses. It is not possible here to do justice to the variety of those responses, which ranged from depictions of the deep emotional bonds individual riders had forged with their animals to the blunt claim that horses were weapons of war whose occasional sacrifice was regrettable but necessary. Although individual riders had significantly different explanations and justifications for what had happened, they each defended their own masculine honor and the noble sacrifices the animals had made on their behalf.[45] What is clear here is that an event that was intended to glorify standards of elite martial masculinity had instead subjected such standards and values to increased public scrutiny. Still, the furor generated by this event did not end the practice of long-distance horse races, much less steeplechases and other races that could also produce horse fatalities. In fact, the Berlin-Vienna Distance Ride was repeated in 1909—but this time with additional safety precautions for horses and riders.[46]

Conclusion

It is clear that the Great Berlin-Vienna Distance Ride of 1892 was a complex cultural ritual: a diplomatic exchange, a military exercise, an international sporting event, a nationalist spectacle, a social gathering, an urban showcase, and an attempt to celebrate elite martial masculinity. Rather than simply affirming cultural norms, however, this event served as a contested text on which rival groups in German society could seek to inscribe their own diverse models of class relations, gender roles, and national belonging. Post-race commentaries complained about the poor performance of German riders and also bemoaned the relative cultural inferiority of Berlin in comparison to its more sophisticated Austrian rival. Critics also used the death and maiming of dozens of horses during the race as a blunt instrument to challenge German social elites and criticize their models of martial masculinity.

Perhaps the best evidence of the complicated legacy of the Great Berlin-Vienna Distance Ride is the fact that several additional racing competitions were staged the following summer between Berlin and Vienna, each intended to mimic the 1892 horse race to capitalize on the publicity it had generated while also showcasing alternative models of what it meant to be a masculine sportsman. These races included a footrace, a cycling race, and even a homing pigeon race—each sponsored by predominantly bourgeois sporting associations. While none of these subsequent races generated the same levels of publicity or controversy as the original distance ride, each was groundbreaking within its own sporting discipline and each provided an opportunity for middle- and lower-middle-class athletes to appropriate and reenact the glory of the original horse race while also emphasizing the superiority of their own bourgeois models of masculine excellence. Like the Great Berlin-Vienna Distance Ride, all of these subsequent races also used the capital city and emerging sports metropolis of Berlin as their symbolic launch point.

Notes

1. Tatsuya Mitsuda rightly singles out the *Distanzritt* (distance ride) as a rich text that is relevant to three separate historiographical fields: animal history, sports history, and military history. See Tatsuya Mitsuda, "Training Horse and Rider for War? Equine Sport, Military Use, and the Industrialisation of Society: Imperial Germany in Transnational Perspective," *Hiyoshi Review of the Humanities*, no. 34 (2019): 236–38, https://koara.lib.keio.ac.jp/xoonips /modules/xoonips/download.php/AN10065043-20190630-0233.pdf?file_id=142956.

2. The Austro-Hungarian side of the story has both similarities to and differences from events in Germany, and local reactions to the event there were tied to the unique political and cultural context of the Austro-Hungarian Empire.

3. William Anthony Young, *German Diplomatic Relations 1871–1945: The Wilhelmstrasse and the Formulation of Foreign Policy* (New York: iUniverse, 2009), 55–56, 78–81. There is substantial recent scholarship on the internationalization of sport and the growth of sports diplomacy in the late nineteenth century. See, for example, Stuart Murray, *Sports Diplomacy: Origins, Theory and Practice* (London: Routledge, 2019).

4. A more detailed account of the festivities below and in E. von Naundorff [Andreas Hugo Elm], *Der grosse Distanzritt Berlin—Wien im Jahre 1892* (Breslau: Verlag J. Paul Lis, 1893), https://archive.org/details/dergrossedistanzoonaun/page/n9.

5. "Nennungen zum Distanzritt Berlin—Wien," *Militär-Wochenblatt* 77, no. 72 (August 20, 1892): 1903–7, https://catalog.hathitrust.org/Record/008607293.

6. For a discussion of this race in the context of changes in military strategy, new views on the art of horsemanship, and alternate priorities for horse breeding, see Mitsuda, "Training Horse and Rider."

7. Heinrich von Rosenberg, "Distanzritt Berlin—Wien," *Militär-Wochenblatt* 77, no. 89 (October 12, 1892): 2265–71, https://babel.hathitrust.org/cgi/pt?id=nyp.33433009268370 &view=1up&seq=359.

8. The Große Armee-Jagdrennen was held annually from 1862 to 1914. The race was praised on its silver anniversary for having improved German *Reitergeist* (riding spirit) to such an extent that it helped guarantee victory against France in 1870. See "Zum Silbernen Jubiläum Des Großen Armee-Jagd-Rennens in Berlin," *Norddeutsche Allgemeine Zeitung*, June 8, 1888, Abend-Ausgabe, 1.

9. See, for example, the 1889 advertisement for the journal *Sportwelt* printed in the *Berliner Börsen-Zeitung*, no. 225, May 15, 1889, Morgen-Ausgabe, 10.

10. Gerd von Ende, *Berliner Hufgeklapper: Pferde als Spiegel der Vergangenheit* (Hamburg: tredition, 2020), 177. On the more general transformations within the Berlin media during this era, see chapter two of Barnet Hartston, *The Trial of Gustav Graef:*

Art, Sex, and Scandal in Late Nineteenth-Century Germany (DeKalb: Northern Illinois University Press, 2017) and the appendix of Barnet Hartston, *Sensationalizing the Jewish Question: Antisemitic Trials and the Press in the Early German Empire* (Leiden: Brill, 2005).

11. Naundorff, *Der grosse Distanzritt*, 123–24. The play at the Burgtheater was *Wilddiebe* (the poachers), a light comedy cowritten by Theodor Herzl. It was most successful play of Herzl's career, written years before his turn to Zionist activism.

12. See a remarkably detailed description of post-race Berlin festivities in Naundorff, *Der grosse Distanzritt*, 143–60.

13. *Berliner Tageblatt*, no. 513, October 9, 1892, Morgen-Ausgabe, 5, http://zefys .staatsbibliothek-berlin.de/list/title/zdb/27646518/.

14. Franz Höfer, *In 74 Stunden von der Donau bis zur Spree: Schilderung meines Rittes als Theilnehmer an dem im Oktober 1892 stattgefundenen grossen Distanzritte "Wien-Berlin"* (Innsbruck: Im Selbstverlag des Verfassers, 1893), 31.

15. Ann Goldberg, *Honor, Politics, and the Law in Imperial Germany, 1871–1914* (Cambridge: Cambridge University Press, 2010), 51.

16. Albin Friedrich Reitzenstein, *Mein Distanzritt Berlin—Wien, Vortrag, gehalten in der militärischen Gesellschaft zu Berlin am 7. Dezember 1892* (Berlin: Ernst Siegfried Mittler und Sohn, 1893), 26.

17. Elm, under the pseudonym E. von Naundorff, wrote his book based on newspaper reports and the riders' own personal accounts of their experiences. See Naundorff, *Der grosse Distanzritt*, 5.

18. Starhemberg won twenty-four major races between 1887 and 1892, including six of thirty-three races run in 1892. See "Oberlieutenant Graf W. Starhemberg," *Allgemeine Sport-Zeitung*, October 9, 1892. Reitzenstein won the prestigious Pressburg Steeplechase in 1892 and 1893, both times using horses bred by the famous horse breeder and racer Niklolaus von Esterházy. See Naundorff, *Der grosse Distanzritt*, 71.

19. See Jakob Vogel, "Military, Folklore, *Eigensinn*: Folkloric Militarism in Germany and France, 1871–1914," *Central European History* 33, no. 4 (2000): 487–504, especially 491–92.

20. "Distanz-Ritt Berlin—Wien," *Berliner Tageblatt*, no. 505, October 5, 1892, Morgen-Ausgabe, 3, http://zefys.staatsbibliothek-berlin.de/list/title/zdb/27646518/.

21. Naundorff, *Der grosse Distanzritt*, 77.

22. *Berliner Tageblatt*, no. 508, October 6, 1892, Abend-Ausgabe, 4, http://zefys. staatsbibliothek-berlin.de/list/title/zdb/27646518/.

23. *Berliner Tageblatt*, no. 510, October 7, 1892, Abend-Ausgabe, 4; *Berliner Tageblatt*, no. 513, October 9, 1892, Morgen-Ausgabe, 3, http://zefys.staatsbibliothek-berlin.de/list/title /zdb/27646518/.

24. "Der Distanzritt Berlin—Wien," *Berliner Tageblatt*, no. 499, October 1, 1892, Abend-Ausgabe, 3, http://zefys.staatsbibliothek-berlin.de/list/title/zdb/27646518/.

25. "Zum Distanzritt Berlin—Wien," *Berliner Tageblatt*, no. 506, October 5, 1892, Abend-Ausgabe, 3, http://zefys.staatsbibliothek-berlin.de/list/title/zdb/27646518/. There is reason to doubt the identification of these men as Zulus since exhibitors of indigenous people often substituted one ethnic group for another if authentic representatives were unavailable. See Angela Zimmerman, *Anthropology and Antihumanism in Imperial Germany* (Chicago: University of Chicago Press, 2001), 20.

26. Zimmerman, *Anthropology and Antihumanism*, 18.

27. Zimmerman, *Anthropology and Antihumanism*, 19.

28. Zimmerman, *Anthropology and Antihumanism*, 25–36. A few years later, Merker returned to German East Africa, where he became a renowned plant-collector and wrote the first ethnography of the Maasai. After the bloody rebellion of Mangi Meli in 1900, Merker sent the skulls of thousands of executed indigenous rebels back to Germany for study. These are among the 5,500 skulls of African men still in the possession of the Stiftung Preußischer Kulturbesitz in Berlin today.

29. This was apparently part of a longer history of disappointing performances by German riders. See Mitsuda, "Training Horse and Rider," 253.

30. *Berliner Tageblatt*, no. 513, October 9, 1892, Morgen-Ausgabe, 5, http://zefys. staatsbibliothek-berlin.de/list/title/zdb/27646518/.

31. *Berliner Tageblatt*, no. 513, October 9, 1892, Morgen-Ausgabe, 5, http://zefys. staatsbibliothek-berlin.de/list/title/zdb/27646518/.

32. Naundorff, *Der grosse Distanzritt*, 53.

33. Reitzenstein, *Mein Distanzritt Berlin—Wien*, 23–25; see also, Naundorff, *Der grosse Distanzritt*, 71–72.

34. At the time, Harden had just founded the weekly journal *Die Zukunft* (the future), which would serve as his long-time mouthpiece. Harden later became infamous for accusing Prince Philipp Eulenburg of homosexuality, which resulted in one of the biggest scandals of the German Empire. See Norman Domeier, *The Eulenburg Affair: A Cultural History of Politics in Imperial Germany*, trans. Deborah Lucas Schneider (New York: Camden House, 2015), 75.

35. Maximilian Harden, "Distanzritt Berlin—Wien," *Die Zukunft*, Band 1 (October 8, 1892): 92.

36. See, for example, the satirical poem "Nachklänge zum Distanzritt," in which an exhausted horse and rider decide it would be better to make a return trip to Berlin by train, in *Kladderadatsch*, no. 42, October 16, 1892, 167.

37. Kirsten Belgum, "Domesticating the Reader: Women and *Die Gartenlaube*," *Women in German Yearbook*, 9 (1993): 92.

38. "Distanzritt Und Humanität," *Die Gartenlaube*, 44 (1892): 740.

39. Verhandlungen des Deutschen Reichstags (May 2, 1893), Aktenstück, no. 217, p. 1173, accessed December 21, 2022, http://daten.digitale-sammlungen.de/bsb00018684 /image_533.

40. "Massgebliches und Unmassgebliches: Der Distanzritt und das Strafgesetz," *Die Grenzboten* 51, no. 4 (1892): 445–46. Harriet Ritvo describes a similar reluctance by the English RSPCA to directly condemn animal cruelty by English elites. She suggests the members of the RSPCA implicitly defined animal cruelty as uncivilized and barbaric, and thus inherently as a symptom of the "dangerous classes" rather than more respectable orders of society. Harriet Ritvo, *The Animal Estate: The English and Other Creatures in the Victorian Age* (Cambridge, MA: Harvard University Press, 1987), 131–35.

41. Verhandlungen des Deutschen Reichstags, December 3, 1892, 143–51, accessed December 21, 2022, http://www.reichstagsprotokolle.de/Blatt3_k8_bsb00018680_00189.

42. Verhandlungen des Deutschen Reichstags, May 2, 1893, Aktenstück, no. 217, 1173, accessed December 21, 2022, http://daten.digitale-sammlungen.de/bsb00018684/image_533.

43. Heinrich von Rosenberg, "Distanzritt Berlin—Wien," *Militär-Wochenblatt* 77, no. 89 (October 12, 1892): 2265–71.

44. Blum was no objective journalist, but a pro-Bismarck publicist who later published laudatory biographical works. Hans Blum, *Ein Tag in Varzin Beim Fürsten Bismarck: Separatabdruck Aus Den Leipziger Neueste Nachrichten* (Leipzig: Herfurth, 1892), https://babel.hathitrust.org/Record/100543542.

45. Tatsuya Mitsuda situates the race in the broader context of cavalry elites seeking to protect their assertion of specialized knowledge and special relationships with their horses—in contrast to non-elite riders and English professional jockeys. See Mitsuda, "Training Horse and Rider."

46. Mitsuda, "Training Horse and Rider," 258.

CHAPTER TWO

Celebrity and Spectacle

Adolf von Guretzki's Influence on Berlin's Early Twentieth-Century Sports Writing

ALEC HURLEY

In a 1909 epistle bemoaning the use of alcohol in competitive strength sports, J. Petersen, an evangelical American reverend and author, cites a prolific assessment of the greatest continental wrestlers that had been compiled by Adolf von Guretzki, a Berlin sportswriter, two years prior.[1] By the time of his citation by Petersen, von Guretzki was an established newspaper columnist and serialist.[2] His detailed reports and occasional dramatic writings on strength sport and Germanness appeared in both leading national sporting weeklies and Berlin dailies throughout the 1890s and the first decade of the 1900s. His credibility as an author within the contemporaneous physical culture community around the turn of the twentieth century was cemented in his first book, *Der Moderne Ringkampf*, originally published in 1907. His overview of turn-of-the-century wrestling depicted the diets, habits, and training methods of the world's biggest wrestling and strength stars.[3] With characteristic analytical tone and straightforward delivery, von Guretzki summed up the training methods of the world's most notable wrestlers, writing that "[they] owe their success to physical agility and muscular strength, regular exercise, and the most temperate living."[4]

Prior to his emergence as a chronicler of the training regimens and accomplishments of continental strongmen, von Guretzki engaged in his own literary wrestling. As Germany, and Berlin in particular, forged itself into a rising power over the late nineteenth century, the populace faced a struggle between a pastoral legacy and an urbanized future. In his capacity as a Berlin-based strength correspondent for the largest German sports newspaper, *Illustrirte Deutsche Athleten-Zeitung*,[5] von Guretzki embodied the cultural unease of his fellow Berliners. His serialized sport novelette—the earliest of its kind—depicted burgeoning urban sport through thrilling spectacle and captivating celebrity, all the while generating a narrative extolling the dynamic traits of urbanism and weaving them alongside an appreciation for Germany's rural traditionalism. Due in part to the newspaper's widespread popularity—a subscribed readership nearing one hundred thousand—his tale provided a compelling case for the acceptance of urbanism, particularly urban sport in Berlin.[6] Von Guretzki's serialized work presents one of the earliest attempts to promote the dynamic and transcultural elements of urbanization over traditional perceptions of rural pastoralism. His success on this front, deftly achieved through a progressive presentation of the urban center without overtly chastising revered rural pastoralism, places von Guretzki's writing in its own esteemed category.

Through his descriptions of his fictional strongman, von Guretzki revealed and elevated the emerging cultural dynamism of Berlin. The metaphorical wrestling between Berlin's energetic urbanism and Germany's poetic rusticism captured in von Guretzki's work mirrored a broader cultural struggle over the place of the city as a central feature of modern Germanness. Defining the urban and the rural in Germany is complicated by their frequently intertwined history. Historian Kristin Poling argues that Berlin's outward expansion in the mid-eighteenth century allowed the city to preserve "a partially rural character well into the nineteenth century."[7] Perceptions of German, and specifically Berlin, urbanism oscillated between utopian projections of a dynamic nation and dystopian visions filled with greedy bureaucrats and disdainful philistines.[8] As politicians and citizens backed their respective visions during the early decades of Imperial Germany, artists—writers especially—embraced the conflicting yet intimately linked notions of the urban and rural in their works.

Rural and folk sport were particularly important to Germans during this period as the legendary German strongmen performers of the mid-nineteenth century mostly hailed from the small villages in the country's bucolic interior. As a result, a mythical narrative emerged that linked the ideas of strength and the countryside together in the public imagination. As the German Empire coalesced over the 1870s and 1880s, sporting traditions became a moderating and unifying pursuit among culturally similar but politically distinct groups.[9] Over the course of the 1890s, the tone of the *Illustrirte Deutsche Athleten-Zeitung*'s coverage of traditional Bavarian and

Austrian sports oscillated between reverence for their cultural heritage and a distaste for their rural and often mountainous isolation. One of the folk games that earned the most coverage was *Raggeln*, a form of folk wrestling from the Tyrol region. Raggeln received extensive front-page coverage by the *Illustrirte Deutsche Athleten-Zeitung*, and its rules and cross-border heritage received in-depth explanations, all with an explicit emphasis on the natural beauty of the game's outdoor setting and traditional dress.[10] Finally, press coverage of Raggeln often highlighted the communal nature of the sport, with its emphasis on community over singular celebrity, to demonstrate the appeal of traditional German values. The allure of urban dynamism proved overwhelming, however, and by the late 1890s, coverage of urban wrestling and lifting matches with outsized personalities overshadowed the coverage dedicated to folk games.

The elevation of the urban as driven by the celebrity and spectacle of the sports world mirrored and glamorized Berlin's late nineteenth-century transformation into a dynamic, urban cosmopolitan center and an increasingly anxious aspirant to the global stage.[11] The elevation of urban sport led to an increase in event coverage and particularly to the meteoric ascent of sport celebrities—especially within strength sport. Although the newly added serialized columns in the *Illustrirte Deutsche Athleten-Zeitung* were slow to cover the proliferation of these strength-sport celebrities, the continued use and content of serialized narratives within the German sporting press demonstrated the importance of celebrity and spectacle to the formation of Berlin's identity at the turn of the twentieth century.

While only one of von Guretzki's athletic novelettes survives, it provides striking insight into the perspectives of and influences upon Berlin urbanites during a transformative period in Germany's history. His four-thousand-word story explores issues surrounding the emergence of the celebrity athlete, the depiction of foreign cultures, and, most crucially, the promotion of urban virtues and values over those of rural traditionalism. His work establishes a revitalized foundation through which to examine the role of sport and its commentators in sociocultural development, especially during times of tremendous cultural transformation. The expansion of the *Illustrirte Deutsche Athleten-Zeitung* during the 1890s mirrored the efforts of the newly unified German Empire as it sought to establish both its own identity and a more significant role within a globalized world. Michelle Murray summarized the public apprehensions surrounding both tasks, writing that "owing to primary identifications to local notions of tradition, loyalty, and belonging, most of the empire's inhabitants struggled to identify as German."[12] In gymnasiums, fields, and circuses throughout the nation, a desire to cling to the national-istic sporting narratives of the *Turner* (gymnast) that had been established by Friedrich Ludwig Jahn in the early part of the century was balanced by a competing desire to place German sport and recreation within a more global—and increasingly urban—community. Those tensions, underscored by the shift of popular focus from rural folk sports to imported and exotic urban sports, were repeatedly addressed within and plastered on the cover of what became the most widely read sports paper of its time.[13]

Operating against the backdrop of the economic, architectural, and artis-tic revolution that consumed newly united Germany in the late nineteenth century, the sports writers of Berlin embraced sport as an embodiment of cultural spectacle. They promoted that spectacle through comparing international competitions to geopolitical struggles and through heroizing present and historic Germanic strongmen. Their most effective tool, however, was the addition of long-running sports tales to industry organs in 1898, particularly in the serialized novelette format.[14] Von Guretzki's serialized novelette was the first to appear in a leading German sport newspaper of the 1890s. It related the fictional adventures of a German strongman in Egypt as he contended with exoticism and celebrity and navigated between Eastern and Western conceptions of modernized urban space. This story is emblematic of many that followed in its portrayal of Berliners' emerging and fluid perceptions of sport as spectacle during the transformative era of the turn of the twentieth century. It demonstrates the allure of the cult of celebrity, the excitement of sporting spectacles, and the fear of the perceived vices of urban expansion as they were experienced by athletic practitioners and audiences alike.

Berlin and von Guretzki through Words and Action

Von Guretzki and his contemporaries were part of an emerging sportswrit-ing profession that accompanied the rise of modern urban centers in the late nineteenth century. The rapid industrialization of Berlin's economic and cultural environment was facilitated through transformative scientific universities and technologically driven economic advances that cemented the city's place among Europe's leading metropolises.[15] The growth of the sportswriting profession was supported by the expansion of an already robust culture of artistic and literary expression.[16] Newspapers offered a textual representation of the cultural paradox of Berlin's rural traditionalism and urban spectacle. Von Guretzki's fictional narrative, serialized over the spring of 1898, was an ambitious attempt to reconcile the values and practices of traditional German strength sports with the growing cosmopolitan emphasis on performance and celebrity.

The first issues of the *Illustrirte Deutsche Athleten-Zeitung* were published at the start of 1893. Based in Munich, the paper began as a social commentary on traditional German strength sports, recreation, and entertainment. While many of its contemporary, sport-specific publications gave significant coverage to international sports, the *Illustrirte Deutsche Athleten-Zeitung* reflected late nineteenth-century German apprehensions toward foreign sports and instead focused its attention on strength sports, including various forms of wrestling (such as Raggeln) and exhibitions of strongmen and -women.[17] Notably, the paper was skeptical of the influence of British and French sports.[18]

Von Guretzki was one of *Illustrirte Deutsche Athleten-Zeitung's* first columnists to embrace the might and celebrity of foreign strongmen who made their careers in Berlin's rival cosmopolitan centers of London and Paris. Importantly, however, he did so by grafting the key features of those showstopping strongmen onto a fictional Berliner. Donner, the protagonist of von Guretzki's story, was modeled on the gentleman-athlete persona that had been made famous by prominent French strength performer Charles Batta.[19] Batta's reputation for pristine manners, dapper dress, and exquisite stage presence earned him a reputation as not only a legendary strength performer but also the epitome of the dynamic urban athlete.[20] Therefore, by employing Batta's persona as the underlying demeanor of his protagonist, von Guretzki invited his German audience to embrace this new iteration of the sport hero. His intentional presentation of Donner as a refined yet powerful urbanite represented a distinctive shift away from the venerated German folk-wrestlers and strongmen of the 1880s. As such, he elevated the virtues of Berlin's urban transformation in a manner palatable to those more inclined to pastoral reverence.

As the cult of celebrity captivated Berlin as it had comparative European metropolises of the era, sports journalism—and more importantly, sport novelization—offered a unique perspective on the cultural perceptions of urban spaces. The *Illustrirte Deutsche Athleten-Zeitung's* ascendance to the six-figure readership mark by the beginning of the twentieth century demonstrated the reading public's sustained interest in pure sports coverage.[21] In 1899, the paper's audience was more than double what the *Spirit of the Times*, one of the leading sports magazines in the United States, had boasted at the peak of its popularity in the 1840s.[22] Furthermore, the *Illustrirte Deutsche Athleten-Zeitung* held its own against the leading men's magazine of the time, Richard Fox's *National Police Gazette*, which averaged roughly 150,000 readers in the United States throughout the last two decades of the nineteenth century.[23]

The prioritization of folk and rural sport remained the dominant theme in sporting presses across Germany and the Western world. Although contemporary international sporting outlets still prominently featured sports like football, cricket, and baseball, those in the United States often highlighted the mythology present in the rural sports of horse racing and cockfighting, and those in the United Kingdom routinely emphasized endurance feats in contests such as pedestrianism and rowing.[24] In late 1898, however, the *Illustrirte Deutsche Athleten-Zeitung* underwent a leadership change. The German Strength Federation formally assumed control of the paper in January 1899, and the result was a weekly publication that functioned as an organ of the federation. The move was not uncommon; plenty of sport publications in the United States and the United Kingdom were funded or more broadly supported by specific sport governing associations at some point during the late nineteenth century.[25]

Since the German Strength Federation favored traditional forms of strength and combat sports, reports on urban spectacles faded from the *Illustrirte Deutsche Athleten-Zeitung's* pages. Von Guretzki, however, stood apart from his fellow writers during this era of transition in his willingness to embrace prominent contemporary urban sporting figures. In fact, his insistence on prioritizing the urban in his writing may well have influenced the *Illustrirte Deutsche Athleten-Zeitung's* later decision to cut down on or out-right eliminate fictional accounts that questioned the pastoral origins of strength sport in Germany and, by extension, their place as signifiers of Germanness. This is ultimately speculative, as responses to von Guretzki serialized work never appeared in the outlet of its publication. Nevertheless, his work—both fictional and expository—ensured that the values of urban sport spectacles were infused into the historical narrative. The focus of his works, both as a journalist and later as an author, centered on the allure of celebrity status as a desirable wish. The positioning of the celebrity as an enviable character was a concept that had not yet been explored by his fellow sportswriters outside Berlin, who contented themselves with traditional folk and rural sport narratives.

One of the reasons von Guretzki saw the celebrity athlete as an aspirational character was that he had covered the densely packed urban shows taking place in dingy theaters throughout the early 1890s and had seen how the facilities and glamour available to athletes increased exponentially as they advanced. By presenting the celebrity athlete as a character striving for a better life, he made the cult of celebrity within a realm that was often perceived of as a vice-filled spectacle palatable to a wide audience. Von Guretzki held the Palast Theater, previously known as the Feen-Palace, in high esteem. The free-standing building was built beside the river Spree in the mid-1880s to serve as a warehouse, but it found its true calling as an entertainment hall in the early 1890s.[26] In its capacity as an entertainment hall, it hosted plays, concerts, and political rallies—most radically those by the nascent Social Democrat Party.[27] Von Guretzki returned to the building in November and December 1904 as an honorary judge for a series of high-profile wrestling matches. He represented the *Illustrirte Deutsche Athleten-Zeitung* in his capacity as a referee and worked the month-long event alongside Carl Jänecke and Robert Röpnack. Several notable athletes who later appeared in his first book, *Der Moderne Ringkampf*, took part in the competition, including runner-up John Pohl (Abs II) and the legendary George Lurich, who placed fourth.

Von Guretzki was able to capture the energy, excitement, fear, and wonder of the urban sport spectacle because he immersed himself in it as both a journalist and an aficionado. During his time as a leading journalist for the *Illustrirte Deutsche Athleten-Zeitung* he also acted as a referee for large-scale wrestling and strength tournaments in Berlin, and throughout the first decade of the 1900s he helped to facilitate the very kinds of urban spectacles he wrote about during the previous decade. When von Guretzki appeared in outlets other than the *Illustrirte Deutsche Athleten-Zeitung*, it was often for his promoting or officiating strength contests or wrestling matches rather than his covering them.[28] In one of his more outlandish promotions, he, in his capacity as a representative of the *Illustrirte Athleten Sportzeitung*, advertised a small wrestling match in Berlin by cleverly placing their event second on the bill beneath the headliner, "The Lion Bride, Miss Heliot and her Twelve Lions."[29] The first competition he is listed as having officiated was a two-day wrestling event that was part of the Schuman Circus in Berlin and took place less than three years after the publication of his first serialized novelette on urban strength sport.[30]

Despite abundant records of von Guretzki as a reporter and match official, little was recorded of his personal life. This is not in itself unsurprising. Strength and circus performers often existed in a world of exaggerated realities and fabricated origin stories. Therefore, to expect any different of the first generation of reporters covering those intentionally mysterious individuals would be presumptuous. Additionally, it was not uncommon for sport correspondents—especially those tasked with creating snarky or novelized pieces—to begin their careers during their teenage years when the financial support of their families often became less reliable.[31] What records do indicate is a significant number of von Guretzkis living in Berlin at the peak of Adolf von Guretzki's professional productivity. Two Berlin von Guretzkis—a Marie Auguste and Franz Anton—were recorded as being born in 1874 and living to 1954 and 1966, respectively. An obituary for a younger boy, Adolf Thomas Guretzki, showed that he was born in Berlin in 1911.[32] The latter provides a tangential, though far from definitive, opening to speculate that the journalist Adolf von Guretzki could have been of child-rearing age by this time. Another piece of circumstantial evidence that places von Guretzki among those listed in genealogical records is his obituary of the German strongman, spiritualist, and pioneer dietitian Theodor Siebert in 1954.[33] In one of his last popular pieces, von Guretzki criticized Siebert for using "profits from the paternal business" to rebrand himself as a restaurateur in the early 1890s.[34] It is likely that von Guretzki would have been familiar with Siebert's restaurant as it was located somewhere between Berlin and Leipzig, well within the area on which von Guretzki would have been actively reporting during that time for the *Illustrirte Deutsche Athleten-Zeitung*.

In Berlin, no singular sports paper—or sports section—ever matched the physical or cultural reach of the *Illustrirte Deutsche Athleten-Zeitung*. Collectively though, by the mid-1920s the Berlin sports media apparatus had become a well-polished operation. The two dailies *B.Z. am Mittag* and *Berliner Tageblatt* both employed a robust staff of sport writers, although the former was the true Berlin sporting powerhouse. *B.Z. am Mittag* was not exclusively a sporting newspaper, but its purchase in 1904 by Berlin newspaper magnate Leopold Ullstein transformed its coverage to provide a greater focus on sports.[35] During its ascent through the sport media ranks, the paper employed between six and twelve full-time sports reporters and, in a revolutionary move, prioritized coverage of football. The foreign influences of the game and its proletariat roots caused the coverage to shift to a more narrative style, with compelling stories buttressing what had once been brief notes of results and fixtures fitted in among advertisements on the back pages.[36] Even then, the widest breadth of circulation *B.Z. am Mittag* ever managed was 125,000 subscribers in 1914. Several rival sporting presses in Berlin dedicated themselves fully to the world of sport. The three most notable were *Sport im Bild, Illustrierter Sport,* and *Sport und Sonne.* Perhaps unsurprisingly, advances in photography made producing more accurate depictions of increasingly accessible live sporting spectacles more feasible. What all these papers had in common was their ability to weave together social analysis, cultural commentary, and celebrity profiles.[37]

As the Berlin sport and newspaper industries evolved into culturally conscious outlets willing to use sport as an expression of the German populace, one of its earliest proponents faded from view. Following World War I, von Guretzki applied his talent for longform writing to the realm of expanded training manuals and athlete diet manifests. In the mid-1920s, his work *Lexicon der Schwerathletik* became an industry standard training manual as well as a reference point for alternative paths to muscle building. One of the methods promoted in *Lexicon der Schwerathletik* was the use of swimming pools. His reputation as an established journalist and insider to the training regimens of the elite strength performers of the prewar era compelled individuals such as Karl Fürst to seek him out to pursue the potential of pools as a new frontier of athletic and social interest.[38] The book was closer in form to a practical training guide than a full monograph, comprising a mere eighty pages including publisher notes. While brevity eventually became one of his more notable attributes as a writer, the full title of his debut work is almost fifty words long, even though the content—profiles of the diet and training regiments of dozens of wrestling champions from 1895 to 1905—covers just under one hundred pages. Von Guretzki went back to this work several times, providing updates and revisions whenever he could. The last of his four revised editions was published in 1923; the bulk of the work, and certainly its emphasis on celebrity and personal betterment, never altered.[39]

Von Guretzki left the arena of fiction writing following his sole endeavor in the spring of 1898. In that brief span of seven installments, he articulated several concepts that came to define Berlin, as well as German sports writing, for the following two decades. His prioritization of urban sport and the intermingling of classes in the audience were loosely inspired by his own travels as a young sports reporter covering elite strength competitions and wrestling matches at the fabled entertainment halls of Berlin.

Serialized Spectacle and Celebrity

The first serialized story to appear in the pages on the *Illustrirte Deutsche Athleten-Zeitung* was titled *"Raad" (Donner)* and described as an "Arabic Tale." The novelette itself, often published on the paper's front-page, ran from January 9 through June 19, 1898. The work was published in seven parts over this six-month period, with a long break between the sixth installment's publication in early March and the conclusion's publication in mid-June.[40] The primary reason for the delay of the finale was the relegation of all non-championship news to the back pages or off the press completely. Despite the logistic hang-ups, however, von Guretzki's piece continued throughout the spring months.

From the start, von Guretzki reinforces the connection between his main character and the emerging ideal of the celebrity gentleman performer. When introducing the story's antagonists, a group of Bedouin bandits, von Guretzki has their leader regale his associates with the origin story of Charles Batta. In a remarkable line toward the end of this story within a story, the leader relates that Batta "traveled in the company of the champion wrestlers of France, but the victories of Arpin, Marseille, and Rabasson left him cold, his ideal was not wrestling, but rather the power of Samson."

Von Guretzki's protagonist, Donner, exhibits similar gentlemanly, Samson-esque qualities. The character is first introduced after having daringly rescued the English leader of the Arabian expedition, which he is then asked to join.[41] When the traveling party is betrayed by their Bedouin guides in the desert at night, it is Donner who relies on his career as a strength athlete to nearly thwart the attempt by lifting a collapsed tent and allowing some of his compatriots to make a feeble escape.[42] Finally, despite his aversion to wrestling—a trait he shared with his real-life inspiration Charles Batta—Donner

The first installment of von Guretzki's serialized work *"Raad" (Donner)* in the *Illustrirte Deutsche Athleten-Zeitung. Obtained from the Milo Steinborn Collection at the H. J. Lutcher Stark Center at the University of Texas at Austin.*

quickly dispenses of a succession of Cairo's wrestling champions before using his prize money to bribe officials into allowing him to break his traveling party out of the prison adjacent to the auditorium.[43]

Thus, in addition to providing a measure of insight into the possibly hollow echoes of athletic fame, von Guretzki's description of Batta's career and the internal struggle of the fictionalized Donner mirrors a passage in the famed work of early strength celebrities. Edmond Desbonnet's 1901 book, *Les Rois de la Force*, used eerily similar language to describe the first gentleman athlete.[44] Celebrity status was quickly becoming more prominent in Berlin by the late nineteenth century. The bygone era of the singular and quasi-mythical German strongman from the countryside à la Hans Beck and Carl Abs was replaced by an increasingly international array of strength-sport stars. These international competitors from Turkey, France, Egypt, and Italy flocked to Berlin in the late 1890s to test and refine their showmanship in front of crowds eager for a display.

The crowds eager for a display in von Guretzki's tale, however, inhabit a world far different from urbane European metropolises. Despite the central location of his story being several thousand miles to the south of Berlin and separated by land, sea, and culture, the imprints of Berlin's sporting scene upon the story's setting are unmistakable. Donner is a longtime circus performer and low-level celebrity contemplating retirement, hoping for one last chance to prove himself. The infrastructure and glamour of the competition facilities are modeled—in character if not in architecture—after those of the great entertainment halls of Berlin. The addition of an otherworldly element to the tale adds a layer of intrigue for a German population eager to place their nation among colonial powers.

At the turn of the twentieth century, serialized novelizations of sport and German cultural spectacle typically featured a resistance to an increasingly global world. Such long-running fictional narratives were the primary vehicles for depicting Middle Eastern and African cultures as mystical and devious. While German Orientalism arguably never reached the breadth of its British or French counterparts, Jennifer Jenkins maintains that the Orient existed within German culture as a form of classical artistic expression. She argued that even though German Orientalism was "never actual" compared to similar European powers, the German idea of the Orient penetrated lyrics, fantasies, and novels throughout the late nineteenth century.[45]

Donner is accompanied on his journey by a supporting cast of several Westerners—a prominent British scholar and his team along with several bumbling Americans—on an excursion in Egypt. The party is eventually betrayed, captured, and imprisoned by their "ruthless" Bedouin guides.[46]

Through a series of defeats and daring escapes, the strongman is eventually able to free his companions by breaking them out of a jail cell through various feats of strength. The tale opens with a description of four Bedouin antagonists who reside just outside the city of Cairo. The bare-footed mercenaries are presented as plainly dressed, with mannerisms clearly intended to convey their maliciousness. The first antagonist to appear, a young man by the name of Ianger, is introduced as someone "whose deviousness and rudeness were evident at first sight."[47] Their weapons, described as "beautifully made," and their "finest breed" of Arabian horses stood in stark contrast to von Guretzki's otherwise dirty descriptions of the Bedouin people. Behind the young Ianger rode the leader Anje Tajeb and two of his followers, Kalil Anub and Osta Ecid.

Throughout the first two chapters of von Guretzki's work, all four are shown to be devious, underhanded, and self-interested. On the surface, his depictions of the Africans in the story fall directly in line with established Orientalist rhetoric of the age. However, von Guretzki eventually complicates his own picture. By the story's end the readers are exposed to urban Egyptians, specifically the wealthy of Cairo, whom von Guretzki describes in glowing terms. Even the emcee and servants presiding over the penultimate strength show are described as elegant, reserved, and polished. Their comparison with the Bedouin guides depicts a more significant contrast along the urban-rural divide than any form of European or Arab Orientalist commentary. The delicacy with which the Egyptians are considered in von Guretzki's work was likely a manifestation of his admiration for the dominant African and Turkish wrestlers who found their way to entertainment halls in Berlin during the 1890s and 1900s. Turkish wrestlers frequently offering the leading German wrestlers their toughest bouts and fostered a measure of reluctant respect among the sporting press in Berlin and other Western countries. In addition to their physical prowess, von Guretzki also adopted the Turkish flair—in terms of colorful clothing and bejeweled training team—in his depiction of the Beaudoin antagonists of his tale. As such, even though they are depicted as the antagonists in his story, they are also a tool through which von Guretzki paid homage to the non-Western wrestlers he counted alongside the continental athletes as the best in the world. In one of three eventual revisions of *Lexikon der Schwerathletik*, von Guretzki wrote that he considered the Turks the finest wrestlers because, although they often lacked "strict training," their abstinence from spirits endowed them with unparalleled strength and stamina.[48]

"Raad" (Donner) takes place in Beni-Suef, a critical port city and chief town of the second province of Upper Egypt during the late nineteenth century. It is located roughly one hundred kilometers south of Cairo along the Nile. Von Guretzki takes plenty of artistic license with the geography and spatial relationships of the region. In reality the two cities are separated by a full day's walk, yet von Guretzki has the captive Europeans moving between them in several hours as part of a Bedouin-style caravan or train.[49] While von Guretzki portrays the Bedouin antagonists in typical Orientalist style, he writes about the urban settings of the various cities in Egypt with the kind of praise usually reserved for European locales.

It is perhaps unsurprising that a story about kidnapped and imprisoned Westerners would present a less than ideal perspective on non-European individuals. However, von Guretzki inverts the typical Orientalist mythologizing with an unusually practical and endearing assessment of Egyptian urban centers. As the captives are brought back to Cairo to be jailed, von Guretzki depicts several cities along their route. Most notable is his description of Memphis, although in his tale, he calls the city *Mitrahenneh*—a Germanization of the Arabic *Mit Rahina*. He writes in awe of the ancient and functioning infrastructure on the legendary city, including the irrigation mill (*sakkiyeh*) and the abundance of sparkling white minarets.[50] He depicts Cairo in even more glowing terms. Understanding the importance of a central city—in terms of both political and cultural influence—von Guretzki is an unlikely narrator to be blown away by the Egyptian capital's grandeur. However, he treats the cultural fulcrum of the East and West with deference. Taking a break from his narration late in the sixth installment, von Guretzki describes the glorious gates of Bab al-Futuh and explains the role they played in Napoleon's expedition nearly a century earlier.[51] Although von Guretzki's assessment is slightly off geographically, the importance of his admiration for the foreign urban environment more than compensates.

In fact, he depicts the Western buildings in Beni-Suef and Cairo, particularly the British and American embassies, as decrepit compared to the Egyptian surroundings. Even the stage where Donner must perform a series of athletic feats and engage in competition is described in unequivocally glowing terms. The climax of the story takes place in a crowded auditorium where an upper-class Egyptian audience watches and gambles on various matches. The space is described as a refined spectacle. The auditorium is spacious and the stage broad enough to accommodate a full complement of professional wrestlers and strongmen. In addition, prior to the start of the contest, a high-ranking Egyptian official lays a purse containing a "great sum of money" on a side table surrounded by four elegantly dressed servants.[52]

The setting is a far cry from the less than ideal infrastructure to which Donner is used from his performance days traveling around Europe. A brilliant performer, Donner is impressed with the scene as he stands off-stage ready to simultaneously perform and negotiate an escape route.[53] The spectacle of the final competition highlights the impressiveness of von Guretzki's storytelling. The *Illustrirte Deutsche Athleten-Zeitung* often paired his story with front-page photos of various German athletic settings, mostly rural, outdoor affairs. The contrast provided in his story lends evidence to the desire among the widespread urban readership of the *Illustrirte Deutsche Athleten-Zeitung* for sport as a celebrity spectacle, an adventure as much as a contest.

Conclusion

The abundance and variety of sports-related newspapers that arose in Berlin following von Guretzki's serialized narrative and decade of correspondence mirrored Peter Fritzsche's description of Berlin as *allerlei*. The term, in relation to a city, can be defined as "a continuous stream of incidents, events, and impressions."[54] Fritzsche argues that the city itself is a spectacle, observed through the movement of crowds and the (occasionally sensationalized) reporting of the press.[55] The sensationalization and paradox of the press are important to adequately reflect the constant fluctuations in urban life. For Fritzsche, the Berlin press made a conscious effort to have their texts be simultaneously orderly and disruptive, invariably regulating ways in which the Berlin public saw and did not see.[56] Von Guretzki's work, at once elevating the celebrity sportsman and the dynamic urban environment from which he came, set the stage for twentieth-century expansions on those themes.

As von Guretzki moved away from the dynamism in the city, so too did later serialized pieces in the *Illustrirte Deutsche Athleten-Zeitung*. The limited appearances of fiction in the paper following *"Raad" (Donner)* focused less on appreciations of the urban spectacle and more on serene depictions of traditional German rural sporting pastimes. This shift tracks with the overall tenor of the paper following its takeover by the German Strength Federation, highlighted by its emphasis on local sport clubs and adherence to Germany's pastoral strength history. The immediate follow-up to *"Raad" (Donner)* was a serialized story authored by a Munich correspondent who drew upon the long tradition of strength sport in Bavaria. The work, *Thierbändiger Marco* written by Bruno Piper, tells the story of a farmhouse in rural southwest Germany that is visited by a prominent strongman traveling incognito.[57] The two works present a contrast in depictions and desires between the rural and urban. Piper presents the rural as an idyllic setting and the urban center as physically, emotionally, and mentally draining and debilitating. In that way, Piper's tale has far more in common with similar tales across cultural boundaries in which praise of rural sporting pursuits and a prioritization of the natural life reign supreme. In contrast, von Guretzki's story disowned the rural. While the extremes of Bedouin capture remain a fantastical element, the urban setting provided depictions of wealth, stability, and redemption.[58] Piper presents the countryside as an idyllic setting—for sport and for life. By extension, the idealization of the urban center, without veering into Orientalist rhetoric, places von Guretzki's work in a category unto itself. These two authors also represent a more metaphorical extension of Germany's search for identity during the last decade of the nineteenth century. Piper's pastoral depiction of Bavarian Germany is delightful but comes across as hackneyed and superficial and von Guretzki's fast-paced and compelling narrative relies upon exaggeratedly devious and heroic characters, but each author is searching for their place in a rapidly changing world. As a product of Berlin and the spectacle of urbanization that consumed the city for the entirety of the second half of the nineteenth century, von Guretzki's urban influence is palpable through his writing. While perhaps of a secondary concern in a sports outlet, von Guretzki's writing reveals Berlin's effect upon the sporting rhetoric of the newly unified German nation. His novelette presented a new way through which Germans could experience celebrity, diversity, and urban space from the perspective of a Berliner.

In von Guretzki's novelette it is never explicitly stated that Donner comes from Berlin. Indeed, he might hail from anywhere in the German-speaking territory. One can extrapolate from this that von Guretzki saw Berlin less as a physical place and more as a cultural phenomenon. Anyone who was willing to take a chance on Berlin, to experience the paradox and dynamism of a city experiencing cultural growth and tumult and survive, could consider themselves a Berliner. In this vein, his writings make it clear that he considered the great Turkish wrestlers who participated in extended tours of the city to be among Berlin's greats. This view of adopted celebrity ran at odds not only with his rurally-oriented contemporaries but also with Germany's modern sports media landscape. In 2018, Mesut Özil—a German-born star football player—left the German national team after facing brutal racist remarks challenging his Germanness.[59] The issues raised by Özil have not been resolved, but rather pushed to the side. At its core, he asked, what does it mean to be a German, a Berliner? In a spectacular story written 125 years ago, a young Berlin sports correspondent laid out an answer.

Notes

1. J. Petersen, "Wrestling and the Use of Alcohol," *Scientific Temperance Journal* 19, no. 1 (1909): 117.

2. "Raoul Le Boucher, 1883–February 13, 1907," Wrestling Epicenter, accessed January 19, 2023, http://www.wrestlingepicenter.com/RIP/RaoulBoucher.html.

3. Adolf von Guretzki, *Der Moderne Ringkampf* (Leipzig: F. W. Gloeckner, 1907), 3.

4. Petersen, "Wrestling and the Use of Alcohol," 117.

5. The name of the newspaper changed several times during the 1890s. The title of the outlet at the time of the publication of Adolf von Guretzki's serialized novelette (from March 28, 1897 to December 25, 1898) was *Illustrirte Deutsche Athleten-Zeitung*, and therefore this is the how the newspaper will be referenced throughout this chapter.

6. That is not to say sport itself was absent from the German literary tradition of the eighteenth and nineteenth centuries. For an example of sport in Goethe's stories and poems, see Michael Fritz Krüger, "Physical Education and Sport between Human Rights, Duties, and Obligations—Observations from Germany," *Societies* 11, no. 4, 127 (2021): 8.

7. Kristin Poling, "Shantytowns and Pioneers beyond the City Wall: Berlin's Urban Frontier in the Nineteenth Century," *Central European History* 47, no. 2 (2014): 247.

8. Robert Springer, *Berlin. Die deutsche Kaiserstadt nebst Potsdam und Charlottenburg mit ihren schonsten und hervorragendsten Monumentum* (Darmstadt: Verlag von Friedrich Lange, 1878), 64.

9. Douglas Booth, "Escaping the Past? The Cultural Turn and Language in Sport History," *Rethinking History* 8, no. 1 (2004): 105.

10. "Der beste Ranggler von Tirol," *Illustrirte Deutsche Athleten-Zeitung*, June 2, 1895. Aspects of the game explicitly covered in this article are its goals and rules, and its outdoor setting is referenced repeatedly.

11. David Hamlin, "Water and Empire: Germany, Bavaria and the Danube in World War I," *First World War Studies* 3, no. 1 (2012): 66–67.

12. Michelle Murray, *The Struggle for Recognition in International Relations: Status, Revisionism, and Rising Powers* (Oxford: Oxford University Press, 2019), 89.

13. Illustration with a calendar captioned "100,000 Subscribers," *Illustrirte Deutsche Athleten-Zeitung*, January 1, 1899, 1.

14. The serialized stories under examination typically ran between four thousand and eight thousand words, placing them just shy of the standard cutoff for the novella category, which is roughly ten thousand words.

15. Woodruff D. Smith, *Politics and the Sciences of Culture in Germany, 1840–1920* (Oxford: Oxford University Press, 1991), 224; Louis Menand, Paul Reitter, and Chad Wellmon, eds., *The Rise of The Research University: A Sourcebook* (Chicago: University of Chicago Press, 2017), 4.

16. Sabine Hake, *Topographies of Class: Modern Architecture and Mass Society in Weimar Berlin* (Ann Arbor: University of Michigan Press, 2008), 267.

17. For an example of the extensive coverage offered to German folk sport in the early days of the newspaper, see "Der beste Ranggler von Tirol," *Internationale Illustrirte Athleten-Zeitung,* June 5, 1895, 1–2. The multipage article addresses the cultural significance of the outdoor setting, along with a review of the rules and goals of the sport.

18. This skepticism can be seen in the paper excluding football from its coverage entirely throughout its run in the 1890s and in the minimal coverage it granted to the first two modern Olympic Games in 1896 and 1900.

19. Conor Heffernan, "Who Is Professor Attila?," Physical Culture Study, April 12, 2021, accessed November 29, 2022, www.physicalculturestudy.com/2021/04/12/who-is -professor-attila/.

20. David Chapman, *Sandown the Magnificent: Eugen Sandown and the Beginnings of Bodybuilding* (Urbana: University of Illinois Press, 1994), 10–11.

21. "Leserzahl wöchentlich 20,000 garantirt[*sic*]!," *Internationale Illustrirte Athleten-Zeitung,* January 1, 1894, 1; illustration with a calendar captioned "100,000 Abonnenten," *Illustrirte Deutsche Athleten-Zeitung,* January 1, 1899, 1.

22. Elliot J. Gorn and Warren Goldstein, *A Brief History of American Sports* (Urbana: University of Illinois Press, 1993), 67.

23. Brett McKay and Kate McKay, "America's First Popular Men's Magazine: The National Police Gazette," Art of Manliness, June 16, 2021, accessed November 15, 2022, https://www.artofmanliness.com/character/knowledge-of-men/americas-first-popular -mens-magazine-the-national-police-gazette/.

24. For attention to the rise of folk sport in Europe and North America, see: Melvin Adelman, *A Sporting Time: New York City and the Rise of Modern Athletics, 1820–70* (Urbana: University of Illinois Press, 1990); Steven A. Riess, *City Games: The Evolution of American Urban Society and the Rise of Sports* (Urbana: University of Illinois Press, 1991); James Riordan and Arnd Krüger, *European Cultures in Sport: Examining the Nations and Regions* (Bristol: Intellect Books, 2003).

25. Alec S. Hurley and Conor Heffernan, "Cartoon as Satire and Source: Jack Nicolle, Physical Culture, and Cartoons in 1920s Britain," *Sport in History* 43, no. 4 (2023): 442–69.

26. *Berlin und Seine Bauten: Bearbeitet und Herausgegeben vom Architekten-Verein zu Berlin und der Vereinigung Berliner Architekten, II und III der Hochbau* (Berlin: Wilhelm Ernst & Sohn, 1896), 511.

27. *Berliner Amusements: originelle und pikante Skizzen über das Leben und Treiben in den Berliner Vergnugungs-Lokalen* (Berlin: F. Cronmeyer, 1895), 25.

28. "Zirkus," *Norddeutsche allgemeine Zeitung,* February 1, 1905, 3.

29. "Unterhaltungen — Das Februar Programm des Winter-gartens," *Norddeutsche allgemeine Zeitung,* February 12, 1905, 2.

30. "Internationalen Ringkampfen," *Berliner Börsen-Zeitung,* February 7, 1901, 8.

31. Hurley and Heffernan, "Cartoon as Satire and Source," 25.

32. Open-access databases on Ancestry.com were used to compile the list of von Guretzkis in Berlin between 1870 and 1970.

33. Bernd Wedemeyer, "Theordor Siebert: A Biography," trans. David Chapman, *Iron Game History* 6, no. 3 (2000): 6.

34. Adolf von Guretzki, "Theodor Siebert 88 Jahre," *Athletik*, 21, no. 7 (1954): 16.

35. Jochen Hung, *Moderate Modernity: The Newspaper Tempo and the Transformation of Weimar Democracy* (Ann Arbor: University of Michigan Press, 2023), 26.

36. Peter Fritzsche, *Reading Berlin 1900* (Cambridge, MA: Harvard University Press, 2009), 81–82.

37. Erik N. Jensen, *Body by Weimar: Athletes, Gender, and German Modernity* (Oxford: Oxford University Press, 2010), 12.

38. Bernd Wedemeyer-Kolwe, *Der neue Mensch: Körperkultur im Kaiserreich und in der Weimar Republik* (Würzburg: Königshausen & Neumann, 2004), 250.

39. Mike Viellard, "Treatise Database—Martial Arts Reconstruction," accessed January 18, 2023, http://www.middleages.hu/english/martialarts/treatise_database.php?values _set=1&sort_order=year&direction=&secondary_sort_order=author&secondary _direction=&limit=1&search_string=Guretzki&ok=Start+search&pagesize=50&sort =year&sortmethod=ASC.

40. The Milo Steinborn Collection at University of Texas at Austin where the newspaper collection is housed is missing one date—June 12, 1898. It is possible there is an eighth installment contained in that edition, but the story can be sufficiently assembled as-is.

41. Adolf von Guretzki, *"Raad" (Donner), Illustrirte Deutsche Athleten-Zeitung*, January 9, 1898, 1.

42. Adolf von Guretzki, *"Raad" (Donner), Illustrirte Deutsche Athleten-Zeitung*, January 23, 1898, 2.

43. Adolf von Guretzki, *"Raad" (Donner), Illustrirte Deutsche Athleten-Zeitung*, June 19, 1898, 3.

44. Edmond Desbonnet, *The Kings of Strength: A History of All Strong Men from Ancient Times to Our Own*, trans. David Chapman (Jefferson, NC: McFarland, 2022), 295.

45. Jennifer Jenkins, "German Orientalism: Introduction," *Comparative Studies of South Asia, Africa, and the Middle East* 24, no. 2 (2004): 97–98.

46. Adolf von Guretzki, *"Raad" (Donner), Illustrirte Deutsche Athleten-Zeitung*, January 16, 1898, 2.

47. Adolf von Guretzki, *"Raad" (Donner), Illustrirte Deutsche Athleten-Zeitung*, January 9, 1898, 1.

48. Petersen, "Wrestling and the Use of Alcohol," 117.

49. Adolf von Guretzki, *"Raad" (Donner), Illustrirte Deutsche Athleten-Zeitung*, March 6, 1898, 1.

50. Guretzki, *"Raad"(Donner)*, March 6, 1898, 2.

51. Guretzki, *"Raad"(Donner)*, March 6, 1898, 2.

52. Adolf von Guretzki, *"Raad" (Donner), Illustrirte Deutsche Atheten-Zeitung*, June 19, 1898, 2.

53. Guretzki, *"Raad"(Donner)*, June 19, 1898, 3.

54. Fritzsche, *Reading Berlin*, 129.

55. Fritzsche, *Reading Berlin*, 223.

56. Fritzsche, *Reading Berlin*, 3.

57. Bruno Piper, *Thierbändiger Marco, Illustrirte Deutsche Atheten-Zeitung*, October 30, 1898, 2. Literally translated, the title reads, "animal-tamer Marco."

58. Adolf von Guretzki, *"Raad" (Donner), Illustrirte Deutsche Athleten-Zeitung,* January 16, 1898, 1.

59. Michelle Martin, "Soccer: Ozil Quits German National Side Citing Racism over Turkish Heritage," Reuters, July 22, 2018, accessed January 19, 2023, https://www.reuters.com/article/us-soccer-germany-turkey/soccer-ozil-quits-german-national-side-citing-racism-over-turkish-heritage-idUSKBN1KC0UQ.

CHAPTER THREE

Power/Play

Sports, Journalism, and Contested Modernity in Weimar Berlin

ERIK JENSEN

When Kurt Doerry, editor-in-chief of the Berlin-based weekly *Sport im Bild* and a former track champion, referred to sports as the "symbol of their times" in a 1926 headline, he was exercising his magazine's power to ascribe cultural, economic, and political meaning to the games and physical contests that it covered.[1] He was also drawing on the fact that Berliners had embraced competitive sports during the Weimar Republic on a hitherto unprecedented scale, in terms of both participation and avid fandom.[2] From the inaugural automotive Grand Prix of Germany on Berlin's Avus racetrack in 1926, which attracted over two hundred thousand spectators, to the crowds that cheered the hometown football club Hertha BSC to six national championship finals in a row, Berliners attended competitions in numbers unrivaled by any other German city. An even larger number of them followed the results of competitions in the pages of the city's proliferating newspapers and magazines, often despite their lack of any genuine interest in doing so. Sports had assumed such a central role in contemporary life—they were so "in"—that many Berliners felt compelled to feign a fashionable interest. When a sports magazine declared in spring 1929 that a person had to stay on top of the latest athletic news "just to be able to carry on a conversation nowadays," it was clearly being self-serving, but it was likely not too far off base, either.[3]

Posers and ardent fans alike turned to the pages of Berlin's sports press not just for the latest athletic results but also for the accompanying essays and commentaries that framed those results within a larger societal context. In this sense, sports writers, too, symbolized their times, an era that closely analyzed every facet of modern life. When the Berlin-based Ullstein publishing house debuted a new sports and culture themed journal in 1929, it heralded the magazine as "the most modern publication in Germany."[4] Aptly titled *Tempo*, its promotional advertising featured a kinetic collage that included horses, racecars, a motorcycle, a female high jumper, and a male tennis player, all recorded by two hands on a typewriter in the lower-right corner of the ad in their own journalistic race against time. The magazine promised to deliver topical content to its readers at the same high speed that the advertisement's images conveyed.

Like the athletes themselves, the sports reporters and commentators symbolized their times in terms of their aggressive competitiveness, fast pace, and stamina, all of which were qualities demanded by urban life in general. Both organized sport and the sports media also shared a propensity for sensationalism and a knack for relentless self-promotion, traits that Germans especially associated with the entertainment and amusement metropolis of Berlin. After a Berlin boxing gym hired the American trainer "Kid" Lewis to transform the city's up-and-coming fighters, for instance, Lewis laid out his vision for German pugilism in a manner designed to appeal to those looking for a hair-raising slugfest. In a 1927 article, he pointedly contrasted "the fine, artistic, stylish boxing" seen in German rings throughout the early 1920s, which he framed as too refined and dull, with his approach, which he described succinctly as "totally combative—just punching and more punching."[5] Lewis, in other words, promised Berlin's fans a spectacle.

Berlin's status during the Weimar Republic as Germany's preeminent sports city, its biggest publishing center, and its foremost showcase of urban modernity makes the metropolis a useful site for exploring how sports reporters—many of them current and former athletes themselves—contested larger transformations in German society via their commentaries about the action on the field. Articles criticizing the constant pressure faced by sprinters or doubles players to improve their performance, for example, served simultaneously as a critique of the competitively driven age in which those athletes lived. As the historian Frank Becker argued in his 1993 book *Amerikanismus in Weimar*, sports rhetoric helped to promote a type of efficiency-minded modernity that many observers in the 1920s associated with America.[6] Sprinters, for example, strived to maximize their performance in part by adapting the techniques of the prewar American industrial engineer F. W. Taylor, whose principles particularly enthralled German business leaders in the second half of the 1920s. These Taylorist techniques, moreover, received wide coverage in the sports press.

The coverage of athletic competitions introduced Germans to key elements of rationalized modernity in a particularly seductive way by connecting those elements to a cultural practice—sport—that already enjoyed broad popularity. When sports reporters and commentators criticized those elements (for example, by raising questions about the consequences of cutthroat ambition or by decrying the decline of playfulness or the rise of mechanization), they had the potential to shift conversations and underline particular concerns. In the last half of the Weimar Republic, the coverage of track and field and women's tennis, in particular, wrestled with the ramifications of increasingly calibrated training and high-pressure competition, by turns embracing these innovations and mourning their ramifications, such as the disappearance of the genteel backhand and the demise of the "natural" sprinter.

Through the Lens of Berlin's Sports Pages

When pioneering sports commentator Willy Meisl pointed out in 1927 that "the names of the top-tier athletes are more well-known than those of the great poets," his comparison proved especially apt because so many athletes at the time were deciding to pick up the pen themselves and write about their disciplines.[7] As the social observer Siegfried Kracauer noted in that same year, "the faster a man runs, the more world-renowned his legs are . . . even the fists or the tennis racket can make one's name"—and publishing pieces in a big-city newspaper could make that name even bigger.[8] In addition to the added celebrity, many athletes turned to journalism as a relatively easy and appealing way to supplement their incomes, pave the way for possible post-competition careers, and shape the development and broader popularity of their sport. For their part, the newspapers and magazines appreciated the athletes' expertise and the allure of their names as a means of boosting sales, at least until a larger cadre of professional sports writers could establish themselves and develop a dedicated readership of their own.

Berlin publishers had already started to cash in on public interest in sport—and the insights of leading athletes—in the late nineteenth century when weekly journals such as Sport im Bild (Sports in pictures) and Sport im Wort (Sports in words) began appearing on newsstands. These weeklies pioneered a formula that presented sports reports alongside an eclectic mix of society gossip, fashion, personality profiles, and plenty of pictures. They treated sport as a modern form of cultural expression, and they crafted athletes into public figures whose accomplishments demanded attention and acclaim. Daily newspapers started to invest more concertedly in sports coverage in 1904, when the Scherl publishing house took over *Sport im Bild* and simultaneously introduced the first sports page to one of its daily Berlin papers, the *Lokal-Anzeiger*. Ullstein, a rival publisher, introduced a dedicated sports page that very same year to its daily *B.Z. am Mittag*, a paper that branded itself as offering a quick midday update in the midst of a busy schedule. Sport fit perfectly within this format, given its easy digestibility and its capacity to fill column space on weekends and Monday mornings when political and economic news was in shorter supply.[9] According to one sport historian, the sports section of *B.Z. am Mittag* sometimes comprised over 50 percent of the entire Sunday newspaper.[10]

As sports pages expanded rapidly in the 1910s and 1920s, newspapers could only meet the demand for content by relying on freelancers who were often former or current athletes themselves, such as Kurt Doerry and Carl Diem. Their intimate understanding of the competitions lent them an authority that compensated for any potential shortcomings as writers, and the fact that they were given bylines at a time when most sports reporters remained anonymous revealed an assumption on the part of publishers that they attracted readers. Doerry, whom Scherl had tapped well before World War I to edit *Sport im Bild*, drew not only on his personal background as a track and field athlete but also on his experience as a ring referee for boxing matches and his familiarity with the English sporting press to inform his decisions on who to hire and what to publish. At the same time, he and other athlete-writers used their journalistic soapboxes to generate support for their disciplines, educate their fans, and push their sports to develop in particular directions.

As professional sports journalists began to establish themselves in the 1920s, they, too, used their positions to advocate for changes and participate in debates. By 1927, professional sports reporters had created an institutional presence—the Federation of German Sports Journalists (Verband Deutscher Sportjournalisten, or VDS), based in Berlin—in order to raise their profile, push for the right to receive their own bylines, and lobby for their interests. Among other initiatives, the VDS began awarding the Sports Press's Golden Sash (Goldener Band der Sportpresse) to the year's top athletes as a way to bolster its members' status and to generate even more interest in the subjects that provided its members their livelihoods.[11] In doing so, the

VDS also further solidified sports reporters' claims to evaluate, judge, and guide the development of the sports that they covered. Female athletes and writers started publishing more of their work in this same period as well, although they remained a distinct minority on the sports pages of the Berlin dailies in the 1920s. Women only comprised about 2.5 percent of all German journalists in 1925, although a few of the leading ones did attract dedicated followings for their coverage in areas such as track and field and tennis.[12]

Track and Field and the Taylorized Athlete

Track and field adopted more principles of Taylorism into its training and coaching regimens, did so more quickly, and became more closely associated with the entire concept of rationalization than any other sport in the Weimar Republic. A 1926 report on the German track and field championships in *Die Leibesübungen*, for instance, made unmistakable reference to Taylor's principles of scientific management when it called for "more technical training! . . . systematic and strict."[13] The article elaborated in terms that any systems engineer would immediately have recognized: "A good many beads of sweat are yet to drip before the athlete has rid himself of all sorts of bad, little habits and adopted the detailed, new improvements." Such minute analysis, a hallmark of scientific management, may have provoked grumbling in the workplace, but, when applied to athletes' bodies, it appeared as an innovative, irrefutable marker of progress whose effects were plain to see. The Berlin sports press regularly called attention, after all, to the streamlined bodies of sports champions as testaments to the benefits of modern training, and it published articles touting science as the key to athletic improvement. At the same time, however, some commentators worried about the pressure-filled and soulless atmosphere on the men's side of the sport and even more about the purported strains and excesses on the women's side.

Because winning times in track and field competitions were often decided by just fractions of a second, even small adjustments to an athlete's start or stride could make a significant difference to their performance. Some of the most celebrated clubs and trainers therefore adopted Taylor's technique of using stop-action photography to locate somatic inefficiencies. Another 1926 article in *Die Leibesübungen* extolled the way in which such photographic analyses enabled coaches to examine the movements "of a start, a baton exchange, or a [discus] throw in all its details."[14] The fact that

Die Leibesübungen, the official organ of the Association of German Turnen Instructors, encouraged the use of Taylor's system to train track and field athletes is noteworthy. *Turnen*, a form of collective gymnastics that had century-old roots in German-speaking Europe, had long harbored hostility toward the competitive sports that Germany had imported from Britain in the late nineteenth century and particularly toward individual sports of measurement, such as track and field, with their relentless drive to set new records.[15] By 1926, however—as both articles underscore—the sharp lines between Turnen and competitive sports had blurred, and even adherents of Turnen had begun to extol the performance benefits that derived from modern training principles.

Track and field athletes embodied a modern sensibility in their Taylorized training practices as well as in their individualistic ethos, which revealed itself in the ambition to beat their previous performances, rise in the rankings, and win meets. Such pursuit of personal accolades seemed to capture the self-interested impulses of the era and stood in contrast to the collective spirit embodied by the earlier generations of Turnen adherents. The sports commentator Walter Schönbrunn even argued in 1930—again in the pages of *Die Leibesübungen*—that the self-assertiveness of track and field competitors exemplified the values of "republican" citizens, while the communal exercises of old-school Turnen only befitted "the subjects of a monarchical government," quiescent and obsolete.[16] Although Schönbrunn did not explicitly connect the personal traits of his republican athletes to the characteristics exhibited by the era's self-made business entrepreneurs, his characterization certainly suggested it. Modern sport stars stood out as very public examples of ambitious self-interest.

Although most commentators and athletes supported track and field's broader ethos of individualism and encouraged its embrace of scientific training, some voices within the sport expressed a degree of ambivalence about both developments. With respect to individual ambition, few writers begrudged the champions their due and none saw any real alternative, unless it meant doing away with titles and medals altogether. Some did, however, wish to reframe participation in track and field as a collective benefit to the nation and, in that sense, a form of communal patriotism. As an undertaking in image management, these commentators downplayed individual aggrandizement in the sport and underscored its contribution to the country's overall fitness. In particular, they zeroed in on the sport's contribution to Germany's military preparedness and sometimes even attributed Germany's defeat in 1918 to poor physical fitness. Doerry, for one, highlighted the ostensible contrast between Britain's athletically trained soldiery and Germany's, and he called on his countrymen to emulate England, which, he claimed, "could muster armies out of nowhere during the World War because it possessed a youth that had been steeled through sport."[17] With the restrictions that the Treaty of Versailles had placed on Germany's freedom to engage in wide-scale military training, Doerry suggested, track and field assumed even greater importance as a permissible substitute.

Even as Taylorist principles and a spirit of individualism were generally gaining ground in men's track and field over the course of the 1920s, the pervasiveness of scientific training methods did prompt some consternation. The sports correspondent Richard Harbott, for instance, chose to write his 1926 article on a special training course for German sprinters as a wistful eulogy for what he perceived as the more instinctive, superior style of bygone days. "The era of the natural runner is over," he lamented in the pages of Die Leibesübungen. "The simple practice of running has intensified into a scientifically taught procedure, whose training alternatives and tactical and technical modifications grow daily."[18] Harbott denounced modern track and field as an invasive extension of the very same industrial engineering from which the sport had once provided an earlier generation of athletes needed refuge. On this point, Harbott joined other Weimar commentators who decried the exhaustive analysis of every last twitch in the runner's gait. Rudolf Hartung, in a 1927 article, distilled the debate over Taylorism in track and field to a clash between two opposing approaches to sport—materialism and idealism. He condemned the former as a sterile, Americanized betrayal of true physical culture, with its reliance on "motion studies, mechanics, technique, [and] measurement." He described the latter, on the other hand, as "expression, verve, [and] competition based on manly instincts," depicting the less trained style of running as sport in its purest, most genuine form.[19]

This nostalgia-tinged skepticism toward scientific training in men's sport, however, mutated into fierce debate when it came to women's disciplines— especially middle-distance running, a subject on which medical professionals also began weighing in. A 1926 essay in Die Leibesübungen titled "Wohin führt der Weg?" (Where is the path leading?) predicted that rigorous preparations for modern competition would, in the quoted words of the former decathlon champion Karl Ritter von Halt, "defame our German girls and make hard, manly bodies out of them." In a sweeping condemnation of the central tenets of competitive sport, Ritter von Halt concluded, "Therefore, do away with the women's championships [and] away with the terrible listing of records for women's performances!"[20] Five months later in an article in the Berlin weekly *Sport im Bild*, discus champion Milly Reuter seemed to sympathize with Ritter von Halt's underlying sentiment that no female athlete should train in a way that resulted in "hard, manly bodies." Reuter denied, however, that competitive women's track and field ever produced such physiques in the first place, and she insisted that the figures of the female athletes whom she had come across at meets all had a "slim, soft musculature." She then claimed that "the body of the female track and field athlete is not athletic but graceful," a statement that seemed keen to renounce the very condition of being an athlete and instead to lend an air of finishing-school refinement to this elite sport.[21]

Debates surrounding the training practices and competitive prepared-ness of women's track and field athletes reached a crescendo on August 2, 1928, after the final heat of the 800 meters at the 1928 Olympic Games. Even though a German middle-distance runner, Lina Radke-Batschauer, had won the gold medal in world-record time, the German press focused less on celebrating her victory than on decrying the sight of two of her competitors, who had collapsed to the ground after crossing the finishing line. The official journal of Germany's governing agency for track and field, *Der Leichtathlet*, immediately sought to shift attention back onto Radke-Batschauer and her admirable preparation for the race by explicitly praising her as "brilliantly trained" and by pointing to her modern regimen as the solution, not the problem.[22] A 1928 commemorative book on the Olympic Games, pub-lished in the closing months of that year, emphasized the value of modern training even more directly. In it, the physician Friedrich Messerli praised Radke-Batschauer's physical condition and competitive strategy, and he insisted that any female athlete could achieve that same balance of stamina and tactical acuity, "as long as [she] seeks to reach her level of performance through rational training."[23]

Most commentators, though, revealed far more ambivalence about the race than Messerli did, and many blamed "rational training" for having pushed female track and field athletes too hard and too fast. Indeed, the sport's governing body decided shortly after the race to eliminate the wom-en's 800 meters from future Olympic Games. In the weeks and months that followed, sports reporters reflected on the ramifications of the race and the International Olympic Committee's subsequent decision to cancel it. Meisl, for instance, ultimately defended the decision of the committee to discontinue the event even as he praised Radke-Batschauer's "clever technique and tremendous ability," two qualities that directly spoke to the benefits of her rationalized training. Nevertheless, Meisl claimed that "almost all of the participants had so exhausted themselves" that officials had no choice but to cancel the 800 meters, and he concluded, "Women's sports are, after all, still so young that it is quite unlikely that they are fully up to the most difficult tasks yet."[24] Meisl's concluding "yet" implied that he could foresee women competing in the middle distances at some future point, but his piece stopped decidedly short of endorsing the sort of comprehensive training that would have enabled the sport to get there.

In November 1928, just as Meisl's reactions appeared in print, Lina Müller-Passavant expressed her own feelings about the race and what it indicated about modern women's sport in Der Leichtathlet. For the most part, Müller-Passavant voiced strong support for women's middle-distance running and the modern training that accompanied it, and she argued that officials should not base a decision about the appropriateness of a given athletic event on the outcome of one race alone. Müller-Passavant also dedicated part of her article to excoriating Berlin's sports reporters, the vast majority of them male, for the manner in which they had covered the 800-meter race and its aftermath. In particular, she singled out the daily Berliner Morgenpost for its evaluation of the physical appearances of the runners after the race, which included one correspondent's protestations of shock at the sight of the women's red, exhausted faces. "In the future, spare us the account of men's reactions to the sight of an athletically competing woman," she admonished.[25] Still, Müller-Passavant did not dismiss the officials' concerns altogether, and she acknowledged her own feeling that women's middle-distance running still required more study, given its newness as a competitive sport and the uncertainties about its long-term effects.

Tennis and the Cultivated Athlete

Similar misgivings about the consequences of rigorous training shadowed elite women's tennis players, as Paula von Reznicek demonstrated in her 1928 book Auferstehung der Dame (Resurrection of the lady). In it, Reznicek—a top-ranked tennis player, whom the literary journal *Der Querschnitt* described in 1932 as "Germany's first and foremost female sports journalist"[26]—included a one-page vignette in which she satirized what she saw as the excessive competitiveness in modern women's tennis. The short piece, the title of which translates to "The record addict," contrasted one fictional player's ostensibly measured approach to the game with another's purportedly obsessive approach to it.[27] Reznicek pointedly referred to the latter's "insane ambition," as indicated by the impossible goal that she had set for herself: to compete at the level of Suzanne Lenglen—the era's dominant women's tennis player—within three weeks. In pursuit of this ambition, she not only pushed herself to train five hours per day but also turned down a film role in order to do so. Reznicek never gave her a name, but instead referred to her simply as "the abnormal one" and depicted her in a way that highlighted Reznicek's own concerns about the direction of the sport and the types of players it supposedly encouraged. "The abnormal one" augured the demise of tennis as an elegant and flirtatious game, in Reznicek's view, and signaled its replacement by an aggressive, relentlessly ambitious, and scientifically engineered contest. Players like "the abnormal one," who continuously strived to improve their game, did more than simply offend Reznicek's sensibilities, of course. They also threatened her, given that they had their sights unmistakably set on overtaking top-ranked players like herself.

Reznicek's books and press commentary revealed a longing for the rapidly disappearing style of play that she had grown up with as the daughter of a wealthy banker who owned an estate just outside of Breslau. Reznicek's critique of the accelerating competitiveness in tennis, along with its lack of grace, also implicitly criticized the increasing social accessibility that had begun to redefine tennis in the Weimar Republic. Her opinions hinted at a nostalgia for the lost entitlements of an earlier German society, entitlements to which she had access not just by virtue of her own wealthy upbringing but also thanks to her first marriage to a fellow tennis player, commentator, and aristocratic bon vivant, Burghard von Reznicek. The couple had built their early journalistic reputations in the mid-1920s by issuing dispatches from tennis tournaments at spa resorts, which they liberally garnished with fashion reports and gossipy details about post-game socializing. Paula von Reznicek's early bylines often appeared below articles such as the one that ran in *Sport im Bild* in 1926 and bore the stately headline "Schlesischer Adel daheim und beim Sport" (Silesian nobility at home and at sport), in which she presented tennis as integral to the life of the landed gentry.[28] Reznicek's later writing continued in this same vein—lingering at least as much on the hobnobbing and romantic trysts that accompanied tennis competitions as on the actual matches themselves. This sensibility suffused *Auferstehung der Dame*, a book lavish with references to tennis as the "white sport" and accompanying illustrations of courtside couples in stately repose.[29]

This closeup of Paula von Reznicek, taken during a match against Cilly Aussem in July 1930, highlights her incredible athleticism. Even as she criticized ambition in women's tennis, Reznicek visibly channeled that quality into the development of her own body. *Getty images.*

Reznicek was not alone in criticizing the competitive trend in women's tennis, as a 1928 article in the Berlin-based magazine *Sport und Sonne* showed. Under the lyrical title "Von der Schönheit und dem Rhythmus der Tennisschläge" (On the beauty and rhythm of tennis strokes), the article argued that players should place just as much importance on an aesthetic style of play as on a winning one: "It may be that the beautiful player is not always the best player, but it should remain a goal just the same to carry out the task as perfectly as possible."[30] Two years later, an article in the same magazine reminded its readers, once again, that in tennis winning counted less than how beautifully one played: "The lesser hero [is] not always the one who loses. To return the cunningly thought-out and most maliciously placed balls of your partner with a spirited, elegant stroke—that is what true sport is all about."[31] This second article not only celebrated gracefulness as a central virtue in tennis but also expressed obvious disdain for those players who purportedly degraded the game by practicing the type of malicious ball placement found in competitive contests. A 1930 article in *Die Leibesübungen* went so far as to demand an end to rankings in women's tennis altogether, because they fueled rivalries between female players. Only "when the women on the courts . . . hit the ball to their partner with no other purpose than sheer enjoyment," the article insisted, could the game of tennis occupy a healthy role in women's lives.[32] Other top-ranked female tennis players privileged the "beauty and rhythm" of the women's game over its competitive aspects, too, including Ilse Friedleben. A regular contributor to *Sport und Sonne*, Friedleben described tennis in a 1928 article for that magazine as such a "light and elegant sport" that it appeared to outside observers as "unmanly and playful," a description that Friedleben seemed to validate rather than debunk.[33]

Such critiques of female competitiveness did not monopolize coverage of tennis in Berlin, however—far from it. Instead, they represented one smaller side in a debate that had emerged in the 1920s over not just the direction of women's sports but also the larger shift in gender norms that had begun during the war. Betty Nuthall, a top British player in the interwar period whose writing appeared occasionally in the Berlin press, called for more ambition in women's tennis, not less. In a 1929 article for *Sport und Sonne*, she traced women's often poor showings in mixed doubles to their lack of confidence. Nuthall complained that, when placed in competitive situations opposite men, women "do not try enough," and she insisted that they could score points against men if only they cultivated a will to do so.[34] In 1931, the same year that she herself reached the finals of Wimbledon, Hilde Krahwinkel praised the transformation in women's play that she had seen during her competitive career. In the pages of *Sport im Bild*, she marveled at the powerful style and aggressive tactics in the women's game in recent years, and she noted that, whereas the game had boasted only a handful of truly great players before the war, by 1931 it could point to a legion of remarkable female athletes, all of whom possessed "a proper, modern stroke technique."[35]

Even Friedleben, who saw nothing wrong with "light and elegant" tennis, nevertheless enthusiastically greeted the first glimmers of Taylorism that she discerned among the German women playing tennis by February 1928.

After offering a glowing appraisal of the up-and-coming German player Cilly Aussem, Friedleben summarized her assessment by underscoring that "Miss Aussem has achieved an astounding, machine-like accuracy in her shots and wonderful footwork through systematic, excellent training."[36] Friedleben's reference to "machine-like" strokes immediately calls to mind the image of a factory floor, and the term "systematic, excellent training" points directly to rationalized coaching and scientifically proven drills. "Every sport develops," the sports commentator Horst Wagner declared in 1927, as he summarized the ways in which tennis had begun to modernize, particularly among the American players. Wagner underscored how scientific research had enabled players across the Atlantic to elevate their play dramatically, and he encouraged Germany to invest similar resources in order to make tennis into "a genuine physical work-out for the first time."[37]

The social backgrounds of the top female players also began to change over the course of the 1920s, in tandem with the growing competitiveness of the sport itself, and Berlin's commentators paid increasing attention to this trend, too. Essays and articles noted, for instance, that some players came from families that had to scrimp and save in order to pay for lessons and court time. The press then interpreted the fact that these players had succeeded in spite of their more modest backgrounds as evidence for a modern, functioning meritocracy in women's tennis. In addition to stories about climbing the social ladder, writers frequently emphasized the social independence and self-determination of the leading female players, pointing out the many areas of their lives—from finances to institutional infrastructure—in which they had taken control. Reznicek, for one, fully embraced this aspect of female ambition, and she applauded the way in which sport had empowered women to create independent spaces for themselves in which the traditional priorities of Kinder, Küche, and Kirche (children, kitchen, and church) did not predominate. All-women's tennis clubs, Reznicek argued, opened up new forms of sociability to their female members and decision-making positions for those with aspirations to leadership:

> Now that we have our clubs, regardless of whether they are for bridge, rowing, golf, gymnastics, or tennis, we . . . make the rules, can do and have done what we want, can come and go without having to ask, "is it still OK to go into this bar?," or "does anyone have anything against meeting the swimmers on the club terrace after supper?" . . . We stand over the situation that we have created![38]

The ambition to train harder may have concerned Reznicek, but the ambition to direct one's own life met with nothing but hearty approval on her part.

Reznicek's fellow tennis player and commentator Nelly Neppach, meanwhile, approvingly called attention to another aspect of female players' independence in the 1920s: their ability to move about on their own. In a 1929 article in *Sport im Bild* on the social aspects of women's tennis, Neppach stressed the fact that the modern player "'naturally' drives herself to the tournament," to which she added, "We women steer our cars, when we have them, with the same sense of entitlement that the men have."[39] Neppach implicitly acknowledged the financial hurdle to car ownership, but she also accentuated the elements of empowerment—"we women steer our cars" to the tournament to compete for laurels as individual athletes. When a 1928 article giddily reported a sighting of Aussem tooling around the French Riviera in her new Mercedes, it signaled the potential for women's tennis to serve as an avenue of financial upward mobility by referring to Aussem as the daughter of a middle-class salesman. The reporter also emphasized Aussem's self-confidence, as demonstrated by her "sure hand" at the steering wheel.[40] Reznicek, meanwhile, cultivated her own reputation for independent automobility—as well as sexual independence—in a short story that she published in Germany's national automobile magazine, in which a male and a female driver engage in a spontaneous road race before striking up a conversation that quickly kindles into a one-night tryst.[41]

The career of the legendary French player Suzanne Lenglen epitomized the association between women's tennis and ambitious self-determination, especially in the wake of her pathbreaking decision to turn professional in 1926. The sports columnist Georg Lehmann immediately sympathized with her unprecedented move, which he framed in the pages of *B.Z. am Mittag* in class terms, given Lenglen's modestly middle-class background. His article bore the headline, "Der dritte Stand der Tennisspieler," (The third estate of tennis players) explicitly evoking the pre–French Revolution distinction between the first two estates—the clergy and the nobility—and the third estate that designated commoners. Underscoring that Lenglen had come from the third estate, without having had the privileges that players from the nobility possessed at birth, Lehmann then stressed the immense time commitment that "modern" tennis required of Lenglen, on top of the time required just to support herself. He even suggested that this commitment was "even greater than the demands of other sports on their elites." He concluded with the rhetorical question, "Who can still achieve top performances in tennis while simultaneously pursuing a career?"[42] His answer, clearly, was no one, thus justifying Lenglen's move to make her tennis performances into her career.

Other journalists compared Lenglen's monetization of tennis to the actions of the oft-heralded "self-made man," while many of the younger players who looked up to her viewed it as a hopeful sign that they, too, could aspire to independent wealth. According to the 1927 article in *Die Leibesübungen* "Was Berufssportler verdienen können" (What professional athletes can earn), Lenglen had taken in almost a million dollars during just one four-month tour, which did not include her public-appearance fees or the royalties derived from articles that she published in newspapers and fashion magazines.[43] Lenglen's unapologetic ambition drew fire from some critics, such as Heinz Lorenz, who in 1927 warned women "not to take a professional athlete as their role model," because she pushed herself too hard.[44] The overall coverage of Lenglen, however, tended instead to commend her decision to capitalize on her tennis skills. *Der Leichtathlet*, for instance, paid tribute in 1928 to both Lenglen and her American rival Helen Wills for having "blazed the trail for women's sports through their incredible achievements, not only in tennis . . . but also in other areas," especially self-marketing.[45] Surprisingly, it was a frequent defender of tennis refinement, Burghard von Reznicek, who, in his 1932 book on tennis, gave some of the most glowing praise to the era's "cult of the individual." Players such as Lenglen, whose personas had fueled that cult, had also, Burghard acknowledged, transformed the "modern female tennis player into a completely different figure than her predecessors."[46] Women's athletic ambitions still provoked hostility in some circles, but commentators such as Burghard both reflected and contributed to the significant, if still contested, change that was underway.

While debates over ambition and competitive training animated the press coverage of women's tennis in the late 1920s, the older, more genteel spirit persisted for far longer in the men's game. This divergence between the two games, and the sporting press's response to it, reveals the persistence of clearly gendered assumptions about masculine aggressiveness and feminine grace, even in the progressive and relatively fluid metropolis of Berlin. While Paula von Reznicek and other writers were satirizing the ambition and competitive zeal of female athletes in the late 1920s, some of those very same sports commentators were actively encouraging male tennis players to channel far more of these qualities into their matches and careers. In a 1926 magazine profile, for example, Friedleben started out by complimenting the male player Heinrich Kleinschroth's "elasticity," his economy of movement, and even the dashing way he "wore his camels' hair coat," but she bemoaned his lack of drive. Longing to see evidence of a competitive instinct on the court, Friedleben ultimately criticized Kleinschroth for having far too many of the very same qualities that she found so praiseworthy in women. "His style in tennis is nearly perfect," Friedleben wrote, but it is "nevertheless a limited perfection, which he . . . never pushes himself to surpass."[47]

When a rare criticism of excessive competitiveness did surface in connection to the men's game, as in the 1932 autobiographical sketch in *Die Leibesübungen* "Mein ehrgeiziger Vater" (My ambitious father), it located that competitiveness in the sport's fans, not in its players. The piece described the relentless pressure placed on a young male player by his father, who pushed him to compete more aggressively. The story angrily concluded, "An entire club could be founded in which only such ambition-driven fathers are members."[48] Here, the ambition of the players themselves posed no concern whatsoever. In fact, the piece focused on the ongoing efforts of an overzealous parent to instill precisely that drive and fighting spirit into the game, since his son's style of play decidedly lacked both.

Given the nearly universal perception that the men's game desperately needed to cultivate more athletic ambition, the sports journal *Sport und Gesundheit* seemed understandably relieved in 1929 when it claimed to have discerned a trend in German men's tennis toward the modern, competitive sport that many German women were already playing. Under the headline "Wandel im Tennis" (Transformation in tennis), the magazine announced that "the man with the racket has transformed himself. The bored gentleman has become a passionate fighter." It went on to describe an aggressive style in the men's game that finally focused more on winning points than on politely keeping the ball in play. "Whereas it was earlier considered unrefined to run after the balls, and unfair to serve the ball with skill so that the opponent could not reach it with his racket," the article scoffed, "now it is played competitively and with every sport-like means available to win. . . . The balls today are unscrupulously sliced, something previously frowned upon."[49] The acceptance of a style of play that the men's game would previously have rejected as "cutthroat" paralleled the sharper elbows that many commentators perceived in German society as a whole in the late

1920s, a period when rationalized restructuring and its attendant stresses signified a more aggressive economic atmosphere. The image of a "bored gentleman" metamorphosing into a "passionate fighter" seemed to align with this development, as well as with the ostensibly meritocratic order of the Weimar Republic, in which individual achievement, rather than familial entitlement, determined one's status.

Conclusion

Throughout the mid-1920s, Franz Diener, the German heavyweight boxing champion, attracted notoriety as a fixture of Berlin's nightlife, where he frequented billiard rooms and dancing clubs. In 1926, the columnist Rumpelstilzchen described Diener, who only trained in the mornings, as "a very animal-like being" and quoted the boxer himself as saying, "It may be good to renounce wine, women, and song, but for starters I'm only going to do without song!"[50] The sports editor Curt Riess later recalled Diener as "a victim of his own lack of discipline and his unsportsmanlike lifestyle," which led to his poor showing in a series of bouts in the United States.[51]

Reznicek may well have sided with Diener, at least when it came to his amorous pursuits. She seemed concerned that the new generation of women's tennis players—and athletes, in general—had stripped the sporting world of its sexiness, of "everything erotic," as she put it in her vignette on the tennis game between "the normal one" and "the abnormal one." Like Diener, too, Reznicek seemed to find discipline overrated, and she certainly felt that too much of it, whether stemming from personal ambition or a regimen of scientific training, detracted from the exuberant elements of play. Her attitudes echoed those in a piece that appeared in the Berlin newspaper *8-Uhr Abendblatt* in 1927, the year before the publication of Reznicek's handbook. That piece had similarly explored the unstable terrain of gender by categorizing contemporary women into types. Instead of "the normal one" and "the abnormal one," however, the 1927 piece referred to the "Gretchen," the "Girl," and the "Garçonne."[52] While the Gretchen conformed to a domesticated ideal of womanhood, the Girl and the Garçonne both made athleticism a central part of their identities. Like "the normal one," however, the Girl leaned partly on flirtation and charm to achieve her goals, while the Garçonne exuded a "masculine" self-assurance that mirrored that of "the abnormal one" and eschewed such efforts to attract the attention of others.

Modern sport demanded discipline, and this became increasingly clear over the course of the 1920s. If one wished to achieve even a modicum of proficiency, let alone a shot at elite competition, then modern sport also demanded an expertly designed training program, adherence to which required some type of motivation, generally in the form of personal ambition. The Berlin sports press wrestled with the roles that these elements should play in modern sport, and it even envisioned its own sports correspondents as teachers and adjudicators. They served not only to explain the sport but also to help decide how best to engage in it. As early as 1919, *Illustrierter Sport* advocated "sportliche Erziehung"—the rearing, as if by parents, of an athletic and athletically literate population. That rearing entailed instruction, but it also implied engagement and debate.[53] Sport, by mirroring its surrounding environment, expressed the same feelings of ambivalence, uncertainty, and occasional resistance that German society at large exhibited toward a whole host of changes at the time. The enforcement of workplace regimens designed by industrial engineers, for instance, found its reflection in a similar trend in sport, which athletes and commentators used the sports pages to debate. Because Berlin supported such a large and self-reflexive press culture, whose contributors acutely analyzed the social and cultural transformations taking place around them, it provides an especially insightful case study for exploring the interrelated, bumpy, and contested establishments of both modern competitive sport and the modern competitive workplace.

Notes

1. Kurt Doerry, "Der Sport als Zeitsymbol," *Sport im Bild* 32, no. 24 (November 26, 1926): 1077.

2. For a good discussion of the intersections between sports and other cultural practices in Weimar Berlin, see Kai Marcel Sicks, "'Der Querschnitt' oder: Die Kunst des Sporttreibens," in *Leibhaftige Moderne: Körper in Kunst und Massenmedien 1918–1933*, ed. Michael Cown and Kai Marcel Sicks (Bielefeld: Transcript, 2005), 33–47.

3. Hans Hädicke, "Sensationssport," *Start und Ziel* 5, no. 4 (April 1, 1929): 100.

4. Advertisement for *Tempo*, *Ullstein-Berichte* (October 1928), digitized on https://www.arthistoricum.net/werkansicht/dlf/87532/2#.

5. Ted Kid Lewis, "Amerika gegen Europa," *Sport und Sonne*, no. 9 (September 1927): 549.

6. Frank Becker, *Amerikanismus in Weimar: Sportsymbole und politische Kultur 1918–1933* (Wiesbaden: Deutscher Universitäts-Verlag, 1993).

7. Willy Meisl, "Das Problem des Amateurismus," *Die Leibesübungen*, no. 5/6 (March 20, 1927): 121.

8. Siegfried Kracauer, "Sie sporten" (1927), reprinted in *Sportgeschichten*, ed. Bernd Goldmann and Bernhardt Schwank (Frankfurt am Main: Insel, 1993), 12.

9. See Peter de Mendelssohn, *Zeitungsstadt Berlin: Menschen und Mächte in der*

Geschichte der deutschen Presse (Frankfurt am Main: Ullstein, 1982), 203. Mendelssohn unfortunately has little to say about early sports coverage.

10. See Birk Meinhardt, *Boxen in Deutschland* (Hamburg: Rotbuch, 1996), 46.

11. Of the seventeen Golden Sashes awarded between 1927 and 1932 (when the award ceased for nearly two decades), only two went to women: Helene Mayer (fencing, 1928) and Cilly Aussem (tennis, 1930).

12. The 2.5 percent figure comes from the Reichsverband der Deutschen Presse, which had only 78 female members, about 2.5 percent of the total membership, in 1925. In 1928, there were 170 female journalists in Germany, of whom 97 were full-time in some capacity and 73 were freelancers. Swantje Scharenberg, *Die Konstruktion des öffentlichen Sports und seiner Helden in der Tagespresse der Weimarer Republik* (Paderborn: Ferdinand Schöningh, 2012), 206.

13. Hans Loose, "Erlebtes und Geschautes anläßlich der Deutschen Meisterschaften in Leichtathletik," *Die Leibesübungen*, no. 18 (September 20, 1926): 429.

14. Albert Conrad-Hansen, "Film und Leibesübungen: Einige Worte über die Bedeutung des Filmes für Turnen und Sport," *Die Leibesübungen*, no. 20 (October 20, 1926): 466.

15. Historian Christiane Eisenberg has even referred to a "culture clash between Turnen and sports." See Christiane Eisenberg, *"English Sports" und deutsche Bürger: Eine Gesellschaftsgeschichte 1800–1939* (Paderborn: Ferdinand Schöningh, 1999), 250–61.

16. Walter Schönbrunn, "Körperliche Ertüchtigung," *Die Leibesübungen*, no. 14 (July 20, 1930): 415.

17. Kurt Doerry, "Der Sport als Zeitsymbol," *Sport im Bild* 32, no. 24 (November 26, 1926): 1077.

18. Richard Harbott, "Die deutsche Sprinterkurs im Frankfurter Stadion," *Die Leibesübungen*, no. 13 (July 5, 1926): 314.

19. Rudolf Hartung, "Männliche Körpererziehung im Lichte der Bodeschen Ausdrucksgymnastik," *Die Leibesübungen*, no. 23 (December 5, 1927): 555.

20. Dr. Karl Ritter von Halt, quoted in Walter Kühn, "Wohin führt der Weg? Eine kritische Betrachtung zur Frauensportbewegung," *Die Leibesübungen*, no. 8 (April 20, 1926): 193.

21. Milly Reuter, "Athletisch oder graziös? Eine zeitgemäße Frauenfrage," *Sport im Bild* 32, no. 18 (September 3, 1926): 791. Reuter placed fourth in the women's discus competition at the 1928 Olympic Games.

22. "Die einzige Goldmedaille für Deutschland: Frau Radtkes Weltrekord," *Der Leichtathlet* 5, no. 32 (August 7, 1928): 9. The press spelled her last name as both "Radke" and "Radtke," although recent biographies clearly favor the former.

23. Friedrich Messerli, "Die Wettkämpfe der Damen," in *Die Olympischen Spiele 1928: St. Moritz Amsterdam*, ed. Julius Wagner, Fritz Klipstein, and Friedrich Messerli (Zurich: Julius Wagner, 1928), 65.

24. Willy Meisl, "Die Leichtathletik," in *Die Olympischen Spiele in Amsterdam 1928*, ed. Deutscher Reichsausschuß für Leibesübungen (Leipzig: Verlag für Industrie und Kultur, 1928), 48.

25. Lina Müller-Passavant, "Der Kampfsport!," a response to an article in *Berliner Morgenpost*, by G. K., *Der Leichtathlet* 5, no. 47 (November 20, 1928): 19.

26. "Sport-Gotha," *Der Querschnitt* 12, no. 6 (June 1932): 431.

27. Paula von Reznicek, *Auferstehung der Dame* (Stuttgart: Dieck, 1928), 148.

28. Paula von Reznicek, "Schlesischer Adel daheim und beim Sport . . . ," *Sport im Bild* 32, no. 23 (November 12, 1926): 1023.

29. Reznicek, *Auferstehung der Dame*, 124.

30. "Von der Schönheit und dem Rhythmus der Tennisschläge," *Sport und Sonne*, no. 28 (August 1928): 481.

31. Gertrud Dagen-Höfer, "Wenn die weißen Bälle fliegen: Vom Siegeszug des Tennisspiels," *Sport und Sonne* 6, no. 3 (March–April 1930): 97.

32. "Ablehnung der Tennisranglisten," *Die Leibesübungen*, no. 22 (November 20, 1930): 676.

33. Ilse Friedleben, "Deutsches Damentennis: Spaziergang unter Meisterinnen," *Sport und Sonne*, no. 2 (February 1928): 84.

34. Betty Nuthall, "Die Frau im Tennis," *Sport und Sonne*, no. 9 (August 1929): 389.

35. Hilde Krahwinkel, "Die Nach uns Kommen," *Sport im Bild* 37, no. 15 (July 28, 1931): 874.

36. Friedleben, "Deutsches Damentennis," 83.

37. Horst M. Wagner, review of *Das Buch vom Tennis*, by Oskar Kreuzer, *Die Leibesübungen*, no. 11 (June 5, 1927): 269.

38. Reznicek, *Auferstehung der Dame*, 146.

39. Nelly Neppach, "Was trägt man zum Tennis?," *Sport im Bild* 35, no. 12 (June 13, 1929): 948.

40. "Zeitlupe," *Sport und Sonne*, no. 4 (April 1928): 237.

41. Paula von Reznicek, "Die ver'herrlichte' Nebenbuhlerin," *Allgemeine Automobil Zeitung* 29, no. 26 (June 30, 1928): 17.

42. Georg Lehmann, "Der dritte Stand der Tennisspieler," *B.Z. am Mittag*, reprinted in *Sport-Chronik am Sonnabend* 3, no. 3 (October 16, 1926): 15.

43. "Was Berufssportler verdienen können," *Die Leibesübungen*, no. 5/6 (March 20, 1927): 132.

44. Heinz Lorenz, "Frauenanmut und Sport": 132–35.

45. Alfred Kremer, "Mädchen im Tempel: Eine Wertung olympischer Frauen," *Der Leichtathlet* 5, no. 51/52 (December 18, 1928): 28.

46. Burghard von Reznicek, *Tennis: Das Spiel der Völker* (Marburg: Johann Grüneberg, 1932), 202.

47. Ilse Friedleben, "Eindrücke vom Territet-Turnier," *Sport im Bild* 32, no. 11 (May 28, 1926): 468.

48. Peter, "Mein ehrgeiziger Vater," *Vossische Zeitung*, reprinted in *Die Leibesübungen*, no. 1 (January 10, 1932): 21.

49. "Wandel im Tennis," *Sport und Gesundheit*, no. 51 (1929): 806.

50. Franz Diener quoted in Rumpelstilzchen, *Mecker' nich!*, collected works, vol. 6, 1925/26 (Berlin: Brunnen, 1926), 347.

51. Carl Riess, "Weltbühne Berlin," in *Alltag in der Weimarer Republik: Erinnerungen an eine unruhige Zeit*, ed. Rudolf Pörtner (Düsseldorf: Econ, 1990), 47.

52. "Drei Frauen stehen vor uns: Die Drei Typen: Gretchen, Girl, Garçonne," *8-Uhr Abendblatt*, June 4, 1927, quoted in Lynne Frame, "Gretchen, Girl, Garçonne? Weimar Science and Popular Culture in Search of the Ideal New Woman," in *Women in the Metropolis: Gender and Modernity in Weimar Culture*, ed. Katharina von Ankum (Berkeley: University of California Press, 1997), 12.

53. "Mehr Selbstbeherrschung bei Boxkampfen," *Illustrierter Sport* 7, no. 35 (December 23, 1919): 687.

CHAPTER FOUR

Rebuilding the Beautiful Game

Occupation, Football, and Survival in Berlin, 1945–1946

WILL RALL

Berlin in May 1945 was a conquered city. The Allied powers seized the capital of the so-called Thousand Year Reich with ambitions to sow seeds of lib-eration and democracy across a landscape of broken buildings, shattered streets, and charred corpses.[1] In the months following Germany's uncon-ditional surrender, the Allies' new order was typified by turmoil, scarcity, and hunger. As historian Tony Judt wrote, "Surviving the war was one thing, surviving the peace another."[2] Berlin's inhabitants struggled to find even the most basic necessities: enough food to eat, shelter for warmth, or even a moment of peace from the chaos surrounding them. What they could find, however, every weekend, in each occupied sector, and in practically every neighborhood across the city, was a game of football.

Allied occupiers promoted football as a tool to build democracy not only in Berlin but also across Germany, and the sport became woven into the fabric of the city's everyday life. Indeed, not three weeks after the end of World War II, the first football matches in postwar Berlin took place in front of thousands of spectators. Occasional neighborhood games invigo-rated Berlin's sporting landscape until, in January 1946, a citywide league kicked off comprised of weekly competitive rounds and culminating in the crowning of a city champion in July. The first city championship included teams representing thirty-six different neighborhoods from all four occupied sectors, uniting fans on terraces of war-damaged stadiums amid material insecurity and existential instability. While all of this was designed to serve the goals of democracy and denazification set out by the Allies at the Yalta Conference even before the war ended, it also created space for ordinary Berliners to publicly confront the continuities between National Socialism and the realities of the material conditions of their postwar lives.

Berlin after World War II was by no means a blank canvas onto which Allied occupiers could easily imprint their geopolitical ambitions. If the Allies hoped to achieve their mission to democratize and denazify the city through sport, they would have to contend with more than logistic and infrastructural challenges to orchestrate a citywide championship. They also had to reckon with the undeniable vestiges of National Socialism that manifested themselves in the people, symbols, and organizations that constituted Berlin's new postwar sporting landscape. Over the course of the first year of occupation, Allied authorities confronted administrative, historical, and material challenges that inhibited their ability to remake Berlin football as they hoped.

Historians have made the case that ordinary Berliners in the first years of postwar life were too concerned with their own survival to engage in much beyond a phototropic existence.[3] Yet recent research has demonstrated that what constituted "survival" often transcended material needs and reached into more existential yearnings for meaning, identity, and community.[4] While some historians have downplayed football's importance to the immediate postwar landscape, Berlin football indeed mattered deeply to the powers who occupied the city, the athletes who played the game, and the spectators who watched the matches.[5] Investigating the ambitions, events, and organization of the first postwar Berlin football league can help access the "below and beyond" of everyday life.[6] It reveals not just the confrontations between Allied occupation and an occupied population but also how Berlin's inhabitants experienced and understood the devastated city.

Football and Postwar Allied Ambitions

Sport occupied a critical space in Allied plans to develop democracy in Germany once they defeated Hitler's armies. Even before the war ended, occupying powers debated their shared concerns about the potential for sporting clubs and associations to foster nationalist fervor while also recognizing them as an opportunity to promote community-building and democratic values. Allies expressed particular concern over activities like fencing and gymnastics (*Turnen*), not only as curricula for military preparedness but also for their perceived historical connection to Germany's nationalistic movements of the nineteenth century. This, weighed against benefits like creating opportunities to help achieve occupational objectives, inspired careful oversight of sport in postwar Germany and ultimately resulted in the creation of policies like Allied Control Directive 23, "Limitation and Demilitarization of Sport in Germany." This policy laid out a framework to regulate sport as a means of achieving the broader aims of demilitarization and denazification, and it empowered Allied authorities to oversee and, in some cases, ban sports that might disrupt their occupational ambitions.[7]

Football was not among the activities initially prohibited by policies like Directive 23. Allied authorities did not perceive it to muster the same latent militaristic threat that, say, yachting and regatta had for the British or skiing had for the Russians.[8] They also did not read the sport's history with the same concern either. The Allies considered football as a modern sport that did not have the same historical connections to German nationalism or militarism as other, more worrisome, athletic endeavors like gymnastics. Football had emerged in Germany at the end of the nineteenth century as an English import, but it only became broadly popular after World War I.[9] During the Weimar Republic, football nudged its way outside of upper-class spaces and into the psyche of the masses, and it was enjoyed by thousands of fans across Germany every weekend.[10]

In the Weimar and Nazi eras, football primarily flourished on a regional level with no regular national league.[11] Germany's most successful football teams played in the south, where 1. FC Nürnberg won no fewer than six national titles during the interwar period. Meanwhile, Berliners enjoyed a football environment that was, if not as prestigious as their southern counterparts, dynamic and energetic. Teams like Hertha BSC and Tennis Borussia Berlin contested a lively local rivalry, but only Hertha claimed any national prestige with its two national championships in 1930 and 1931. Consequently, Berlin existed more as a ceremonial capital rather than a football powerhouse, especially once the new Olympic Stadium unveiled during the Third Reich became the preferred venue for national championship matches.

Football's close administrative ties to National Socialism meant that the Allies carefully scrutinized its institutions. Much like everything else in Nazi society, football clubs were swept into the state apparatus through the process of coordination (*Gleichschaltung*), and all sports associations were obliged to join the Reichsbund für Leibesübungen, the office that oversaw sport and physical education. This effectively meant that every football association in the country, including traditional clubs like Hertha BSC and Tennis Borussia Berlin, had been a part of the Nazi state and were summarily dissolved under Allied occupation in an effort to eliminate the Nazi Party and all associated organizations.[12] Along with local clubs, administrative organizations like the German Football Federation (Deutscher Fußball-Bund, DFB), which oversaw the administration of German football on a national level, were also eliminated. In their place emerged community sports associations (*Sportsgemeinschaften*, SG) organized through local neighborhood sports offices. In Berlin, the Berlin Magistrat's newly formed Sports Office (Hauptsportamt), comprised initially of ten Berlin sport functionaries and run by German Communist politician Franz Müller, administered these associations.[13] Thus, when Berliners picked up the newspaper, they read about teams like SG Gesundbrunnen against SG Mariendorf or SG Charlottenburg versus SG Prenzlauer Nord. Where the Southern League in the American-occupied zone saw the return to competition of perennial champions 1. FC Nürnberg, along with FC Bayern München, Eintracht Frankfurt, and VfB Stuttgart, soon after the war ended, traditional names did not return to Berlin until 1948 (and then only on the Western side) when political ties between East and West Berlin frayed beyond repair.[14]

Through these administrative reworkings, Allied occupiers hoped to accomplish the goals they had articulated before the end of World War II. As well as affecting the game's political connections, these new policies had a profound impact on its symbolic orientation. Teams vanished, players moved, and badges changed. Rivalries shifted, and allegiances turned. In other words, football simply looked different in Berlin under Allied occupation. Few examples demonstrate these changes better than the story of Heinrich Schmidt, who had been a stalwart of Berlin football for decades.[15] Born in 1909, Schmidt grew up in the north of Berlin and began his football training at a local neighborhood club, Alemannia 1890. At a young age he already showed considerable promise as an athlete, and his abilities earned him a place at Tennis Borussia Berlin, which required him to move across the city but allowed him to intensify his training. Schmidt was neither physically imposing nor did he have an abundance of speed, but his unmatched guile meant that he secured a regular starting position at Tennis Borussia Berlin by age nineteen and earned ten selections to Berlin's all-star team.[16] With a deft touch, a clever flick, a slick feint, he could not just dance past defenders but also charm his fans, who adoringly called him "Heini" or "Micky-Maus."[17] Schmidt cemented his place in the hearts of Tennis Borussia Berlin fans when he scored a vital goal against Minerva Berlin that won his team the 1932 Berlin championship.

Heini Schmidt had become one of Tennis Borussia Berlin's biggest heroes, but Allied occupiers had no reverence for the city's football pantheon. Occupational policies meant that when the thirty-seven-year-old Schmidt decided to play in the city's first postwar football championship, he could not return to the same club that he had previously led to a championship. Tennis Borussia Berlin did not exist anymore. Moreover, Magistrat policy required athletes to participate in the sports association of the district in which they resided, so Schmidt played the season representing SG Prenzlauer Berg West from the Soviet sector. This realignment was just one marquee example of several other similar moves that demonstrate the wide-reaching consequences of Allied occupation on defeated Berlin.

When Allied authorities established a framework to oversee sport in occupied Berlin, they imagined a mutualistic relationship with a sympathetic football administration that would promote the occupational objectives of demilitarization and denazification. The Allies aimed to sever football's administrative connections to National Socialism by reorganizing clubs as neighborhood associations while maintaining the broad, mass appeal that could breathe new life into the postwar game. Such administrative realignment certainly had consequences and affected the way the game looked in Berlin. New teams, under the supervision of a new government, now suddenly had new players with new allegiances, fundamentally changing the traditions and the symbols of Berlin's football pantheon.

Revitalized Sports in Postwar Berlin

Under the administrative oversight of first Soviet and then combined Allied occupational forces, sports and football grew quickly in the immediate aftermath of World War II. Diverse opportunities to participate in sports initially emerged in local settings and developed into larger citywide endeavors in the latter months of 1945. Despite Allied commitments to sever Berlin's football administration from its very recent and violent past, however, the lasting fingerprints of National Socialism upon the sport became all too apparent. While responses were swift, efforts to denazify Berlin's burgeoning sports environment in the first year of occupation ultimately proved ambiguous at best.

Sport was a constant in the postwar lives of Berliners. Even before American or British troops had reached the city, Berliners played their first postwar football matches on May 20, 1945. Not three weeks after the end of the war, the Soviet-backed *Berliner Zeitung* reported that "10,000 football-crazy fans" visited stadiums in Lichtenberg and Weißensee, which had been repaired and made match-ready thanks to the local municipal authorities in Lichtenberg.[18] These games were not isolated incidents. In the weeks and months that followed Germany's unconditional surrender, Berlin's newspapers regularly featured reports not just on football events but also on a broad and active sports environment throughout the city. Berliners had opportunities to play handball, basketball, and hockey. They organized horse races at the Karlshorst racecourse.[19] They ran track and swam laps. They even participated in novelty competitions like newspaper-delivery bicycle races.[20] Adults, adolescents, and young children could all find their own place in sport should they wish. Both men and women, boys and girls, were active, but not in all sport. Women and girls competed primarily in handball, field hockey, and, once teams emerged, basketball but remained glaringly absent from any media coverage of football—a seeming continuation of an entrenched sentiment within Germany's sporting institutions that vehemently opposed women playing football.[21]

The burgeoning sports scene was buttressed by a reemerging media voice that served as a reliable resource to access football coverage in occupied Berlin. Popular football publications like the Nuremberg-based *Kicker Sportmagazin* ceased its operations in Autumn 1944 and did not return to press until 1951. Indeed, Allied authorities had a hard enough time marshaling the resources to rehabilitate a reliable daily press that expansion into more specialized journalistic endeavors seemed like a distant dream. Along with most material goods, paper and ink—not to mention infrastructure and editorial staff—proved in short supply.[22] The *Berliner Zeitung*, aligned with the German Communist Party, was among the earliest newspapers to press and published its first issue on May 21, 1945. Readers only had to wait until the second issue to find coverage of football.[23]

As Berlin's presses returned to print across all sectors of the city, so too did the coverage of city sports. Papers like *Neues Deutschland* in the Soviet sector and *Der Tagesspiegel* in the American zone all featured regular, if not daily, sports coverage. Certainly they were closely monitored by their corresponding occupying power and represented regular organs for announcing policies and communicating directives. Newspapers, however, represented not only the official voice of the occupiers but also an effort to build trust with German populations. Indeed, newspapers relied on German editors and journalists to present trustworthy and accessible voices to their readership.

They also created a venue for heated debates about the legacies of Nazism, the rebuilding of Germany, and postwar experiences.[24] While this was no doubt a strategy of the Allied occupation to build relationships with the German people, it also meant that football coverage was far from perfunctory and offered readers a lively window onto the field. Sport calendars communicated a regular schedule, but more interested readers could also find matchday previews ahead of each round of the city championship as well as weekly reports summarizing the action. Papers occasionally featured player profiles, offered editorial opinions, or even included photographs that helped to bring the sport from the field to their readers.

Through this active media coverage and a lively sports environment, Allied authorities hoped to use football to promote their mission to denazify Berlin and promote antifascist and democratic ideals among the population. Some of these initiatives featured more overt political messaging than others. For example, neighborhood sports offices hosted educational lectures and informational sessions to emphasize the connection between sport and democracy, like a three-part sports lecture series that included presentations entitled "The Rebuilding of Berlin" and "The Renewal of the Democracy of Europe."[25] Other political demonstrations relied on matches to commemorate victims of the Nazi regime. One such game memorialized Paul Zobel, a Weimar-era sports editor and member of the German Communist Party who died as a political prisoner in Dachau in 1944. The match featured a selection of players from Wedding in the French sector and Charlottenburg in the British sector, and it took place at a sports ground near the train station Gesundbrunnen in the French sector.[26] In other more subtle interventions, football quietly underpinned educational initiatives and reclamation projects. Many children played football in neighborhood day care centers where they stayed while their guardians returned to work. The Youth Office in Neukölln even organized an initiative for both office staff and local children to restore the nearby Karstadt-Sportsplatz in anticipation of a youth football exhibition at the end of May 1945. It was not uncommon for Soviet newspapers to celebrate the early collective "joyful effort" of Berlin's inhabitants to rebuild local sporting spaces.[27]

Early Allied efforts in divided Berlin to commemorate the victims of political persecution at the hands of the Nazis often overlooked Jewish victims. Commemorative initiatives ignored athletes like Simon and Fritz Leiserowitsch, Jewish brothers who played for Tennis Borussia Berlin alongside Heinrich Schmidt in the 1920s and 1930s and were expelled because of the club's collaboration with Nazi policy. After playing his last football match in Berlin on May 7, 1933, Simon fled to Palestine. His younger brother remained in Berlin with his wife and daughter until the family was captured and deported to Auschwitz.[28] Once competitive league play resumed in Berlin in January 1946, these brothers, like countless other players, administrators, and spectators who had been targeted by systemic violence under the Nazis, could not reclaim their place in Berlin's sporting pantheon, and Allied authorities demonstrated little interest in commemorating them.

Beginning first as a hyperlocalized initiative, football eventually provided the impetus to bring together a city divided by modern warfare and conquest. One notice published in the *Berliner Zeitung* captures the local scope of these associations. It instructed that "athletes, coaches, and youth leaders who would be interested in building a community sports association" in the neighborhood of Osloer Straße (an area in the Soviet sector designated as the short stretch "between Prinzenallee and Oskarplatz") to meet at the restaurant Dabbert, located at Schulstraße 66, "for conversations about logistic measures."[29] As local sports offices established teams, neighborhoods started to offer more than just showcase exhibition events and to discuss more structured competitions. By August 1945, for example, districts from northern Berlin formed the Northern Division (Abschnitt Nord) that brought together sixteen teams from the French- and Soviet-occupied sectors for regular matches.[30] Similarly, the Eastern Division (Abschnitt Ost) included twenty teams from both Soviet and American sectors.[31] Competitions included all levels of play and were not just for the most talented players, as some neighborhoods included second-choice teams as well as adolescent (*Schüler*) and youth (*Jugend*) squads. By grouping together teams from different sectors, football divisions started to sketch their own maps of Berlin irrespective of the political lines drawn by the Allied occupation.

Perhaps one of the earliest and most ambitious interventions to coordinate sports across Berlin came in June 1945 when Johannes "Hanne" Sobek organized the citywide Großkampftage. Along with serving as one of ten committee members for the Berlin Sports Office, Sobek was also one of Berlin's most beloved football personalities. His athletic talent and his personal charm—punctuated by his carefully manicured coiffure—made him a revered figure not just in sports circles but also in Berlin's broader popular culture. Hertha BSC's brightest star during its most successful period in the

1930s, Sobek helped the team win no fewer than eight city championships from 1925 to 1938 and to win back-to-back German national championships in 1930 and 1931. He was selected to the Berlin all-star team over one hundred times, and he represented the German national team on ten occasions.[32] After his playing career ended, Sobek remained active in Berlin's football scene and worked as a sports presenter during the Third Reich.

In the lead-up to the Großkampftage, a writer from the *Berliner Zeitung* visited Sobek to discuss the upcoming events. The journalist was captivated by a "strong, healthy, and tanned" Sobek regaling coworkers with stories from his playing days. Sobek described the events of the weekend, which included football matches in Gesundbrunnen, track and field events in Charlottenburg, and cycling through Mitte, among many other displays. The main attraction, Sobek insisted, would take place at the British sector's Poststadion where a Berlin all-star football team would play a selection of players from the Red Army.[33] Sobek believed the match would attract double the stadium's forty-thousand-person capacity. Local sports competitions would animate excitement across the city. "You will be able to see on Sunday," he said, "Berliners' love of sports [will] once again run wild."[34] These were precisely the kinds of athletic events that Allied authorities hoped to promote: bringing together communities and knitting together the city through healthy and spirited competition.

Yet Sobek—this charming face of Berlin football, charged by Allied authorities as a founding member of the Berlin Sports Office with the express mission to denazify the game and democratize the community—soon revealed that he had been a member of the Nazi Party. Consequently, soon after the Großkampftage Sobek was deposed from the Berlin Sports Office and replaced by Karl Koppehel, who had been a prominent Berlin football functionary during the Weimar Republic.[35] According to his denazification hearings that began in April 1946, Sobek alleged that he had been compelled to join the party in 1940 to advance his career and preserve his standing as a sports-radio personality after his playing career ended.[36] By accounts offered on his behalf, Sobek harbored no admiration for the Nazi Party or the ideology of National Socialism and indeed had rebuffed multiple earlier attempts by Nazi officers to persuade him to join the party. A Berlin denazification hearing confirmed that while Sobek had been a member of the Nazi Party, he was "not actively committed to goals of National Socialism."[37] Sobek was only declared denazified in August 1948, however, and soon after resumed an active football career as a manager.[38]

Sobek's association with the Nazi Party might not have been as nefarious as those of some of his football-playing contemporaries, but he nevertheless represented a very public and clear connection to the fallen regime that undermined Allied occupational objectives.[39] The gears of Soviet denazification purged him from local administration only after he had been promoted as a relatable and popular face of a sports festival as well as a prominent member of a new administrative body in Berlin's new government.[40] By the time American, French, and British forces arrived in the city to set up their denazification apparatuses, the swift expansion of Berlin's football landscape complicated Allied authorities' capacity to monitor and evaluate other administrators and participants in the league. One such player was Rudolf Kippel, the captain of SG Wilmersdorf, who appeared before a denazification panel October 30, 1946.[41] By that time, Kippel had already captained his team to an undefeated season and captured Berlin's first city championship. He was pictured in a photo spread in *Neue Berliner Illustrierte* receiving a trophy from Berlin mayor Arthur Werner.[42] By the time his relationship with National Socialism had been scrutinized, Kippel had become a prominent and celebrated fixture of Berlin's football resurgence no matter the findings of the committee. Much like Sobek, Kippel had been expressly connected with the Allies' reimagining of Berlin football.

Under Allied stewardship, Berlin developed a sprawling football atmosphere that grew from locally organized initiatives. The game found its way into various dimensions of postwar life: as a spectacle for fans, as physical education for athletes, as public commemoration for political victims and, consequently, as a popular and connective tissue that bonded the physically and administratively fractured city. While Allied authorities imagined football as a vehicle to sever ties with National Socialism, the quick spread of the sport across the city, coupled with the slow and uneven implementation of denazification policies, meant that the results of this plan were ambiguous at best and largely reflected the ambivalent conclusions drawn about Allied denazification efforts.[43]

The First Postwar City Championship in Berlin

Despite their ambitions to utilize sport as a transformative force in Berlin society, Allied occupiers could not impose their values through sheer force of will. Staging a citywide football league required considerable coordination since food shortages, material scarcities, and destroyed infrastructure did not provide the most conducive conditions. For the league to succeed, organizers, players, and spectators had to negotiate the challenges of postwar life. Perhaps much more than a mechanism for accomplishing Allied occupational goals, then, the Berlin city championship instead confronted ordinary Berliners with the challenges of postwar life and reminded them of the limits of Allied administration.

Berlin's first postwar citywide football championship kicked off on January 6, 1946, with characteristically winter weather. The forecast for the day predicted cold and damp conditions, and that was precisely what players and fans encountered as they attended matches. In his journal for that day, US major general John Maginnis described a "miserable, ice-stormy morning."[44] The *Berliner Zeitung* also lamented that the weather conditions interfered with the abilities of the athletes and ultimately dampened the spectacle of the game, reporting that "almost no technically outstanding play was seen."[45] Nevertheless, on that dreary winter Sunday—amid one of Berlin's bitterest winters—individuals made decisions to compete on the field and to watch from the terraces. Those decisions and actions that made the league possible also brought Berliners into a new postwar landscape as they became familiar with the city's new networks and ultimately made space to include football in everyday lives that, in January 1946, could largely be characterized by scarcity. Berliners might not have known whether their local store could honor their ration card or where they might find fresh vegetables. Yet, for weeks to come, Berliners knew where they could find competitive football at 2:30 on Sunday afternoons.

From January through July, teams, administrators, and fans crisscrossed the city, traversing occupied boundaries and overcoming material challenges so that they might watch a football match. Thirty-six teams represented different neighborhoods from across the city and were divided into four separate groups (*Staffeln*). The groups were not divided along occupied sectors, and geography seemingly played no role in the organization of the league at all. Soviet-, American-, and French-sector teams competed in all four groups while the British sector only had teams in Group A and Group C. Teams competed in nineteen rounds of games to determine the champion of each group. The four group champions then competed against each other in a championship round (*Endrunde*) to crown Berlin's first city champion after World War II.

Athletes battled over league position during the same historical moment when they also struggled to secure regular sources of food. The Magistrat's commitment to equitable distribution of food ultimately failed as the city's different sectors experienced various levels of access to food.[46] Even so, some Allied sectors only permitted a fraction of the requisite calories (itself a politicized concept) needed to sustain an average adult.[47] Pervasive scarcity gave way to widespread starvation and disease that resulted in rising death rates in the first months of Allied occupation.[48] Malnutrition at the hands of Allied occupiers led not only to widespread public health crises in Berlin but also to the proliferation of perceptions among Germans of their own victimization, and consequently access to rations became a highly politicized issue.[49] Obtaining enough calories required not only searching for sufficient food but also struggling to claim justice in the wake of cataclysmic violence and destruction.[50] Even if individuals could secure a ration card, that did not mean that they would actually be able to claim their entitled portion, and ration access continued to haunt Berliners as both an omen of persistent vulnerability as well as a signal of Allied judgment.[51]

This context serves as a stark reminder that most football players in Berlin had to navigate particularly precarious lives immediately after World War II because football was not a professional sport in Germany and, consequently, football players could not be eligible for a ration card as such.[52] Indeed, the Berlin Sports Office reiterated its commitment to amateurism in football by declaring that "no one who is a part of the leadership of Berlin sports supports professional football," and they continued to indulge in the idealism of amateurism.[53] Players had to work alternative jobs to be eligible to claim their ration in hopes they might be fit and fueled enough to participate in training throughout the week and to compete in weekly matches. This physical strain put players at such risk that they jeopardized their health to both earn rations and play football. For example, Rudolf Kippel, captain of SG Wilmersdorf, suffered a "work-related injury" that kept him out of competition for several matches.[54]

The search for calories and nutrition was only part of the larger material struggle of staging the season. The games themselves required leather for equipment like balls and shoes, fabric for uniforms, not to mention space and time—all notably scarce in first years of postwar Berlin life. Shoes proved an especially elusive commodity, illustrated by the forum moderated on the pages of the *Berliner Zeitung* entitled "Wie steht es mit den Schuhen?" (What is going on with shoes?) that solicited questions from readers writing for solutions on how to find shoes or even learn where or how to repair shoes. Local Berlin shoemakers wrote responses, including one master shoemaker from Treptow, in the Soviet sector, who replied exasperatedly, "There are no nails, there is no leather for soles, no thread and no needles for the sewing machine. How am I supposed to carry out repairs?"[55] Even when shoes were available, people could hardly afford their exorbitant prices. In one instance of price gouging reported by the *Berliner Zeitung*, a retailer in Charlottenburg attempted to sell a pair of athletic shoes for RM 220, a price deemed so excessive that local authorities levied a fine of RM 2,000 against the store owner.[56] Efforts to circumvent shortages and price gouging led some Berliners to post want ads in hopes of negotiating trades. One ad posted in *Neue Zeit* sought a pair of women's athletic shoes and offered to purchase them or trade with a women's overcoat.[57]

Fabric and textiles, too, were strictly rationed, with a considerable supply available on the black market for exorbitant prices.[58] It has been suggested that scavenging for uniform fabric resulted in a proliferation of teams wearing red and black, since an abundance of Nazi flags had suddenly become unfashionable to fly.[59] Access to materials might have been limited, but competing football teams found ways to produce a wide array of uniforms that, in many ways, reflected the undeniable historical complexities of the league. Some uniforms were simple. SG Tempelhof, for example, wore an all-white kit with a simple blue *T* drawn on the chest. These nondescript uniforms could have been worn by any team in any historical moment, and these kinds of monochromatic schemes would have been easy to cobble together from mismatched clothes or other scraps of fabric. Similarly, SG Stadtmitte lined up with black shirts, black shorts, and black socks. It seems fitting that SG Stadtmitte, a sporting association formed in occupied Berlin, wore a kit as aesthetically blank as their competitive legacy. However, that kit, potentially woven from remnants of Nazi regalia (and possibly suggestive of the stains of fascism on Europe), meant that even a team with no sporting history could evoke complex historical ambiguities. In many ways, this dynamic was emblematic of the league as a whole.

Other clubs, however, wore more elaborate jerseys. Ahead of their clash on June 2, SG Prenzlauer Berg West and SG Stadtmitte, both teams from the Soviet sector, had an opportunity to seize control of Group D on the last day of the regular season. In their all-black, blank uniforms, Stadtmitte's kit contrasted sharply with Prenzlauer Berg's flashier design with two-toned sleeves, an angular, outlined collar, and a distinctive patch with a circled *P* on the left chest. This patch did not exist before May 1945 because SG Prenzlauer Berg West did not exist before May 1945. In some respects, the circle *P* badge represented unconditional surrender and was a stark reminder to players and spectators that football in Berlin now played out under occupied terms. Simultaneously, it expressed a reckoning with the realities of the present and a willingness to usher in a new moment in Berlin football.

Contrastingly, SG Wilmersdorf from the British sector took a different approach that gestured toward a continuity with the recent past that Allied restructuring efforts attempted to sever. Rather than wearing a blank uniform or creating a new insignia, Wilmersdorf uniforms carried the small striped flag of Berliner Sport-Verein 1892.[60] Berlin football fans would recognize it as the same badge worn by the team when it had won three Berlin championships during the Third Reich. Also harkening back to the past, SG Charlottenburg wore the distinctive violet and white colors that had earned its predecessor, Tennis Borussia Berlin, the nickname "die Veilchen" (the Violets). These material hints toward the past kept the spirit of pre-1945 associational life alive in a postwar world.

These were the kinds of historical nuances that spectators encountered when they attended matches. Some Berliners could access the stadium experience more easily than others. Individuals living near stadiums like the Exerstadion in Prenzlauer Berg or Zastrowstraße in Tempelhof could access a regular schedule of league football in their own neighborhood. Most other fans had to rely on a public transportation system that was slowly resuming. Berlin's public transportation system, consisting of several overlapping networks of buses, trains, trams, and even ferries, had been a target for Allied bombing during World War II. By June 1945, only the bus system had marginally come back to some semblance of regular service; large stretches of the underground train (U-Bahn) remained out of service due to damage from aerial bombing and underground flooding.[61]

The questionable reliability of public transportation was one challenge for Berlin football to overcome. Another was the logistics of the actual travel itself. Some teams, like SG Staaken and SG Oberschöneweide, lay on opposite ends of the city. On March 3, during the eighth round of the championship, SG Staaken traveled from the western end of the British sector to Köpenick, a borough in the eastern reaches of the Soviet sector, to play SG Oberschöneweide at Sadowa stadium. The morning began damp and cold and, while the clouds broke later in the afternoon, the temperatures never rose much above freezing. SG Staaken was a strong team and sat comfortably atop Group C. By all accounts, they were expected to win comfortably against SG Oberschöneweide—perhaps the most arduous test they faced that Sunday was the train journey. Because Köpenick lay on the eastern outskirts of Berlin, stadiums like Sadowa remained largely unharmed by Allied bombing and could be used with minimal refurbishing soon after the end of World War II. Staaken itself was nestled safely on the western banks of the Havel River in the crook of the Königswald; traveling between the two locations pushed the logistic capacity of postwar Berlin's public transit system to its limits and, for most, might simply have been impossible. Indeed, the *Berliner Zeitung* even lamented that matches held at the field adjacent to Bahnhof Staaken wrought the "most unfavorable travel conditions" for the Berlin football community.[62]

Even though a journey from Staaken to play against SG Tiergarten at Poststadion in the center of Berlin might have been logistically more manageable, it would have confronted players and spectators with the visceral wounds of war that haunted Berlin's streets. More than just the rubble and the destruction, football spectators living on the edges of Berlin would have seen how spaces now worked differently than they had before the end of the war. Any travelers who transferred through Alexanderplatz—a bustling hub in the Soviet sector that by September 1945 could facilitate travel further south to areas of Neukölln or west to Stadtmitte and Charlottenburg—would have navigated one of Berlin's more active black market spaces and glimpsed a new perspective on scarcity and survival. The regular reportage in local newspapers about black market raids and racketeering reflected lived experiences that not only showed Berliners their postwar city but also reminded them of the limits of Allied authority.

In this way, the Berlin football championship was more than just a stadium experience. It was more than just the defined values and objectives that Allied occupiers had embossed onto it. It represented, instead, a unique lens through which participants could learn about the mechanisms of Allied authority and the complexities of postwar life. Certainly Berliners did not need a football league to remind them that scarcity pervaded or disease abounded. The signs were unavoidable. Yet, through the game, Berliners could familiarize themselves with the tactics of navigating postwar life and understand the limits of Allied occupation.

Conclusion

The competition to determine the first postwar Berlin football champion concluded in spectacularly dramatic fashion. On the final day of the season, SG Wilmersdorf from the British sector faced SG Prenzlauer Berg West from the Soviet sector with the title on the line. Wilmersdorf had finished the regular season undefeated, but a surprise loss to SG Staaken in the penultimate game of the championship round had journalists questioning whether they could finish the job.[63] Nearly twenty thousand spectators visited the Hertha-Platz in Gesundbrunnen in the French sector to watch the season's final match.[64] A scoreless first half was reportedly not without incident as admirable technical play was interrupted by "incompetent" decision-making from the referee, Lausch, who made a controversial decision to disallow Prenzlauer Berg's opening goal.[65] The simmering crowd became increasingly rowdy, and soon after Wilmersdorf took the lead through a ferocious strike from Niedzwiadek, which sent the entire stadium into a frenzy. As the fans became more agitated the players too became more aggressive, culminating in unsportsmanlike play from Prenzlauer Berg's forward Heinz Behnke that led to his dismissal from the game. Behnke responded by attacking the referee, and the spectators invaded the pitch to join the fray. Only after the police arrived could order be restored, but play did not resume. The match was abandoned, and in such unceremonious circumstances a 1–0 victory awarded to SG Wilmersdorf and with it the first postwar football championship in Berlin. Wilmersdorf's captain, Rudolf Kippel, spoke of his disappointment, saying, "The joy of our well-earned championship has been overshadowed by the regrettable incidents of the day."[66] This calamitous end to the season was in many ways a fitting encapsulation of the relationship between Berlin football and Allied occupation in the first year after World War II. Wilmersdorf left the field as the first postwar champion of Berlin through an unsatisfying resolution and to popular resentment, much in the same way that Allied occupiers might claim to have achieved their collective goals to assert authority over Berlin.

The championship match between SG Prenzlauer Berg West and SG Wilmersdorf was abandoned when fans stormed the field after Prenzlauer Berg's forward Heinz Behnke attacked the match referee following a series of contentious decisions. Wilmersdorf was awarded a 1–0 victory and the first Berlin football championship after World War II. "Das Ende vom Endspiel," *Neue Berliner Illustrierte*, no. 27, August 1946, 6. *Courtesy of Center for Research Libraries.*

However, the Allied perspective only represents a narrow glimpse into a richer landscape. Peering beyond their ambitions, a fuller image slowly emerges of the first league season of postwar football in Berlin. The unruly and violent spectators demonstrated just how much football mattered in 1946 and served to emphasize the emotional dynamics that the game could evoke. Football created a public venue where ordinary Berliners could express their emotions, about the simple events of the game or, perhaps, the subtle (or overt) inflections of historical nuances encapsulated by it. The efforts required to play the game—to endure the cold, gather the resources, sacrifice the time and energy—themselves represented collective acts to learn about and engage with the physical and historical contours of postwar life in Berlin. By July, the Berlin Sports Office confirmed the second season of the city championship would begin on September 22 in a new, expanded league system that would include over one hundred different teams divided into three different tiers.[67] This expanded new league, with its new players, administrators, and fans, would draw in more and more participants to experience postwar Berlin, its scars, and its boundaries. More importantly, the game created spaces where Berliners might imagine what could be—a goal, a victory, a championship, a future—before the geopolitical conflict of 1949 ultimately rendered these visions impossible.

Notes

1. Richard Bessel, *Germany 1945: From War to Peace* (New York: Harper Collins, 2009); Konrad Jarausch, *After Hitler: Recivilizing Germans, 1945–1955* (Oxford: Oxford University Press, 2006); Harald Jähner, *Aftermath: Life in the Fallout of the Third Reich, 1945–55* (New York: Knopf, 2021); Monica Black, *Death in Berlin: From Weimar to Divided Germany* (Cambridge: Cambridge University Press, 2010); Paul Steege, *Black Market, Cold War: Everyday Life in Berlin, 1946–1949* (Cambridge: Cambridge University Press, 2007).

2. Tony Judt, *Postwar: A History of Europe since 1945* (New York: Penguin, 2005), 21.

3. Bessel, *Germany 1945*, 297; Steege, *Black Market*, 19.

4. Black, *Death in Berlin*, 145–86.

5. Rene Wiese, "Hertha BSC im Kalten Krieg (1945–1961)," in *Sportstadt Berlin im Kalten Krieg*, ed. Jutta Braun and Hans Joachim Teichler (Berlin: Christoph Links Verlag, 2006), 97; Ulrich Hesse-Lichtenberg, *Tor! The Story of German Football* (London: WSC Books, 2002), 130–31.

6. Heather L. Dichter, Robert J. Lake, and Mark Dyreson, "New Dimensions of Sport in Modern Europe: Perspectives from the 'Long Twentieth Century,'" *The International Journal of the History of Sport* 36, nos. 2–3 (2019): 123–30.

7. Heather L. Dichter, "'Strict measures must be taken': Wartime Planning and the Allied Control of Sport in Occupied Germany," *Stadion* 34, no. 2 (2008): 193–217.

8. Dichter, "'Strict measures,'" 200.

9. Perhaps it is no coincidence that an English sport was deemed permissible by the Allies.

10. Wolfram Pyta, "German Football: A Cultural History," in *German Football: History, Culture, Society*, ed. Alan Tomlinson and Christopher Young (New York: Routledge, 2006), 3–5.

11. Each region organized its own league. In Berlin, the Verband Berliner Ballspielvereine oversaw the Berlin league until it was dissolved in 1933 when soccer operations in Germany were taken over by the Deutscher Fußball-Bund (DFB). Only regional champions qualified to play for a national championship.

12. "6. Magistratssitzung vom 11. Juni 1945," in *Die Sitzungsprotokolle des Magistrats der Stadt Berlin, 1945/6*, vol. 1, ed. Dieter Hanauske (Berlin: Verlag A Spitz, 1995), 122–24.

13. "Sportamt der Stadt Berlin gebildet," *Berliner Zeitung*, June 21, 1945, 4.

14. "Sportamt," 4.

15. "Ein Berliner Fußballerleben," *Berliner Zeitung*, July 7, 1946, 4.

16. Wiese, "Hertha BSC," 102.

17. Wiese, "Hertha BSC," 102.

18. "Hiiiiinein . . . ! Fußballkämpfe im Stadion Lichtenberg," *Berliner Zeitung*, May 23, 1945, 4.

19. "Neues Leben auf dem 'Grünen Rasen,'" *Neue Zeit*, July 22, 1945, 4; "Ein 80,000-Mark-Rennen der Traber: Stichfahren in Karlshorst am 12. August," *Neue Zeit*, August 2, 1945, 3.

20. "Morgen nachmittag: die Meisterschaft der Zeitungsfahrer," *Berliner Zeitung*, July 20, 1945, 4.

21. Gertrud Pfister, "The Future of Football Is Female!? On the Past and Present of Women's Football in Germany," in *German Football: History, Culture, Society*, ed. Alan Tomlinson and Christopher Young (New York: Routledge, 2006), 97–100. The DFB in West Germany would not recognize women's football until 1970. The first women's football team was founded in East Germany in 1968.

22. Wolfgang Schivelbusch, *In a Cold Crater: Cultural and Intellectual Life in Berlin, 1945–1948*, trans. Kelly Barry (Berkeley: University of California Press, 1998), 154; Burghard Ciesla and Dirk Külow, *Zwischen den Zeilen: Geschichte der Zeitung "Neues Deutschland"* (Berlin: Das Neue Berlin, 2009), 28–29.

23. "Fußballwettkampf," *Berliner Zeitung*, May 22, 1945, 4.

24. Jähner, *Aftermath*, 237–43; Schivelbusch, *In a Cold Crater*, 154–60.

25. "Sportkalendar," *Berliner Zeitung*, August 20, 1945, 4.

26. "Fußball am 2. September," *Berliner Zeitung*, September 2, 1945, 4; Wolfgang Eichel, *Geschichte der Korperkultur in Deutschland, 1945–1961* (Berlin: Sportverlag, 1965), 19.

27. "Jugend schafft fur die Jugend: Ein Jugendpfleger berichtet," *Berliner Zeitung*, May 24, 1945, 4.

28. Matthias Hörstmann, ed., *Verlorene Helden* (Berlin: 11Freunde Verlag, 2014).

29. "Fuß-, Hand-, und Hockeyspiele," *Berliner Zeitung*, May 28, 1945, 4.

30. "Fußballabschnitt Nord," *Neue Zeit*, August 10, 1945, 3.

31. "Fußball am 2. September," *Berliner Zeitung*, September 2, 1945, 4.

32. Hardy Grüne, *Von Kronprinz bis zur Bundesliga, 1890 bis 1963* (Kassel: Agon Sportverlag, 1996), 258; Wolfgang Hartwig and Gunter Weise, *100 Jahre Fussball in Berlin* (Berlin: Sportverlag Berlin, 1997), 244.

33. It is worth noting that the Poststadion is the same stadium where Adolf Hitler infamously watched Germany lose to Norway during the 1936 Berlin Olympics.

34. "Großkampftage Gespräch mit Hanne Sobek," *Berliner Zeitung*, June 1, 1945, 4.

35. "Sportkalendar," *Berliner Zeitung*, August 19, 1945, 4.

36. Daniel Koerfer, *Hertha unter dem Hakenkreuz: Ein Berliner Fußballclub im Dritten Reich* (Gottingen: Verlag Die Werkstatt, 2009), 67.

37. Landesarchiv Berlin, Entnazifierungsakte Sobek, April 8, 1946, quoted in Koerfer, *Hertha unter dem Hakenkreuz*, 73.

38. "Hanne Sobek entnazifiziert," *Berliner Zeitung*, August 6, 1948, 4.

39. For example, Otto "Tull" Harder, a player for Hamburg Sportverein during the first half of the twentieth century, joined the SS and served as a camp commandant at the Ahlem concentration camp, a satellite camp to the Neuengamme system. He and four of his former subordinates were tried for war crimes by British authorities and sentenced to fifteen years in prison while another defendant formerly under his supervision was sentenced to death.

40. Jarausch, *After Hitler*, 50; See also Timothy Vogt, *Denazification in Soviet-Occupied Germany: Brandenburg, 1945–1948* (Cambridge, MA: Harvard University Press, 2000), 80–81.

41. "Verhandlungstermine der Entnazifizierungskommission," *Berliner Zeitung*, October 10, 1946, 4.

42. "Berlin: Ein Hohepunkt im Sportleben," *Neue Berliner Illustrierte*, November 1946, 15.

43. Jarausch, *After Hitler*, 49–52.

44. John Maginnis, *Military Government Journal: Normandy to Berlin* (Amherst: University of Massachusetts Press, 1970), 326.

45. "Überraschende Ergebnisse in der Berliner Fußballmeisterschaft," *Berliner Zeitung*, January 7, 1946, 4.

46. Steege, *Black Market*, 37.

47. Jähner, *Aftermath*, 166; Nick Cullather, "The Foreign Policy of the Calorie," *American Historical Review* 112, no. 2 (2007): 337–64.

48. Black, *Death in Berlin*, 147.

49. Jessica Reinisch, *The Perils of Peace: The Public Health Crisis in Occupied Germany* (Oxford: Oxford University Press, 2013), 104; Alice Autumn Weinreb, "Embodying German Suffering: Rethinking Popular Hunger during the Hunger Years (1945–1949)," *Body Politics* 2, no. 4 (2014): 463–88.

50. Atina Grossmann, "Grams, Calories, and Food: Languages of Victimization, Entitlement, and Human Rights in Occupied Germany, 1945–1949," *Central European History* 44, no. 1 (2011): 123.

51. Grossmann, "Grams, Calories, and Food," 125; "Leser schreiben an 'Neues Deutschland,'" *Neues Deutschland*, May 5, 1946, 4.

52. "Erhohung der Lebensmittelnormen," *Neues Deutschland*, July 14, 1946, 1.

53. "Berufsfußball in Berlin?" *Berliner Zeitung*, March 15, 1946, 4. In November 1946, in the American-occupied zone in southern Germany, football players in Baden-Württemberg were permitted to create a union to explore the development of professionalization in football. "Die Bildung einer Fußballvereinigung deutscher Berufsspieler," *Berliner Zeitung*, November 11, 1946, 4.

54. "Fußball-Städtekampf: Berlin-Zwickau," *Berliner Zeitung*, September 20, 1946, 4.

55. "Wie steht es mit den Schuhen? Was unsere Leser zu dieser Fragen zu sagen haben," *Berliner Zeitung*, May 17, 1946, 2.

56. "Preichwucher in Charlottenburg," *Berliner Zeitung*, May 17, 1946, 2.

57. "Damen-Sportschuhe," *Neue Zeit*, June 2, 1945, 5.

58. Steege, *Black Market*, 55.

59. Hesse-Lichtenberg, *Tor!*, 106.

60. "Berlin: Ein Hohepunkt im Sportleben," *Neue Berliner Illustrierte*, November 1946, 15.

61. "Hurra, der Omnibus fahrt wieder!" *Berliner Zeitung*, June 1, 1945, 2.

62. "Auftakt zur Berliner Stadtmeisterschaft," *Berliner Zeitung*, June 14, 1946, 4.

63. "Schafft es Wilmersdorf?" *Berliner Zeitung*, July 27, 1946, 5.

64. "Fußballmeisterschaft mit Krach," *Neue Zeit*, July 30, 1946, 4.

65. "Ein nie dagewesener Fußball-Endspiel-Skandal," *Berliner Zeitung*, July 30, 1946, 5. Media outlets could not agree whether the goal was rightfully disallowed or not. The *Berliner Zeitung* reported the goal was correctly ruled out while the *Neue Zeit* indicated that the goal should have stood.

66. "Ein nie dagewesener Fußball-Endspiel-Skandal," *Berliner Zeitung*, July 30, 1946, 5.

67. "Berliner Fußballplane: Zwei Pokalwettbewerbe und neue Meisterschaft," *Neue Zeit*, July 18, 1946, 4.

CHAPTER FIVE

United Sport in Divided Berlin

Negotiating the 1964 All-German
Olympic Team Trials Venues

HEATHER L. DICHTER

As soon as World War II ended in 1945, Berlin emerged as a focus of international political tensions and negotiations, first between the four Allied powers and then between the two new German states. In sport, however, the city did not become a flashpoint until the 1960s. West German sport leaders wrote in 1960 to Avery Brundage, the International Olympic Committee (IOC) president, asking him to provide a statement that West Berlin belonged to the Federal Republic and thus jurisdiction for sport in that part of the city fell under their National Olympic Committee while East Berlin belonged to East Germany so sport there fell under East Germany's National Olympic Committee.[1] Brundage did not provide as detailed a statement as requested, but his reply acknowledged that "it is generally considered internationally that West Berlin is part of the Federal Republic of Germany, and East Berlin is part of the German Democratic Republic," thus "the International Olympic Committee must consider that the Nationales Olympisches Komitee fur [sic] Deutschland has jurisdiction over West Berlin and the Nationales Olympisches Komitee der Deutschen Demokratischen Republic has jurisdiction over East Berlin." He then ended his letter by commenting that he was "astonished that such a question has been raised and I point out again the necessity of keeping sport free from politics."[2] Although Brundage fervently hoped to keep Cold War politics out of sport, this proved impossible. The division of Berlin became the focal point in negotiations and threatened the Olympic movement's effort to overcome the division of Germany.

The status of the two Berlins and the two Germanys in the eyes of Brundage and the IOC reflected the significant role played by the IOC in recognizing and legitimizing nation-states in the twentieth century. Newly independent states, such as the European countries that emerged from the collapse of several empires in 1918 and the new African and Asian states that emerged throughout the post-1945 wave of decolonization, immediately sought recognition by the IOC. Additionally, the Soviet Union joined the IOC in 1951, thus guaranteeing the Olympics as a site for Cold War conflicts between East and West. Even with this expansion of the Olympic movement as the result of global politics, however, Brundage continued to insist that sport was completely separate from politics.

Brundage's rejection of the German division within Olympic sports set up the conflict between a unified ideal and the concrete existence of two separate and distinct political entities. By 1951 the Federal Republic had resumed the place of "Germany" within the IOC and affiliated international federations.[3] While some international federations granted separate recognition to the German Democratic Republic, others followed the IOC's lead and only granted provisional membership to East Germany. The IOC therefore insisted on the creation of an all-German team for the Olympic Games in the 1950s and 1960s, with athletes and officials from both German states coming together as a single Olympic team. Brundage praised sport's ability to transcend politics and called the establishment of the all-German Olympic team "a tremendous victory for sport in accomplishing something the politicians have been unable to do."[4] Even though East German sport leaders actively participated in the all-German Olympic team negotiations, they nonetheless still pushed for their own separate Olympic team.[5] East German political leaders fought for international recognition outside of the Soviet bloc on many fronts, including the establishment of formal diplomatic relations, the welcoming of ships flying the East German flag into foreign ports, and the acceptance of travelers carrying East German passports.[6] Yet due to the significant global visibility and popularity of Olympic sports, the East German government made sport its most prominent diplomatic tool in its quest to gain international recognition.

The special status of Berlin made the sport diplomacy of West Germany, East Germany, and the IOC particularly challenging. Berlin's unique place during the Cold War was a legacy of its postwar occupation. The quadripartite powers had divided and occupied Berlin as they had the rest of

Germany. When in 1949 the American, British, and French occupation zones merged to form the Federal Republic of Germany (West Germany) and the Soviet zone became the communist German Democratic Republic (East Germany), Berlin's sectors were likewise consolidated into West Berlin and East Berlin. The city's location in the heart of the Soviet occupation zone meant that, after 1949, West Berlin provided a Western outpost behind the Iron Curtain. The Federal Republic of Germany provided additional support to West Berlin in the form of extra financial assistance and tax breaks, and its male residents were exempt from military service.[7] East Germany and the Soviet Union frequently limited freedom of movement and threatened West Berlin as a way to remove an area of Western democracy and capitalism in Eastern Europe.[8] The construction of the Berlin Wall in 1961, which put a stop to freedom of movement, exacerbated tensions between East and West Germany. These tensions transferred over to the world of sport during the preparations for the 1964 all-German Olympic team.

Despite West Berlin and East Berlin belonging to two separate states, in the 1950s and 1960s the IOC viewed these territories as representing the single entity of Germany and insisted on an all-German Olympic team. This requirement necessitated competitions to select the athletes for the German Olympic team. It was out of this context that the West German sport leaders' 1960 letter to Avery Brundage emerged. Because of West Berlin's status as a free city completely surrounded by East Germany, the East Germans did not want events to take place there, while the West Germans actively sought to hold events in West Berlin to reinforce the city's position as part of the Federal Republic. The consideration of Berlin as a host city for the all-German Olympic trials did not pertain to all sports, as some required specific outdoor terrain that Berlin could not accommodate. For the remaining sports, however, both East and West Berlin provided numerous possible venues for Olympic trials. For individual sports, athletes from both East and West Germany would compete in the Olympic trials and the top finishing athlete(s) would represent Germany at the Olympics.[9] For team sports, however, the East German team would play against the West German team and the winning side would be selected for the Olympic Games. Instead of the best football players from both East and West Germany playing on a single side, or the best rowers selected to form the strongest four or eight, athletes from only one German state formed the Olympic squad for each team sport.

German sport leaders repeatedly met to negotiate the location for these qualifying events and went back to the international federations and the IOC when they could not agree. This process turned a seemingly intra-German matter into a major problem for the IOC and international sport federations that required them to become involved in what should have been the concern of national—not international—sport leaders. After the erection of the Berlin Wall in 1961, Berlin's place as a site for Olympic trials in preparation for the 1964 Olympics in Innsbruck, Austria, and Tokyo, Japan, became even more contentious. The broader Cold War issues of freedom of travel and West Berlin's status directly affected sport as Berlin became a contested space within German-German negotiations during the preparations for the 1964 all-German Olympic team, as both East and West German sport leaders sought to use the status of sport in Berlin to accomplish their governments' broader Cold War diplomatic aims.

West Berlin's Status after the Wall

In August 1961, just days after the East German government laid out the barbed wire and sandbag fencing that soon became the concrete Berlin Wall, the Federal Republic's sport leaders met and agreed to end all German-German sport relations.[10] East German athletes lost additional opportunities when, in response to the wall, the Federal Republic's NATO allies tightened travel restrictions to prevent East German athletes representing national teams from entering their borders.[11] These actions, and particularly the West German decision not to engage in any sport competitions with East Germans, threatened the viability of the all-German Olympic team for 1964. Further complicating matters, East Germany argued that West Berlin should have its own Olympic Committee and team separate from West Germany, which would thus disqualify West Berlin as a potential site for the all-German Olympic trials. Both East and West German Olympic Committees sought to use Berlin as part of their broader diplomatic efforts to assert their position vis-à-vis the other German state. The fight against West Berlin as a site for selection events for the all-German Olympic team, including the outlandish idea that the city have its own Olympic team, became yet another strategy by which East Germany hoped to achieve its diplomatic goals and remove West Berlin from the Federal Republic's control during the Cold War.

What remained of Berlin's interwar sporting infrastructure after 1945 was spread across East and West Berlin, providing several venues that could host Olympic qualification events on each side of the city. The 1936 Olympic stadium complex was in West Berlin and stood in what had been the British sector of the city where the British military forces had used it during the occupation period and for the next two decades.[12] The Sportpalast, a famous indoor arena that opened in 1910, was also in West Berlin. East Berlin had the Exer, a nineteenth-century military training ground that eventually became sport fields and the first playing grounds for BFC Hertha 1892 (later Hertha BSC). In the 1950s the German Democratic Republic had expanded this area into a major site for sporting activity and renamed it the Friedrich-Ludwig-Jahn-Sportpark.

After the creation of the Berlin Wall, travel and freedom of movement became points of conflict within the city of Berlin and hampered the ability of the two German Olympic Committees to work together. Because thousands of East German citizens had fled East Germany through West Berlin prior to August 1961, East German officials feared that and holding events there would re-open that escape route for additional East Germans.[13] Once the IOC persuaded both sides to resume negotiations for the 1964 Games, West Berlin, now completely surrounded by a visible border, became one of the most frequently discussed points. The East German effort to isolate West Berlin from the Federal Republic was both physical, with a concrete wall, and rhetorical, with claims that West Berlin was not in fact part of the Federal Republic. In October 1962, more than a year after the Berlin Wall appeared and German-German sport stopped, the IOC invited the two National Olympic Committees to a December meeting in Lausanne, Switzerland, to start preparations for the 1964 all-German Olympic team. The IOC acknowledged in its letter to both committees that "the erection of the wall in Berlin and the stop of the free personal traffic between both parts of Germany are regarded as a fundamental change of the situation in Germany in many parts of the world."[14] The IOC recognized the drastic change in Germany as a result of the Berlin Wall and realized that this action that had nothing to do with sport had in fact impacted sport and had the potential to affect the Olympic Games.

Although the IOC acknowledged the changed reality with the Berlin Wall, they nonetheless "insist[ed] on the formation of a combined German team for the Olympic Games in 1964," proposing six points that should form the basis of the preparations for the all-German Olympic team. The third point specifically addressed the ability of both East and West Berlin to host the selection events.[15] When the two German National Olympic Committees met with the IOC in December 1962, both sides agreed to accept Berlin as a site for Olympic selection events. However, the East Germans did not want Berlin to be the host for every event, and suggested, for example, Leipzig for swimming since the city had been the site of the recent European championships. The minutes from the meeting note that "disagreement arose when discussing the notion of free circulation," with the West German delegates demanding "that the press, broadcasting companies and interested sportsmen must have the possibility to attend the events freely and everywhere." The minutes do not record the nature of the disagreement, just noting that the East German delegates "also wish free circulation" and that "sport has not erected the wall and neither wished it."[16] Both sides nominally agreed to all six points, but when they next met in February 1963 the supplemental details to the location of Olympic selection events did not mention Berlin. In his statements to the press, however, Brundage acknowledged that not all events would take place in Berlin, with Leipzig and Dresden hosting some of them.[17] Although the East German sport leaders were officially saying that they would accept West Berlin, they spent the next year attempting to thwart those efforts.

The West German sport officials had their government's support in pushing for West Berlin as the location for these events. The Auswärtiges Amt, the Federal Republic's foreign ministry, reported to its American, French, and British colleagues that holding Olympic trials in Berlin served two political purposes. First, it prevented East German political officials from having access to West German territory. The West German government tried to prevent politically affiliated East Germans from traveling to the Federal Republic and fomenting unrest. All high-ranking East German sport officials held some level of political standing (otherwise they could not hold these high-level sport leadership roles). By holding events in West Berlin, the West German government did not have to worry about East German officials causing problems in the Federal Republic as their ability to do so was significantly diminished by West Berlin's special status and its residents' lack of support for East Germany. Second, holding events in Berlin could have a positive benefit in providing "a pretext to increase relations between the two parts of the old capital."[18] East Germany's enclosure of West Berlin with the construction of the wall immediately ended the ability of people to move between the two parts of the city for virtually any reason, including employment, shopping, or sport. With the West German Olympic

Committee's insistence on free travel not only for the media but also specta-tors, holding events in West Berlin would help to resume a small amount of the free movement that the wall had stopped in August 1961. The *Frankfurter Allgemeine Zeitung,* one of the Federal Republic's largest newspapers and based in the same city as the National Olympic Committee, emphasized this point as the federations started finalizing their plans. By holding these events in Berlin, the paper wrote, athletes "are helping their sport friends in West Berlin, who have been boycotted by the zone for years."[19]

With both National Olympic Committees agreeing that Berlin should host Olympic qualification events, the matter appeared to be resolved.[20] However, the relationship between the two National Olympic Committees soured again two months later, renewing the battle over Berlin. In late May 1963, newspapers around the world reported on the plans of West Berlin mayor (and future West German chancellor) Willy Brandt and the West German Olympic Committee to propose all of Berlin, both East and West, host the 1968 Olympic Games. They made this proposal with the knowl-edge of the federal government in Bonn, which hoped to achieve a new diplomatic breakthrough in the German-German Cold War relationship. The East German Olympic Committee declared that it had never heard of these plans and blamed the West Germans. Without full support from all German sport leaders (and for other reasons as well), the IOC's executive committee rejected the Berlin bid in early June.[21]

In response to West Germany attempting to politicize Berlin through the supposedly apolitical proposal for the 1968 Olympics to be held across all parts of the city, the East Germans pushed back against West Berlin hosting the all-German Olympic team trials, arguing instead that West Berlin should have its own Olympic team. On June 10, 1963, Heinz Schöbel, president of the East German National Olympic Committee, held a press conference to denounce the West German efforts to put forward a Berlin bid for the 1968 Summer Olympics. A reporter from the wire agency UPI noted that Schöbel had said "that West Berlin was not part of the Federal Republic." The reporter then asked him, "Do you think that the NOC [National Olympic Committee] of the Federal Republic is not responsible for the West Berlin athletes and therefore a third Olympic Committee, in other words a West Berlin Olympic Committee, should be formed?" Schöbel replied that it would be the IOC's right to recognize an Olympic Committee in West Berlin, noting that they had done so previously for Saarland, and that "West Berlin was not part of the Federal Republic under constitutional law."[22] His comment referenced the French efforts in the early 1950s to cleave Saarland from the Federal Republic, which resulted in Saarland's own Olympic team in 1956. However, Saarland residents had already declared their desire to return to Germany, leaving 1956 an anomaly within sport.[23] By using the IOC's precedent with Saarland and proposing this idea for West Berlin, Schöbel strengthened East Germany's claims for separate recognition and its own Olympic team, while at the same time reinforcing the German Democratic Republic's official view that West Berlin was not part of the Federal Republic.

The West German Olympic Committee countered these claims immediately, arguing that West Berlin and its sport system were part of the Federal Republic, a position reinforced by the government. Willi Daume, president of the West German Olympic Committee, wrote a letter to Schöbel that West German newspapers published in full. After reviewing the East German actions with respect to sport shortly before and after the Berlin Wall's construction, Daume reiterated that West Berlin sport clubs have been members of the West German sport federation since its founding in 1949. West Berlin's athletes therefore "belong to the representative teams of the Federal Republic. The affiliation of West Berlin sport clubs to sport organizations of the Federal Republic is based on the free decision of the West Berlin athletes." Furthermore, Daume noted that Schöbel had "never questioned this free decision of West Berlin sport in the past; it has been recognized by all international federations and expressly confirmed as legal by the IOC for the Olympic field. Irrespective of all political views, the sporting status of West Berlin is absolutely clear, both legally and practically."[24] The West German sport leaders needed to reaffirm West Berlin as part of the Federal Republic from both a sporting and legal standpoint. The West German government supported its National Olympic Committee's position because of the political implications of reinforcing West Berlin's position. At the two-day conference of Federal Republic interior ministers a week later, the ministers noted the need to have nothing threaten the talks to revive the German-German sport relationship—including the boycott of West Berlin sport. The interior minister for North Rhine Westphalia also served as the chair of his province's sport federation and was tasked with developing points to encourage the relationship between the two German states.[25] Continued East German discrimination against West Berlin athletes would thus threaten the resumption of the German-German sporting relationship, including the status of the all-German Olympic team for 1964.

The IOC's rejection of Berlin's bid for the 1968 Olympics, a proposal made by West Germany without support from East Germany, ultimately demonstrated West Berlin's position as part of the Federal Republic. The IOC's consideration of the bid, presented by the West Berlin mayor and the president of the West German Olympic Committee, reiterated Brundage's earlier statement that West Berlin was part of the Federal Republic, at least in the eyes of the IOC. The East Germans thus had to accept that fact, if only from a sporting perspective.[26] Combined with the IOC's rejection of the outlandish East German idea that West Berlin have its own Olympic team, the efforts of both German states to use Berlin as part of their diplomatic positioning against each other failed when the IOC did not accept either claim and continued to insist on an all-German Olympic team.

The 1964 All-German Olympic Trials

With the failure of East Germany's efforts to break West Berlin from West German sport, the country had no choice but to resume the efforts to create the all-German team for the Olympic Games the following year. In the summer of 1963, the negotiations between the two National Olympic Committees and their respective national governing bodies increased in intensity, especially as the winter sport federations needed to finalize these plans before athletes started their competition seasons. Berlin continued to be the point of contention. West German sport officials wanted Berlin to host all of the qualification events (with the exception of sports such as skiing where that was not possible) to reinforce West Berlin's position as part of the Federal Republic. They also recognized that West Berlin events would provide East German spectators an opportunity to flee to the West. In addition, holding events in East Berlin would provide an opportunity for disaffected East Germans to show their support for West German athletes—and thus the Federal Republic. This West German demand for West Berlin to host so many events, and the East German efforts to prevent that entirely, continued to place the divided city at the center of the preparations for the all-German team, frequently requiring the IOC and international federations to intervene in this German-German problem.

In football, for instance, the two federations had agreed in May for the games to take place in September in Karl-Marx-Stadt and Hanover, but when the two National Olympic Committees met again in early July, the Federal Republic delegates refused to confirm these locations because the Western host city was Hanover and not West Berlin. The East Germans interpreted the West German refusal to accept Hanover as evidence that the West German Olympic Committee's actions were following its government's political line of playing up West Berlin's importance.[27] *Neues Deutschland,* the East German state newspaper, placed all of the blame on Daume, claiming that he was "not guided by sporting considerations, but unfortunately by the politics of the Bonn revanchists."[28] The West Germans eventually honored their original agreement, with the two games taking place in Karl-Marx-Stadt and Hanover in September.[29]

The concerns about Berlin as a host city ran in both directions. For the track and field qualification events, the East Germans agreed to the Olympic Stadium from the 1936 Olympic Games, located in West Berlin, for the first of the events, in recognition of the facility's capabilities. However, the East Germans did not want the second qualification event in East Berlin but instead in Leipzig, Dresden, or Karl-Marx-Stadt. The *Frankfurter Allgemeine Zeitung* interpreted the East German request as political, claiming that the East German sport leaders feared that the East Berlin crowd would give the West German athletes a great welcome "that would be tantamount to a political demonstration."[30] Many East Germans watched the West German national football team on television (often illegally) and celebrated their victories, including the 1954 FIFA World Cup, demonstrating that many East Germans did not support the regime.[31] The newspaper also claimed the East German regime not only feared that its citizens would protest if the Berlin Wall prevented them from attending a football match in West Berlin but also that they did not trust their own population "about the communist way."[32] In contrast, speculated the *Frankfurter Allgemeine Zeitung,* the other cities had been without freedom longer than East Berlin and were thus better for the Olympic qualification events, which is why the East German sport leaders proposed alternative cities while arguing that East Berlin did not have enough facilities to host track and field events.[33] The *Frankfurter Allgemeine Zeitung* covered the National Olympic Committee's meetings and actions since they were based in the same city, and with this close relationship the paper had the ability to publicly call East German actions political without having to quote the West German sport leaders who clearly shared these sentiments (and provided the newspaper with information about the negotiations).

For the Winter Olympics, only the skating events took place indoors and were thus the only events that had the possibility of taking place in Berlin.

When the two ice skating federations met, the East Germans claimed their athletes' safety could not be guaranteed at the West Berlin Sportpalast. They also claimed that the venue was too small, which the West Germans said was the "most unserious argument the Eastern delegation was able to find" since the venue had, since its opening before World War I, hosted numerous large events including the 1961 European Figure Skating Championships.[34] British diplomats in Berlin called this meeting between the two ice skating federations "even more fruitless" than the meetings between the National Olympic Committees, noting that the skating federations could not even agree on the formal statement about their failure to agree.[35] The British noted that the *Neues Deutschland* article emphasized the East German claims that the Sportpalast's ice dimensions were significantly different from those of the rink in Innsbruck where the Olympics would be held. The British report back to London noted that if the point about the rink size was accurate, then the East Germans would "no doubt be in the stronger position in an appeal to international sporting organisations who are likely to take more account of practical than political arguments."[36] These battles continued throughout the summer as the East and West German leaders for each sport met to discuss the Olympic qualification events, with the lack of agreement over host cities—often Berlin—reported in newspapers in both German states. Both East and West German papers claimed the other side was politicizing the issue over Berlin hosting the Olympic trials while their own German sport leaders' actions were not, which reinforced each side's overall position regarding German-German sport more broadly.

Frustrated at the repeated East German efforts to prevent West Berlin from hosting Olympic trial events, the West German Olympic Committee held an emergency meeting in early August 1963. As Daume explained in the press conference after the meeting ended, the Federal Republic only considered "sport and practical reasons" and not political motivations for proposing West Berlin.[37] East Germany, on the other hand, "was apparently prepared to renege" on the pledge made at the meeting with the IOC in December 1962 regarding the preparations for the all-German Olympic team.[38] Since agreements could not be made regarding West Berlin, Daume and the West German Olympic Committee requested that the IOC president make the final decisions.[39] Brundage and a few other IOC members met with representatives from both National Olympic Committees, including Daume and Schöbel, on August 20 in Lausanne to try to resolve the impasse with the all-German team preparations. Interest in this meeting was great, with the press asking Brundage questions before he traveled to Lausanne. Brundage kept his answers general, particularly in response to a direct question about events taking place in West Berlin.[40] Shortly after the meeting began, the issue of venues, and especially West Berlin, became "the main object of dissension." After listening to both German views, Brundage established three principles for the preparation of the all-German team. First, "The interest and welfare of sport must prevail over any other consideration in the selection of the location of try-outs," and the national governing bodies "will suggest the only places that are best fitted" for their sports. Second, West Berlin could host these events "if no better location may be proposed," but that "a concentration of try-outs in West-Berlin is to be avoided." Last, when these events took place in East or West Berlin, arrangements must be made so that "all selected athletes and officials, as well as the spectators of the other area may come to attend the meetings."[41] Brundage and the IOC hoped these principles would result in the rest of the negotiations for the all-German Olympic team running smoothly, allowing for the continuation of their solution, which they claimed rose above Cold War politics.

Both German states focused on the aspects of this meeting's outcomes that aligned with their arguments. The East German press highlighted Brundage's decision that the Olympic trial events would not be concentrated in Berlin.[42] The West German press focused on both sides compromising, with the German Democratic Republic recognizing West Berlin as a place to hold the Olympic trial events, and with the Federal Republic not insisting on West Berlin alone as the preferred site.[43] The *Frankfurter Allgemeine Zeitung* emphasized that Brundage's decision that West Berlin could host the Olympic trial events handed the East German sport leaders a big loss, as they had wanted West Berlin to have its own Olympic committee.[44] British diplomats again reported on the matter, noting that the formal press release "does not, of course, refer directly to the real point at issue—the number of matches to be played in West Berlin. Because of this, the West German press can point triumphantly to the confirmation of the right of West Berlin while 'Neues Deutschland' can hail the outcome as a blow to the Bonn revanchists." The report also commented that "the West German National Olympic Committee will reluctantly accept those agreements already concluded by various sporting associations which do not provide for a match in West Berlin."[45] With this resolution, the negotiations for the Olympic qualification events returned to the national governing bodies to resolve.

Even with this directive, however, the inability of the Germans to come to a consensus regarding some venues and events in Berlin left Brundage to provide the final decision, such as whether the Sportpalast in West Berlin was suitable for figure skating (he agreed it was).[46] Heinz Schöbel protested this decision, but Brundage was unmoved.[47] The same problems arose in the spring of 1964 over the location of some of the qualification events for the summer games, with Brundage again needing to make final decisions.[48] The boxing federations were able to agree for their events to take place in Schwerin and West Berlin, although the *Frankfurter Allgemeine Zeitung* noted that more top-level East German boxers came from East Berlin clubs than Schwerin and suggested that East German officials continued to fear that all-German sporting events in East Berlin "could become public demonstrations for the solidarity between West and East."[49] When the track and field competition took place in the Olympic Stadium in West Berlin, the Norwegian diplomat in Berlin noted that the crowd of forty-five thousand was entirely West German, calling it "a strange spectacle."[50] On the other end of the spectrum, when the West German ice hockey team won the second game in the Seelenbinder Halle in East Berlin, the five thousand fans in the arena, from the fifty thousand people who wanted tickets, were selected based on their political leanings, with 75 percent of the spectators wearing the communist logo.[51]

In the end, despite East German efforts, both East and West Berlin hosted some of the all-German Olympic team trial events for Innsbruck and Tokyo. The arguments repeatedly raised from both sides over Berlin hosting Olympic qualification events reinforced the geopolitical importance of the city. Holding events in West Berlin reiterated the city's connection to the Federal Republic, while allowing East Germans—if they could attend the events—a chance to demonstrate their dissatisfaction with the communist state of the German Democratic Republic. The efforts to exclude West Berlin from hosting qualification events were attempts by East Germany to prevent more of its citizens from voicing their support for the Federal Republic by cheering for its athletes or by using the event to flee to the West. These actions also aligned with East Germany's broader effort to remove West Berlin from the Federal Republic's orbit.

Jürgen Kalfelder of West Germany, left, and Hans-Ulrich Schulz of East Germany, right, both ran the 400 meters at the all-German Olympic team trials at the Olympic Stadium on August 23, 1964. © dpa. *Courtesy of picture-alliance.*

Conclusion

From a German perspective, the 1964 Olympics are often considered the last time an all-German team appeared, remembered for the acrimony between East and West German sport leaders during the Olympic Games themselves. This bitterness was most visible when the two National Olympic Committees could not even agree on a flagbearer when the teams arrived at the Olympic Village in Tokyo—seen in a sad photograph of the German team marching behind a sign but not a flag, an image reproduced in newspapers worldwide.[52] The numerous problems with the all-German Olympic team directly contributed to the IOC finally agreeing the following year to East Germany's separate recognition. The team at the 1968 Winter Olympics in Grenoble, France, was only nominally a combined team because of the host country's NATO membership; the IOC granted East Germany complete autonomy for its Olympic team at its session on the eve of the 1968 Summer Olympics in Mexico City.[53] The formal recognition of East Germany as a separate country with its own Olympic team brought détente to sporting relations before West German chancellor Brandt ushered in the era of political détente.

During the preparations for the 1964 all-German Olympic team, the city of Berlin was one of the most contentious points of negotiation, requiring the IOC and international federations to intervene. Logistically, holding events in both East and West Berlin within twenty-four hours of each other made more sense than traveling longer distances across both German territories, as *Frankfurter Allgemeine Zeitung* once noted.[54] Instead of that simple solution, especially when many East German athletes were based in Berlin, the city became a contested place within the negotiations. Each set of national governing bodies determined the sites for the Olympic qualification events, and the international federations and IOC intervened when the Germans could not agree on locations, making this issue one which numerous sport leaders had to confront. Berlin thus repeatedly became the place over which both East and West German sport officials promoted their government's official position regarding the divided city within the wider landscape of the Cold War. East Germany frequently attempted to isolate West Berlin and claim that it was not officially part of the Federal Republic, a strategy demonstrated in sport with the claim that West Berlin should have its own Olympic committee and not be used as a site of Olympic qualification events. The Federal Republic, on the other hand, wanted as many events in both West and East Berlin as possible to overcome the stark limits to the freedom of movement imposed by the Berlin Wall. These negotiations over where the qualifying competitions for the all-German Olympic team would take place went beyond simple event logistics to become part of the broader efforts of each nation to achieve their diplomatic goals.

The IOC's continued demand for the creation of a combined German team forced both German states to interact through their National Olympic Committees even after relations deteriorated with the construction of the Berlin Wall. These German-German negotiations over the all-German Olympic team, requiring the involvement of the IOC and international federations, demonstrates how international sport serves as a venue for diplomacy—both as a site for diplomatic negotiations and for reinforcing a state's international goals. Holding events in West Berlin forced the German Democratic Republic to acknowledge that West Berlin was, in fact, part of the Federal Republic. Free travel across the two parts of the city remained limited, as demonstrated by crowds being entirely from one side of the city or the other. While on the surface these squabbles appeared petty and repeatedly forced the IOC to get involved, the fight over venues in East and

West Berlin hosting qualification events for the all-German Olympic team brought the Cold War and its problems directly into sport and, because of sport's popularity, to both German publics. Berlin was a symbol of the Cold War from its beginning with the air lift through the end with the fall of the Berlin Wall, and during the heightened tensions of the 1960s, the German problem became an international matter with the IOC's involvement as sport venues across the city became contested spaces.

Notes

1. Willi Daume to Avery Brundage, January 15, 1960, German Question—W. Germany & E. Germany 1945–1969, Box 129 (Reel 71), Avery Brundage Collection (hereafter ABC), University of Illinois Archives, Champaign, Illinois (hereafter UIA).

2. Avery Brundage to Willi Daume, January 18, 1960, German Question—W. Germany & E. Germany 1945–1969, Box 129 (Reel 71), ABC, UIA.

3. Heather L. Dichter, "Sporting Relations: Diplomacy, Small States, and Germany's Postwar Return to International Sport," *Diplomacy & Statecraft* 27, no. 2 (2016): 340–59.

4. Avery Brundage to Roy E. Moore, November 23, 1955, Federation Internationale de Gymnastique, 1946–63, Box 215 (Reel 125), ABC, UIA.

5. The East German actions during the negotiations over the all-German Olympic team in 1952 frustrated the IOC and led to only West Germans competing in the 1952 Winter Olympics in Oslo and Summer Olympics in Helsinki. Uta A. Balbier, *Kalter Krieg auf der Aschenbahn: der deutsch-deutsche Sport, 1950–1972: eine politische Geschichte* (Paderborn: Ferdinand Schöning, 2007); Karsten Lippmann, "... und für die Ehre unserer Nation(en)": *Olympische Deutschlandpolitik zwischen 1960 und 1968* (Hildesheim: Arete, 2017).

6. William Glenn Gray, *Germany's Cold War: The Global Campaign to Isolate East Germany, 1949–1969* (Chapel Hill: University of North Carolina Press, 2003).

7. David Clay Large, *Berlin: A Modern History* (London: Allen Lane, 2001), 417; Jeremi Suri, "The Cultural Contradictions of Cold War Education: The Case of West Berlin," *Cold War History* 4, no. 3 (2004): 5.

8. Dennis L. Bark and David R. Gress, *A History of West Germany, vol. 1, From Shadow to Substance, 1945–1963* (Oxford: Basil Blackwell, 1989), 210–27, 435–40, 462–70; Patrick Major, *Behind the Berlin Wall: East Germany and the Frontiers of Power* (Oxford: Oxford University Press, 2010).

9. Translation, Record of Resolutions of the Joint Session of the Representatives of the National Olympic Committee of the German Federal Republic and the National Olympic Committee of the German Democratic Republic, August 27, 1955, Box 127, Nationales Olympisches Komitee fur Deutschland 1945–1952 (Reel 70), ABC, UIA.

10. H. Passlack, Deutscher Fußball-Bund to FIFA, September 1, 1961, Correspondence with National Associations GER (FRG) 1955–1961, FIFA Archives, Zurich, Switzerland; Statement of the Presidium of the NOC of the German Democratic Republic, August 19, 1961, Republique Democratique Allemagne, Correspondance 1951–1962, Olympic Studies Centre, Lausanne, Switzerland (hereafter OSC).

11. Heather L. Dichter, *Bidding for the 1968 Olympic Games: International Sport's Cold War Battle with NATO* (Amherst: University of Massachusetts Press, 2021).

12. J. C. C. Bennett, Bonn, to J. S. Whitehead, Foreign Office, January 21, 1963, Foreign Office (hereafter FO) 371/169325, The National Archives, London (hereafter TNA), London, UK.

13. Mike Dennis, *The Rise and Fall of the German Democratic Republic 1945–1990* (Abingdon: Routledge, 2000), 90–93, 101; Rudy Koshar, *German Travel Cultures* (Oxford: Berg, 2000), 176; Major, *Behind the Berlin Wall*.

14. Otto Mayer to Nationale Olympische Komitee für Deutschland and Nationale Olympische Komitee der Deutschen Demokratischen Republik, October 22, 1962, Nationales Olympisches Komitee fur Deutschland 1945–1952, Box 127 (Reel 70), ABC, UIA.

15. Mayer to Nationale Olympische Komitee für Deutschland and Nationale Olympische Komitee der Deutschen Demokratischen Republik, October 22, 1962.

16. Protocol, Conference Held between a Delegation of the International Olympic Committee and Representatives of the two German Olympic Committees, December 8, 1962, German Question—W. Germany & E. Germany 1945–1969, Box 129 (Reel 71), ABC, UIA.

17. Minutes, Meeting Regarding the German Problem, Lausanne, February 6, 1963, Allemagne General, Reunion C.N.O. Allemands President Brundage, 1962–1963, OSC; "Gesamtdeutsch—bestimmt Avery Brundage," *Süddeutsche Zeitung*, February 8, 1963, 22.

18. Telegram 1656–57, Courson, Bonn to Diplomatie Paris, February 28, 1963, 105PO/1, Box 9, Centre des Archives diplomatiques de Nantes, Nantes, France (hereafter CADN).

19. "Qualifikationen in Berlin," *Frankfurter Allgemeine Zeitung*, May 31, 1963, 7. West German papers typically refused to acknowledge the German Democratic Republic and still referred to the country as the Soviet Occupied Zone.

20. "Erstes Olympiagespräch zufriedenstellend verlaufen," *Frankfurter Allgemeine Zeitung*, March 11, 1963, 11; "Im „Hilton"-Hotel siegte die Vernunft," *Neues Deutschland*, March 11, 1963, 3; "Fekkes tysk lag til OL neste år," *Aftenposten*, March 11, 1963, 12.

21. Heather L. Dichter, "The Diplomatic Maneuvering against the Short-Lived 1968 Berlin Olympic Bid," *Contemporary European History* 33, no. 2 (2024): 514–28; Noel D. Cary, "Olympics in Divided Berlin? Popular Culture and Political Imagination at the Cold War Frontier," *Cold War History* 11, no. 3 (2011): 291–316.

22. "Gemeinsamkeit weiter möglich?" *Neues Deutschland*, June 13, 1963, 2; "Die Sowjetzone will den Schwarzen Peter loswerden," *Frankfurter Allgemeine Zeitung*, June 11, 1963, 7. The British and French diplomats in Berlin reported on this press conference and news story. Telegram 66, Berlin to Bonn, June 13, 1963, FO 371/169325, TNA; Telegram 67, Berlin to Bonn, June 13, 1963, FO 371/169325, TNA; Despatch 204, Jean Le Roy to Ministre des Affaires Etrangères—Direction d'Europe, June 14, 1963, 105PO/1, Box 9, CADN.

23. Wolfgang Harres, *Sportpolitik an der Saar 1945–1955* (Saarbrücken: Saarbrücker Druckerei und Verlag, 1997).

24. "Gesamtdeutscher Sport nur mit West-Berlin," *Frankfurter Allgemeine Zeitung*, June 15, 1963, 11; "Willi Daumes Brief an Manfred Ewald," *Süddeutsche Zeitung*, June 15–17, 1963, 24.

25. "Die Innenminister sind für gesamtdeutschen Sportverkehr," *Frankfurter Allgemeine Zeitung*, June 23–24, 1963, 10.

26. P. C. H. Holmer to J. A. Robson, July 15, 1963, FO 371/169325, TNA; "Warum das Protokoll nicht bestätigt wurde," *Neues Deutschland*, July 12, 1963, 6.

27. Bericht über die Verhandlungen zwischen den beiden deutschen NOK am 8.7.1963 in Berlin, Hotel „Johannishof," July 15, 1963, Stiftung Archive der Parteien und Massenorganisationen der DDR (SAPMO) DR 510/407, Bundesarchiv, Berlin, Germany (hereafter BArchB).

28. "Warum das Protokoll nicht bestätigt wurde," *Neues Deutschland*, July 12, 1963, 6.

29. "Ost-Berliner Risiko," *Frankfurter Allgemeine Zeitung*, July 20, 1963, 11; "DFB-Amateure gewinnen zweite Olympiaqualifikation," *Frankfurter Allgemeine Zeitung*, September 22, 1963, 9.

30. "Ost-Berliner Risiko," *Frankfurter Allgemeine Zeitung*, July 20, 1963, 11.

31. Simon Kuper, "Cheering the Enemy," *Index on Censorship* 29, no. 4 (2000): 77–83.

32. "Berlin," *Frankfurter Allgemeine Zeitung*, August 6, 1963, 8; "Sportliche Gesichtspunkte," *Frankfurter Allgemeine Zeitung*, July 26, 1963, 7.

33. "Ost-Berliner Risiko," *Frankfurter Allgemeine Zeitung*, July 20, 1963, 11.

34. "Unsinnige Behauptungen gegen West-Berlin," *Frankfurter Allgemeine Zeitung*, July 29, 1963, 8; Willi Daume to Otto Mayer, October 2, 1963, D-RM01-ALLEM/006—Equipe unifée allemande aux JO: correspondance et PV 1962–1964, OSC.

35. P. C. H. Holmer to J. A. Robson, July 29, 1963, FO 371/169325, TNA.

36. Holmer to Robson, July 29, 1963; "Westdeutschsr Eissport vorband ließ Vorhandlungon scheitern," *Neues Deutschland*, July 29, 1963, 1.

37. "Daume: Wir halten an Berlin fest," *Frankfurter Allgemeine Zeitung*, August 2, 1963, 7.

38. "Germans Renew Debate Over Olympics Trails Site," *New York Times*, August 2, 1963, 21.

39. "Daume: Wir halten an Berlin fest," *Frankfurter Allgemeine Zeitung*, August 2, 1963, 7; Telegram, Willi Daume to Heinz Schöbel, August 3, 1963, SAPMO DR 510/407, BArchB.

40. H. F. Stierer to J. A. Robson, August 19, 1963, FO 371/169325, TNA; "Brundage: Beide deutsche NOK gleichberechtigt," *Neues Deutschland*, August 19, 1963, 3.

41. The requirement to ensure the press could attend those events, while discussed at the meeting, disappeared between the draft of the meeting minutes and the final version. Minutes, Meeting of the two German Olympic Committees presided over by Mr. Avery Brundage, August 20, 1963, Allemagne General, Reunion CNO Allemands President Brundage, 1962–1963, OSC.

42. Klaus Ullrich, "Konzentration von Ausscheidungen," *Neues Deutschland*, August 21, 1963, 8.

43. "Olympia-Ausscheidungen nun doch in West-Berlin," *Frankfurter Allgemeine Zeitung*, August 21, 1963, 7.

44. "Mit leeren Händen," *Frankfurter Allgemeine Zeitung*, August 22, 1963, 7.

45. H. F. Stierer to J. A. Robson, August 22, 1963, FO 371/169325, TNA.

46. Avery Brundage to Willi Daume and Heinz Schöbel, October 28, 1963, SAPMO DR 510/142, BArchB.

47. Heinz Schöbel to Avery Brundage, November 8, 1963, SAPMO DR 510/142, BArchB; Avery Brundage to Heinz Schöbel, November 20, 1963, SAPMO DR 510/142, BArchB.

48. "Ein trügerisches Protokoll," *Neues Deutschland*, April 12, 1964, 8; "Die Sowjetzonen-Funktionäre zu Kompromissen bereit," *Frankfurter Allgemeine Zeitung*, April 13, 1964, 8.

49. Despatch 422/EU, Le Nail to Ministre des Affaires Etrangères—Direction d'Europe, October 28, 1963, 105PO/1, Box 9, CADN; "Boxverbände einigten sich," *Neues Deutschland*, October 28, 1963, 4; "Boykott Ost-Berlins," *Frankfurter Allgemeine Zeitung*, November 2, 1963, 11; Airgram A-829, R. Glynn Mays Jr., USBER, Berlin, to Department of State, June 6, 1964, Record Group 59, Department of State, Central Foreign Policy Files, 1964–66, POL 2 GER E, Box 2201, National Archives, College Park, Maryland.

50. Oddvar Aas to Kgl. Utenriksdepartement, August 25, 1964, 74.10/113. Tyskland: Idrett og sport. Bind II. Fra 1/1 1960–31/12–69, Utenriksdepartement, Oslo, Norway.

51. "5000 ausgesuchte Plätze in der Ost-Berliner Seelenbinderhalle," *Frankfurter Allgemeine Zeitung*, December 10, 1963, 3.

52. "Dispute on German Team Dampens Olympic Flag Ceremony in Tokyo," *New York Times*, October 3, 1964, 23.

53. Dichter, *Bidding for the 1968 Olympic Games*, 159–201.

54. "Sportliche Gesichtspunkte," *Frankfurter Allgemeine Zeitung*, July 26, 1963, 7.

CHAPTER SIX

Beyond Integration

Amateur Football among People of Turkish Backgrounds in Berlin since the 1960s

JEFFREY JURGENS

Berlin's reputation as a cosmopolitan metropolis rests, in no small part, on its lengthy history of migration, and no immigrant or minoritized group is more closely associated with the city than people from Turkey and their descendants. According to recent estimates, more than two hundred thousand people of Turkish backgrounds currently live in Berlin, and their impact on the city's built environment and public life is hard to overlook.[1] Significantly, though, some of the city's most prominent Turkish diasporic institutions are not political organizations, restaurants, businesses, or mosques, but rather amateur football clubs. In fact, one 2008 study found that Türkiyemspor (My Turkey Sport), a club established in 1978, was the most recognized Turkish diasporic association in Berlin, and journalistic accounts commonly cite it as one of Germany's most prominent immigrant organizations.[2] This situation, far from being a mere curiosity, points to the central role that football, especially amateur football, has played in processes of migration, settlement, and incorporation in the Federal Republic of Germany (FRG). It also suggests that Berlin, with its extensive array of clubs established by people of Turkish backgrounds, is an apt place to examine them.

Although Ottoman subjects and Turkish citizens have resided in Berlin since the late eighteenth century, most people of Turkish backgrounds who now live there can trace their presence to the 1961 bilateral recruitment agreement that brought so-called guest workers from Turkey to the FRG. These recruited workers arrived in a city that had been decisively shaped by the Cold War division of Germany into two states in 1949 and the construction of the Berlin Wall in 1961. This latter event, in particular, cut off employers in West Berlin and other parts of West Germany from one of their major sources of wage labor: citizens of the German Democratic Republic (GDR) who left the socialist state in order to secure a more satisfying life in the FRG. According to the logic of the agreements that West Germany signed with Turkey and other circum-Mediterranean countries, the guest workers would only remain in the FRG as long as their presence contributed to the country's economic expansion. Indeed, the FRG formally ended labor recruitment in November 1973, when a global economic recession, growing family migration, and increasing labor activism led West German officials to conclude that these workers' ongoing presence was no longer worthwhile.[3]

Contrary to general expectation, however, many people of Turkish backgrounds did not return to Turkey but instead remained in the FRG and, in the case of West Berlin, came to inhabit the city in ways that defied their previous characterization as guest workers.[4] In particular, they established a variety of institutions that gave shape to a cultural-political field that was simultaneously local and transnational. Tellingly, some of the most prominent of these organizations were amateur sports clubs, above all football clubs, that catered to immigrants' desires not only for athletic competition but also for companionship and solidarity in an environment marked by racialized exclusion. At least in their early years, these clubs were comprised almost exclusively of players, coaches, administrators, and spectators who were either immigrants from Turkey or their children, and most if not all included specific references to Turkey in their names.

In its effort to trace the history of amateur football among people of Turkish backgrounds in Berlin, this chapter draws on prior scholarship, relevant mass media coverage, and ongoing ethnographic research.[5] In particular, it is informed by my fieldwork with Gençlikspor, one of the oldest clubs established by people of Turkish backgrounds in Berlin, as well as by a recent interview with Mehmet Matur, the current vice president for social responsibility of the Berlin Football Association (Berliner Fussball-Verband).[6] Perhaps unavoidably, the analytical emphasis falls on the participation of boys and men. Because football typically involves strenuous physical competition in public space and a specific sartorial presentation (i.e., players wear uniforms that leave their head, neck, and parts of their arms and legs exposed), it tends to be most easily reconciled with norms for cisgender men. As a result, the sport is a distinctly gendered pastime in Germany, Turkey, and the Turkish diaspora that remains strongly associated with boys, men, and masculinity.[7]

The ethnonational self-definition of immigrant-established clubs has been a consistent site of public anxiety and scholarly inquiry in the FRG. Much of the debate has hinged on the implications of these clubs for societal processes of integration.[8] Some commentators have insisted that these clubs promote immigrants' incorporation into wider German society, sometimes in line with the notion that sports have the capacity to transcend cultural and other collective differences.[9] Others, by contrast, propose that such clubs tend to segregate immigrants from mainstream German institutions and thereby contribute to societal fragmentation or even the formation of parallel societies (Parallelgesellschaften).[10] These debates become especially pointed when discussion turns to immigrant-established clubs' reputation for emotional outbursts, aggression, and violence directed at opposing players, coaches, spectators, and referees.[11] Instances of misconduct among players and clubs of Turkish backgrounds commonly draw unfavorable media attention, and several academic studies have documented that they are overrepresented in disciplinary actions undertaken by both referees and the sport courts (Sportgerichte) maintained by local- and state-level football associations.

Ultimately, this dominant understanding of integration presumes a linear process of adjustment whereby people of immigrant backgrounds become full members of the German nation-state by abandoning those norms and practices that distinguish them from the putatively monolithic and stable host society.[12] As a result, it cannot grasp the more complex transformations that many if not most football clubs in Berlin, not just those established by people of Turkish backgrounds, have undergone over the past five decades. On the one hand, the prevailing discourse of integration does not capture the varied ways immigrant-established clubs have experienced significant shifts in their demographic composition and reworked their cultural and geographic frames of reference even as they have gradually become less prominent within the city's sports landscape. On the other, it cannot account for the growing number of players and coaches who, even as they continue to define themselves in relation to Turkey in meaningful ways, play for clubs that cannot trace their origins to migration from that country. In the end, then, the amateur football landscape in contemporary Berlin is marked by a remarkable degree of fluidity: although one might have plausibly distinguished ostensibly "German" clubs from "Turkish" and other "foreign" ones into the 1990s, such ethnicized distinctions have grown less tenable over the past two decades, even as racist sentiments and practices continue to target Black people and people of color, including people of Turkish backgrounds. As a result, there is a pressing need to move beyond the discourse of integration, with its presumption of enduring native and immigrant collectivities, in order to pay more nuanced attention to historically contingent practices of marking ethnonational differences.[13]

The Formation of "Turkish" Clubs

Although football initially emerged in the British Isles in the twelfth century, it was not until the 1860s that public school administrators codified the rules of the game and established the sport's first governing body.[14] In its early years, football was a decidedly bourgeois pursuit, and English entrepreneurs, engineers, intellectuals, and university students were chiefly responsible for bringing the game both to Germany and to the late Ottoman Empire. Football gained a mass following in Germany after army officers encouraged enlisted soldiers to play the sport as a means of physical training and diversion in World War I.[15] In Turkey, meanwhile, football steadily moved beyond its center of gravity in the middle classes of Istanbul and Izmir as the Republic consolidated its secularist social order from the 1920s through the 1950s.[16] Thus, by the time guest workers from Turkey began to arrive in West Berlin in the 1960s, many of them were already familiar with the sport and eager to play. Because of persistent discrimination and exclusion, however, it took more than a decade for people of Turkish backgrounds to establish their own clubs. When they did so, they typically cast them as distinctly "Turkish" organizations that differed from the city's long-standing "German" clubs.

Upon their arrival in West Berlin, boys and men of Turkish backgrounds initially played informal pickup games with relatives and friends they knew from their hometowns in Turkey or from their neighborhoods and workplaces. It did not take long, however, for many of them to seek out more regular competition with a wider range of opponents. Their opportunities to do so were initially rather limited. When boys and men of Turkish backgrounds approached established football clubs in the city, they often met with indifference, if not overt resistance, from players, coaches, and club administrators. Several clubs were unwilling to offer membership to boys and men from Turkey because they feared a supposed flood of foreign players, while others were reluctant to grant them significant playing time or a meaningful role in club management. People of Turkish backgrounds understandably interpreted experiences like these as moments of discrimination and exclusion. Moreover, many players of Turkish backgrounds struggled to reconcile their moral and religious commitments with these clubs' activities: the prospect of attending a club-sponsored Christmas party, or of consuming beer and bratwurst, or of showering naked with one's teammates was rather discomfiting for a significant number of otherwise eager boys and men.[17]

In response to such encounters, men of Turkish backgrounds sought to establish their own clubs as an alternative route into the amateur leagues managed by the Berlin Football Association. These efforts, which began in the mid-1960s, were halting at first. On the one hand, it took time for recruited workers and their families to acquire the German-language competence and institutional knowledge necessary to establish a club and secure its legal recognition as a registered association (*eingetragener Verein*). On the other hand, local political officials and association functionaries were reluctant to recognize these clubs' existence. Many institutional gatekeepers regarded these clubs as unnecessary: after all, the common presumption went, recruited workers and their families would eventually return to Turkey. Slightly more receptive officials, meanwhile, adopted an assimilationist stance that foresaw sports clubs for people of Turkish backgrounds (and other ethnonational groups) as an exceptional short-term solution. While the formation of such clubs might be necessary in certain instances to prevent so-called over-foreignization (*Überfremdung*), they reasoned that players of non-German nationalities should eventually merge with mainstream West German society by joining established "German" clubs.[18]

Indeed, the earliest clubs founded by immigrants could only find their footing with the support of Turkey's General Consulate in West Berlin and Workers' Welfare (Arbeiterwohlfahrt), the West German social service organization that worked closely with people who had migrated from Turkey. Even then, it often took years for these clubs to be allowed entry first into the lowest level of play, the free-time league (*Freizeitliga*), and then the association's regular amateur leagues.[19] These clubs were also at a disadvantage when it came to the allocation of football fields, which were particularly scarce in

Kreuzberg, the district of West Berlin with the largest number of immigrants from Turkey. In the face of these obstacles, immigrant-established clubs cooperated with the Turkish General Consulate in 1978 to found the Turkish Sports Association (Türk Spor Birliği), which aimed to establish a football league for people of Turkish backgrounds that would operate separately from West Berlin's existing institutional structure. Given the prospective division of the city's sports landscape along ethnonational lines, Berlin's State Sports Association (Landessportbund) negotiated an agreement in 1983 that allowed for the full incorporation of the immigrant-established clubs into the city's (and the FRG's) amateur leagues.[20] With this agreement in place, twenty-eight clubs established by people of Turkish backgrounds had obtained official recognition by the mid-1980s.[21]

Significantly, these clubs initially defined themselves as explicitly "Turkish" organizations distinct from the established "German" clubs they played against. This seemingly self-evident divide was certainly due to the persistent exclusion these clubs experienced during their early years. Yet it was also a product of the transnational attachments they maintained with the Republic of Turkey. The names of many of the clubs established through the 1990s, for example, included Turkish-language references to Turkey (e.g., Türkspor, Ay Yıldız), to specific cities and towns (e.g., Ağrıspor, Samsunspor), or to Turkish professional football clubs (e.g., Marmara Gençlik, Galatasaray Spandau).[22] In other instances, the clubs aligned themselves with prominent political and cultural-religious currents in Turkey and the Turkish diaspora. Hür Türk and Türk El (which later merged to form Hürtürkel) were affiliated with right-wing Turkish nationalism, for example, while Al-Spor and Dersimspor (which later merged to form Al-Dersimspor) were affiliated with Turkey's Alevi and Kurdish minorities respectively.[23] Finally, Hilalspor was (and still is) known as a religious club whose members combine their enthusiasm for football with their devotion to Sunni Islam.[24]

Gençlikspor fits comfortably within this broader context. The club's first members, most of whom hailed from villages in eastern Anatolia, worked as guest workers at the electronics company Siemens in the late 1960s and early 1970s, and its founders were affiliated with the Turkish Workers' Association, an organization that acted as a liaison between recruited laborers and West German unions. In political terms, the club's profile was resolutely social democratic and leftist: one of its founding figures was an avowed socialist

Türkiyemspor before its match on June 18, 1988. The club had only been established ten years before, but as the sizable block of fans in the background indicates, it already enjoyed a significant following among Berliners of Turkish and other backgrounds. *Photo courtesy of IMAGO.*

who referred to the club as a "workers' and villagers' association" (*işçi köylü birliği*), and much of its membership sympathized with the left-leaning political forces that squared off against right-wing nationalists in Turkey in the 1970s. In its early years, Gençlikspor played informally in a company league against teams of other Siemens employees during the week and against teams of other recruited workers on weekends. It was not until the late 1970s that the club officially became a registered association, the legal status that allowed it to join West Berlin's amateur leagues. During my field-work in 1999–2001, the club's adult membership remained overwhelmingly men of Turkish backgrounds, and most members routinely referred to Gençlikspor as a "Turkish club," albeit one that disavowed an exclusionary definition of Turkish nationhood and welcomed players of Alevi and Kurdish backgrounds. The club's members thereby aligned themselves with other "Turkish clubs" in relation to the "German clubs" against whom they played most of their matches. This Turkish/German divide was so entrenched that it appeared beyond question: any club that Gençlikspor might encounter, it seemed, could be slotted into one of these two categories.

The Question of "Turkish Aggression"

Such practices of ethnic differentiation remain a common feature of Berlin's amateur football scene, and historically they have taken on particular salience in moments of on-field conflict. It is important to note that the vast majority of the matches played by clubs of Turkish and other backgrounds, both in Berlin and throughout the FRG, have proceeded peacefully over the past five decades. Nevertheless, players of Turkish backgrounds have acquired a distinct reputation for excessive emotional outbursts, fouling, aggression, and violence. The consequences of this reputation for immigrant-established clubs, and for people of Turkish backgrounds more broadly, have been manifold. On the one hand, players and clubs of Turkish backgrounds, as a number of studies have demonstrated, are overrepresented not only in conflicts on the field, but also in the disciplinary penalties imposed by referees and sport courts.[25] On the other hand, players, coaches, and spectators of Turkish backgrounds have been framed in local and national mass media portrayals as unduly volatile and aggressive in ways that have shaped wider perceptions of this population and the racialized difference it purportedly embodies.[26] Members of clubs established by people of Turkish backgrounds have been keenly aware of their stigmatization and have sought to acknowledge, dispute, and mobilize it in a variety of ways. In sum, the question of "Turkish aggression" highlights the degree to which amateur football participates in wider debates over pluralism and the terms of national (non)belonging.

These themes can perhaps be most vividly broached by way of an ethnographic vignette. During my fieldwork with Gençlikspor, I regularly played with the first men's team, which was composed almost entirely of men in their twenties and thirties whose families had migrated from Turkey in the late 1960s and 1970s. (The two exceptions were one white German man and myself, a white American man.) On one Sunday in May 2000, our team suffered a frustrating loss to Hellas-Nordwest, a club primarily composed of white German men. Several members of Gençlikspor were upset by the referee's decisions, and as he entered the team's changing area, a number of players approached him to discuss the matter. Most of the conversation revolved around the contest's pivotal stretch: one of Gençlikspor's players, Hasan, had gotten into a shoving match with an opponent from Hellas, and the two of them had collided soon thereafter while competing for a loose ball. Hasan had cried out in (exaggerated) pain as he grabbed his leg and fell to the ground, but the referee had not called a foul. Hasan had been able to keep playing, but a few minutes later, he had tripped another opposing player near Gençlikspor's goal. This time, the referee had not merely called a foul but issued Hasan a yellow card and awarded a penalty kick. Hasan and several of the team's other elder players had complained vigorously, both before and after Hellas scored, but to no avail.

Now it was one of the team's younger members, Erdal, who approached the referee. He tried to dispute the decision on technical grounds—Hasan's tackle had not been as dangerous as it looked, it had occurred outside the penalty area—but the referee was having none of it. It was at this point that the team captain, Ahmet, tried a different tack: "you know, ref, we are after all southerners [*Südländer*]. Can't you understand that we might be somewhat more aggressive than other teams?" Without apparent irony, Ahmet urged the referee to show some sensitivity [*Fingerspitzengefühl*] to this aggressive inclination and to tailor his decisions accordingly. In effect, Ahmet was engaged in a moment of strategic self-typification in order to make the case for culturally relativist or even ethnically appropriate officiating.

Strikingly, the referee rejected Ahmet's argument but basically agreed with the terms in which he had framed it. "You [*ihr*, second person plural] may be more temperamental," he replied, "but you're not more aggressive. And I *did* show sensitivity—I'm a southerner too, but from Yugoslavia, not Turkey. Do you know how many yellow cards I could have given?" The referee thereby implied that the members of Gençlikspor could be thankful that he had not been more severe. Still, even as he disputed just how aggressive or temperamental the team might be, the referee subscribed to the notion that such a thing as "southern temperament" existed, and that Gençlikspor's players, as men of Turkish backgrounds, embodied it. Ahmet, who had presumed that the referee was "German" and had not reckoned with the possibility that he would be a fellow "southerner," was unprepared for the way the referee neatly turned his argument against him. As it became clear that the debate was not going his way, he wondered aloud, "We always have problems with the referee—why is that?" While Ahmet's question was apparently addressed to no one in particular, the irritated glance he shot at the departing referee made his primary target clear. Judging from Ahmet's accusatory tone, he thought discrimination was at the root of our team's problems.

Incidents and conversations like the ones depicted here have indeed occurred with some frequency since immigrant-established clubs joined Berlin's amateur football leagues. So, to echo Ahmet, why do they arise? Observers of the city's sporting scene have tended to offer two main lines of explanation. The first attributes conflict to the mentality (*Mentalität*) that ostensibly prevails among players, coaches, and spectators of Turkish and other immigrant and minoritized backgrounds. According to this argument, people of Turkish and other backgrounds are predisposed to be more emotional and undisciplined than their "German" counterparts and more likely to engage in aggressive conduct. Significantly, this reasoning is not exclusively articulated by the opponents of immigrant-established clubs but by people of Turkish and other backgrounds as well. Both Ahmet and the referee, for example, were ready to characterize Gençlikspor's members as southerners with volatile emotional inclinations. In doing so, they invoked and sought to mobilize an identity category with a lengthy genealogy in German migration history. In the 1960s FRG state officials characterized guest workers from Spain, Italy, Greece, Turkey, and Yugoslavia in particular as southerners with a problematic, excessive, even irrational attachment to their patriarchally organized families. Although the officials sometimes alluded to this attachment to justify the reunification of families in the FRG, they also frequently employed it to explain why guest workers would violate the terms of their labor contracts (i.e., they were inordinately determined to live and work in proximity to their kin). Workers' attachments to their families, in short, threatened to disrupt the optimization of the labor supply that the bilateral recruitment agreements were supposed to achieve.[27]

The second line of explanation, on the other hand, regards racialized animus on the part of "German" clubs and referees as the ultimate source of conflict. Over the past several decades, members of immigrant-established clubs have regularly accused opposing players, coaches, and spectators of deliberately insulting them in order to provoke aggressive and violent responses.[28] Moreover, they have frequently charged referees either with failing to take racist attacks seriously or with officiating against them in prejudicial ways (as Ahmet did). Significantly, this argument does not necessarily dispute that clubs of Turkish and other immigrant and minoritized backgrounds engage in aggressive and even violent modes of conduct. It tends, however, to interpret such conduct as an unfortunate but understandable response to discrimination, perhaps especially when players lack the linguistic command of German to defend themselves verbally. In other words, this line of explanation suggests that aggressive responses are one means for people, especially men of Turkish and other backgrounds, to (re)assert their individual and collective dignity.

Accusations of discrimination have taken on additional specificity in the years since Germany's reunification. Particularly in the early 1990s, the former East Berlin and GDR witnessed a dramatic increase in incidents of harassment and violence directed against asylum applicants, recent immigrants, and long-resident Black people and people of color. Although overt racism was by no means absent in western Berlin and other parts of the former West Germany, many people of Turkish backgrounds, like the members of other racialized groups, came to regard the former East Berlin and the new states (*neue Bundesländer*) as areas where racism was particularly pronounced.[29] This perception of the former GDR has given further definition to perceptions and experiences of on-field discrimination among people of Turkish and other backgrounds. Indeed, for many immigrant-established clubs, the fall of the Berlin Wall marked a turning point in their institutional histories: for the first time, these clubs were expected not only to play against formerly East German teams but also to leave the familiar confines of western Berlin for away matches in the former East Berlin and GDR. In the ensuing years, players, coaches, and spectators of Turkish and other backgrounds have frequently faced insulting, discriminatory, and violent treatment at the hands of clubs and referees in the former GDR, and many have come to greet encounters with clubs from these areas with at least some degree of anxiety. During my 1999–2001 fieldwork, the members of Gençlikspor regarded both home and away matches with clubs from former East Berlin with a certain trepidation. Even today, the incidents of racialized antagonism reported to the Berlin Football Association continue to involve clubs from the former GDR to a disproportionate degree.[30]

Taken together, these two lines of explanation frame a discursive landscape in which a range of subtle interpretations and judgments are possible. Indeed, the two main lines of explanation are not mutually exclusive: Ahmet's reasoning managed to attribute an inherently aggressive disposition to "Turkish people" and other "southerners" even as it imputed prejudice to a referee whom he had initially presumed was "German." At the same time, at least some members of immigrant-established clubs and other observers adopt critical stances that dispute the idea that aggressive conduct is either an intrinsic feature of Turkish mentality or the byproduct of racist discrimination alone. In particular, it is not unusual for people of Turkish and other backgrounds to perceive in some but not all of their compatriots a certain oversensitivity (*Überempfindlichkeit*): that is to say, an anticipatory readiness to see insulting or discriminatory treatment in most any encounter with an opponent or referee and to respond with reflexive belligerence.[31] Interestingly, this interpretation was not absent from the conversation after the Hellas-Nordwest match either. Once he was out of earshot, one of Gençlikspor's other players, Levent, observed that Hasan all too often confronted opposing players, reacted aggressively to supposed slights, and committed costly fouls. "Every game is the same with him," Levent grumbled. "It's slowly getting on my nerves."

Once again, then, the discourse surrounding "Turkish aggression" reveals the degree to which on-field conflicts intersect with wider debates about ethnoracialized difference and racist discrimination in Germany. Far from being isolated or irrelevant, amateur football is instead an animated field of societal interaction that exposes persistent fault-lines in the terms of German citizenship. It thereby reveals the extent to which Berlin, more than three decades after the fall of the wall, remains divided in a host of complex ways.

Beyond Ethnonational Self-Definition

Yet even as references to "Turkish," "German," and other ethnicized categories remain prevalent in the city's football scene, it would be a mistake to assume that their significance has remained fixed and immutable. In fact, the past two decades have witnessed dramatic shifts not merely in the demographic composition of Berlin's clubs but also in their orientation to local, national, and transnational contexts. On the one hand, the number of clubs with overt connections to labor migration from Turkey (and elsewhere) has gradually decreased, and those that remain are marked by a more heterogeneous range of members as well as a more Berlin-specific orientation. On the other hand, growing numbers of players of Turkish backgrounds play for ostensibly "German" clubs that previously lacked any relationship with postwar migration history, and in some cases people of immigrant or minority backgrounds have assumed key administrative positions within long-established clubs. As a result, it has become increasingly difficult to identify unambiguous ethnonational affiliations within the city's football landscape.

To be sure, a certain number of clubs, including a few recently established ones, remain marked in ethnonational terms, not least because Berlin continues to be a site of racialization, migration, and displacement. In 2008, for example, Yaw Donkor, a man born in Ghana but raised in Berlin, founded 1.

FC Afrisko, the first African football club in Berlin and, indeed, Germany.[32] In its early years, Afrisko's membership was primarily composed of Afro-German and African immigrant players, coaches, and administrators, many of whom had sought out the club as an opportunity for camaraderie and solidarity in the face of persistent anti-Black racism. In addition to athletic competition, Afrisko organized and participated in workshops, artistic events, and sociopolitical gatherings that situated the club within the larger field of antiracist politics and African diasporic life.[33] Following the outbreak of war in Syria, meanwhile, a group of refugees established Syrischer (Syrian) SV, a club that drew as many as fifty Syrian boys and men to its practices after it began official league play in 2015.[34]

Such ethnonational and racialized affiliations, however, should not divert attention from a range of deeper transformations. At perhaps the most basic level, fewer clubs possess names that unambiguously refer to their connections with Turkey (or other countries of origin) and Germany's history of postwar migration. Indeed, whereas twenty-eight clubs included references to Turkey in their names in West Berlin in the mid-1980s, only eleven clubs in Berlin did so during the 2021–2022 season.[35] In the intervening years, many clubs established by people of Turkish backgrounds have simply dissolved when they could no longer field teams, secure sponsors, or pay for uniforms, referee fees, field permits, fines, and other expenses. A number of clubs have also merged (as previously noted) in an effort to maintain their financial viability and healthy membership base.[36] Finally, in a few cases, clubs established by people of Turkish backgrounds have adopted new names that do not include overt references to Turkey but instead allude to localized attachments within Berlin. Two key illustrations of this trend are Rixdorfer SV (which was known as Göktürkspor until 2011) and FC Kreuzberg (which was established as Karadenizspor in 1978, became Samsunspor in 2003, and took on its current name in 2011).[37] Both of these clubs changed their names to avoid the stigma of conflict associated with "Turkish clubs," while FC Kreuzberg also sought to assert its identification with the district of Kreuzberg and its pluralist, cosmopolitan appeal. In the latter case, the new name was as much an expression of pride as it was an effort to evade derogatory associations.

At the same time, many clubs are becoming more diverse in demographic terms. On the one hand, the youth teams of many clubs increasingly draw their players from their local environs without regard for those players' ethnonational backgrounds. Hence, many ostensibly "German" clubs have a significant number of players from a range of immigrant and minoritized backgrounds, just as many of the clubs established by people of Turkish backgrounds have a growing proportion of young white German players. These shifts are evident, for example, at Hansa 07, a one-time "German" club in Kreuzberg whose youth teams are now quite heterogeneous, as well as at Türkiyemspor, whose youth teams are among the most diverse in Berlin.

On the other hand, many adult players of Turkish backgrounds have joined clubs that have until recently lacked any strong connection with the FRG's postwar migration history. During our interview, Mehmet Matur outlined a scenario that has recently played out with a number of long-standing clubs struggling with administrative and financial issues:

> You can see the transformation with clubs—original, 130-year-old German clubs—that now have a hard time finding volunteers and sponsors. They're really on the edge of the abyss and need to dissolve. And they can't find young people either—the people on the board are all men over seventy and their wives. Many clubs . . . just can't do it anymore. And then some young people of Turkish or Arab background arrive and say, "Is there any way we can help the club?" And they [the elder administrators] reply, "Can you talk with [potential] sponsors?" Then a sponsor appears and takes over the club's debts, which might be something like ten or twelve thousand Euros. And then they [the club's membership] elect him [the sponsor] chairman.[38]

The telling detail that Matur leaves implicit is that the young people who initially approach the club secure a new sponsor who is also of Turkish, Arab, or some other background. Once this sponsor becomes chair and takes over the club's management, in turn, the club tends to become more receptive and attractive to both youth and adult players of immigrant and minoritized backgrounds, with the result that the club becomes more heterogeneous even when its name and other identifying markers (like its insignia and team colors) remain intact. One noteworthy example of this shift is Berliner Athletik Klub (BAK) 07, a club first established in 1907 that, in the mid-2000s, elected multiple chairs of Turkish backgrounds and merged with BSV Mitte, a club that was itself the product of an earlier merger between the immigrant-established clubs BFC Güneyspor and Fenerbahçe Berlin. BAK 07's first men's team, which currently plays in one of Germany's fourth-tier regional leagues, is one of Berlin's most successful amateur teams and is known for recruiting players from a wide range of immigrant and minoritized backgrounds.[39]

Thanks to these dynamics, the contemporary football landscape in Berlin is much more varied and fluid than the frequent references to ethnicized categories would suggest. Indeed, it no longer makes sense to character-ize most clubs in the city as "German," "Turkish," or "immigrant" in any straightforward way. Even clubs with explicit ethnonational references have not been immune to these shifts. In 2022, 1. FC Afrisko merged with CSV Olympia 1897, which had been the oldest football club in Charlottenburg.[40] The outcome of that fusion, CSV Afrisko, now fields boys' and men's teams with players from a range of African, Afro-German, white German, Turkish, and other backgrounds. Syrischer SV and its partner club FC Karame, meanwhile, have become long-term homes for some players from Syria while acting as springboards for others: a number of their players have since joined other clubs, including Türkiyemspor. Finally, Türkspor, the oldest club established by people of Turkish backgrounds in Berlin, merged in 2017 with Hellas-Nordwest, the same club that Gençlikspor faced in May 2000. The fusion of these two clubs was orchestrated by Metin Yılmaz, a man of Turkish background who played for Türkspor in the 1970s but more recently became Hellas-Nordwest's chair. The new club has retained the name Türkspor but moved from its previous headquarters in Kreuzberg to Hellas-Nordwest's facilities in Charlottenburg.[41] Türkspor currently plays in Berlin's highest amateur league, fields teams with players from a range of backgrounds, and draws fans from across western Berlin.

In the end, then, the membership base of many clubs is simply too heterogeneous for facile ethnonational characterizations to hold much purchase, and the clubs themselves do not frame their affiliations and activ-ities in relation to any single locality, region, or nation-state. Moreover, it is difficult to discern within the immigrant-established clubs in particular any consistent process of integration, in the sense of a linear shift in cultural orientation from the country of origin to the host society. In fact, a growing number of clubs, whether or not they can trace their origins to postwar migration, reject ethnonational designations and instead define themselves as diverse (*vielfältig*) or multicultural (*multikulturell*) organizations. In some cases, this self-definition is framed as a matter of moral and political principle: a significant number of the city's clubs have taken explicit stands against racism, antisemitism, and homophobia, for example, by featuring the insignia of activist organizations on their uniforms or by participating in the anti-discrimination campaigns sponsored by the Berlin Football Association.[42] Yet, the commitment to diversity is also decidedly pragmatic. As Matur pointed out, the proportion of young people of immigrant and minoritized backgrounds born or raised in Berlin will only continue to grow in the years ahead. Hence, the city's clubs will need to draw players from a range of backgrounds if they hope to remain viable and competitive. This trend is already evident, Matur noted, in the clubs whose teams play in the higher echelons of Berlin's league system: they are consistently more heterogeneous than those clubs that compete in the lower tiers.[43]

Conclusion

Following the FRG's recruitment of guest workers, people of Turkish backgrounds in Berlin founded a significant number of football clubs that were largely if not entirely composed of immigrant boys and men. The clubs affiliated themselves with prominent political and cultural-religious currents in the Republic of Turkey and the Turkish diaspora, and their names included Turkish-language references to locales and teams in Turkey as well as to the Turkish nation-state more broadly. While these clubs responded in part to the exclusion that people of Turkish backgrounds experienced at the hands of established clubs, local officials, and association functionaries in Berlin, they also expressed their members' ongoing transnational attachments with Turkey. The formation of these clubs thereby contributed to a seemingly obvious distinction between "Turkish" and "German"—one that continues to be invoked in the city's amateur football scene, perhaps especially when players, coaches, and spectators of Turkish backgrounds are perceived to engage in excessively emotional or violent conduct. While some observers have attributed such an aggressive disposition to the mentality that purportedly characterizes people of Turkish and other "southern" backgrounds, others have regarded it as a plausible, if regrettable, response to racist discrimination. For many people of Turkish backgrounds, such discrimination was and still is particularly prevalent among clubs and referees in the former East Berlin and GDR.

Since approximately the early 2000s, however, Berlin's football landscape has witnessed a number of shifts that complicate the seeming self-evidence of ethnonational categories. On the one hand, the number of immigrant-established clubs whose names refer to Turkey have gradually declined, and the ones that remain are marked by a more complex range of cultural and geographic affiliations as well as a more heterogeneous range of players, especially in their youth ranks. On the other hand, many players of Turkish backgrounds have joined clubs that previously lacked a robust connection with Germany's postwar migration history. Moreover, a growing number of established clubs are now led by coaches and administrators of Turkish and other immigrant and minoritized backgrounds even as they retain their long-standing names and identifying markers. Taken together, these transformations not only highlight how ethnonational self-definition, while not entirely irrelevant, has grown less salient as an organizing principle of the city's football scene but also underscore the inadequacy of received conceptions of integration, which presume a linear trajectory of cultural incorporation into a stable host society. Ultimately, it is Berlin's amateur football landscape in its entirety, not simply its immigrant-established clubs, that is now in flux.

One recent event may point toward the future to come. In June 2022, the Turkish Sports Center (Türk Spor Merkezi), the successor to the Turkish Sport Association mentioned above, resuscitated the Atatürk Cup after a four-year hiatus. Named after the Republic of Turkey's first president, Mustafa Kemal Atatürk, the tournament has historically been an annual one-day competition that seeks to determine Berlin's best "Turkish" men's team. Several of that day's events did point to ongoing transnational connections between Berlin's amateur football scene and the Turkish nation-state: the Republic of Turkey's Berlin-based ambassador and consul general presented medals and trophies to the first-, second-, and third-place teams, while the tournament's organizers honored Teoman Gündüz, a young Berlin man who had recently been named to Turkey's under-eighteen national team. Yet several of the eighteen participating teams did not represent clubs traditionally associated with migration from Turkey, and the championship match featured teams from FC Brandenburg, a club based in Charlottenburg that was founded in 1903, and SFC Veritas, a club based in Spandau that was founded in 1996.[44] Although both clubs have a significant number of players, coaches, and administrators of Turkish backgrounds, neither is clearly marked in ethnonational terms. In the end, then, the "Turkish club" of the 1970s and 1980s may be a thing of the past. If the most recent Atatürk Cup is any indication, however, people of Turkish backgrounds will continue to play football in Berlin for decades to come.

Notes

1. Although the phrase is admittedly imperfect, "people of Turkish backgrounds" refers throughout this chapter to people who migrated to the Federal Republic of Germany (FRG) from Turkey and to their descendants who were born and raised in the FRG. They may possess German, Turkish, or dual citizenship, and they may define themselves as Kurds, Alevis, or members of other minoritized groups in Turkey at least as much as they identify with Turks as an ethnonational collectivity.

2. Floris Vermeulen and Maria Berger, "Civic Networks and Political Behavior: Turks in Amsterdam and Berlin," in *Civic Hopes and Political Realities: Immigrants, Community Organizations, and Political Engagement*, ed. S. Karthick Ramakrishnan and Irene Bloemraad (New York: Russell Sage Foundation, 2008), 177. For one example of relevant press coverage, see Dénes Jäger, "Türkeistämmige Fussballvereine in Berlin: Mehr als Özil," *taz*, August 13, 2019, accessed August 9, 2022, https://taz.de /Tuerkeistaemmige-Fussballvereine-in-Berlin/!5618134/.

3. Jennifer A. Miller, *Turkish Guest Workers in Germany: Hidden Lives and Contested Borders, 1960s to 1980s* (Toronto: University of Toronto Press, 2018), 135–61; Lauren Stokes, *Fear of the Family: Guest Workers and Family Migration in the Federal Republic of Germany* (Oxford: Oxford University Press, 2022), 19–100.

4. Sarah Thomsen Vierra, *Turkish Germans in the Federal Republic of Germany: Immigration, Space, and Belonging, 1961–1990* (Cambridge: Cambridge University Press, 2018).

5. In keeping with anthropological conventions, this chapter makes occasional reference, through the use of the first-person *I* and *my*, to my role as ethnographic researcher. These usages are intended to mark my status as a "positioned subject" whose biographical circumstances and social location inevitably shape the tenor of ethnographic fieldwork and interpretation. For one early and influential statement on ethnographers' positioning, see Renato Rosaldo, *Culture and Truth: The Remaking of Social Analysis* (Boston: Beacon Press, 1989).

6. I conducted fieldwork with Gençlikspor from September 1999 to June 2001, with follow-up research occurring in July 2006. *Gençlikspor* (Youth Sport) is a term that commonly figures in the names of sports clubs in Turkey and the Turkish diaspora. Like almost all of the names of individuals that appear here, it is a pseudonym that is intended to offer a measure of confidentiality to research participants. My interview with Mehmet Matur occurred in August 2022. Given his prominence as a public commentator on football-related matters within and beyond Berlin, I use Matur's actual name.

7. While a few immigrant-established clubs (i.e., Ağrıspor, Al-Dersimspor, and Türkiyemspor) have fielded girls' and women's teams, the vast majority have only provided sporting opportunities to boys and men. Clubs established by people of Turkish backgrounds are not particularly distinctive in this regard: the same can be said of all amateur football clubs in Berlin and the FRG more broadly. On the gendered dimensions of football in Germany, see Gertrud Pfister, "The Future of Football is Female!? On the Past and Present of Women's Football in Germany," in *German Football: History, Culture, and Society*, ed. Alan Tomlinson and Christopher Young (London: Routledge, 2006), 93–126.

8. Dirk Halm, "Turkish Immigrants in German Amateur Football," in *German Football: History, Culture, and Society*, ed. Alan Tomlinson and Christopher Young (London: Routledge, 2006), 74; Silvester Stahl, *Selbstorganisation von Migranten im deutschen Vereinssport: eine soziologische Annäherung* (Potsdam: Universitätsverlag Potsdam, 2011), 184–225.

9. Frank Kalter, *Chancen, Fouls und Abseitsfallen: Migranten im deutschen Ligenfußball* (Wiesbaden: Westdeutscher Verlag, 2003); Gunter Gebauer, "Fußball ohne Weltbürgertum geht nicht! Gunter Gebauer im Gespräch mit Diethelm Blecking und Gerd Dombowksi," in *Der Ball ist bunt: Fußball, Migration und die Vielfalt der Identitäten in Deutschland*, ed. Diethelm Blecking and Gerd Dembowski (Frankfurt am Main: Brandes und Apsel, 2010), 43–46.

10. One stark example is Wilhelm Heitmeyer, "Gesellschaftliche Desintegration und ethnisch-kulturelle Konflikte," in *Ethnisch-kulturelle Konflikte im Sport*, ed. Marie-Luise Klein and Jürgen Kothy (Hamburg: Czwalina, 1998), 15–30.

11. The convergence of these themes is perhaps most visible in Marie-Luise Klein and Jürgen Kothy, eds., *Ethnisch-kulturelle Konflikte im Sport* (Hamburg: Czwalina, 1998). For similar journalistic commentary, see Jörn Lange, "Wie Migrantenvereine durch Abgrenzung Integration behindern," *Berliner Morgenpost*, September 26, 2019, accessed June 21, 2023, https://www.morgenpost.de/sport/article227206751/So-macht-Integration-wenig-Sinn.html.

12. For example, Thomsen Vierra, *Turkish Germans in the Federal Republic of Germany*, 10–11.

13. On practices of ethnic differentiation, see Fredrick Barth, *Ethnic Groups and Boundaries: The Social Organization of Cultural Difference* (London: Allen & Unwin, 1969); Andreas Wimmer, "The Making and Unmaking of Ethnic Boundaries: A Multi-Level Process Theory," *American Journal of Sociology* 113, no. 4 (2008): 970–1022.

14. Tony Mason, "Großbritannien," in *Fußball, soccer, calcio: Ein englischer Sport auf seinem Weg um die Welt*, ed. Christiane Eisenberg (Munich: Deutscher Taschenbuch Verlag, 1997), 22–26.

15. Christiane Eisenberg, "Fußball als globales Phänomen: Historische Perspketiven," *Aus Politik und Zeitgeschichte* 26 (June 2004): 9–10.

16. Dağhan Irak, *Football Fandom, Protest, and Democracy: Supporter Activism in Turkey* (London: Routledge, 2019), 9–14.

17. Stefan Metzger, *Das Spiel um Anerkennung: Vereine mit Türkeibezug im Berliner Amateurfußball* (Wiesbaden: Springer, 2018), 63–68.

18. Metzger, *Das Spiel um Anerkennung*, 70–74.

19. Metzger, *Das Spiel um Anerkennung*, 70–71. Berlin's oldest immigrant-established club, Türkspor, offers a revealing illustration: although it was founded in 1965, it was only accepted into the association's leagues in 1977.

20. Metzger, *Das Spiel um Anerkennung*, 74–76.

21. Dieter Romann-Schüssler and Thomas Schwarz, *Türkische Sportler in Berlin zwischen Integration und Segregation* (Berlin: Der Senator für Gesundheit, Soziales und Familie Ausländerbeauftragter, 1985), 13.

22. *Ay Yıldız* (Moon and Star) refers to the icons on the Republic of Turkey's flag.

23. The prefix *Al-* is an abbreviation of *Alevi*, while *Dersim* refers to the city and province of that name in southeastern Anatolia. The city of Dersim was the site of a major Kurdish uprising against the Turkish central government in 1938 that aimed to challenge the state's efforts to create an ethnically homogeneous Turkish nation. After the uprising was violently repressed, the central government officially renamed the city Tunceli. Hence, the very use of *Dersim* in the club's name alludes to a contested history of oppression and struggle.

24. *Hilal* (crescent moon) refers to a common symbol of the Islamic tradition.

25. For an overview, see Andreas Zick, Judith Scherer, and Martin Winands, "Der Fußballplatz und das Sportgericht als ethnische Kampfarena," in *Der Ball ist bunt: Fußball, Migration und die Vielfalt der Identitäten in Deutschland*, ed. Diethelm Blecking and Gerd Dembowski (Frankfurt am Main: Brandes und Apsel, 2010), 133–39. For the situation in Berlin specifically, see Silvester Stahl, *Sportgerichtsurteile im Berliner Fussball-Verband 1999–2009* (Potsdam: Universität Potsdam, 2009).

26. See, for example, "Messer im Stutzen," *Der Spiegel*, March 9, 1997, accessed September 14, 2022, https://www.spiegel.de/sport/messer-im-stutzen-a-44043211 -0002-0001-0000-000008674879; Dennis Betzholz, "Das Märchen vom guten Spiel," *Der Stern*, June 6, 2013, accessed September 17, 2022, https://archiv.reporter-forum.de /fileadmin/pdf/Reporterpreis_2013/frei/Betzholz_Dennis_0558.pdf; Lange, "Wie Migrantenvereine durch Abgrenzung Integration behindern."

27. Stokes, *Fear of the Family*, 23–26.

28. Some of these insults target immigrant-established clubs in overtly racist terms, while others target members' family members, above all mothers, in gendered or sexualized terms. The latter insults seek to injure the sense of honor (*Ehre*) that is stereotypically associated with families of Turkish, Arab, and broadly Muslim backgrounds. For a trenchant analysis of the dominant discourse surrounding Muslim men in Germany, see Katherine Pratt Ewing, *Stolen Honor: Stigmatizing Muslim Men in Berlin* (Stanford: Stanford University Press, 2008).

29. On experiences of racialized violence among Black people and people of color in the former GDR, see Damani Partridge, *Hypersexuality and Headscarves: Race, Sex, and Citizenship in the New Germany* (Bloomington: University of Indiana Press, 2012), 2–16, 50–71.

30. Interview with Mehmet Matur, August 4, 2022.

31. Metzger, *Das Spiel um Anerkennung*, 118–19.

32. Alina Schwermer, "Migrantische Sportvereine: Kick it like Donkor," *taz*, March 18, 2018, accessed August 9, 2022, https://taz.de/Migrantische-Sportvereine/!5489405/.

33. For a glimpse of the club's activities, see its previous webpage at https://www.facebook .com/fcafrisko, accessed June 21, 2023.

34. Tom Mustroph, "Syrischer SV in Berlin: Soziales Lernen beim Fussball," *taz*, June 15, 2017, accessed August 9, 2022, https://taz.de/Syrischer-SV-in-Berlin/!5416583/. Syrischer SV recently merged with FC Karame, another club with ties to the Arab Middle East. See the club's webpage at https://www.facebook.com/FCKarame78Berlin/, accessed June 22, 2023.

35. In addition to these eleven clubs, about a dozen others possessed names that allude to their historical connections with migration from Albania, Croatia, Italy, Greece, Poland, Serbia, Latin America, and the Arab Middle East. The approximately twenty-four clubs with references to regions of migratory origin represent a fraction of the 389 total clubs registered with the Berlin Football Association in 2022. These figures are based on information available on the webpages of the Berlin football publication *Fußball-Woche* (https://www.fussball-woche.de, accessed July 16, 2022) and the Berlin Football Association (https://www.fussball.de, accessed September 12, 2022).

36. These patterns of dissolution and merger are not distinctive to clubs established by people of Turkish backgrounds. Rather, they are evident across the range of amateur clubs in Berlin and other parts of the former FRG.

37. For a fuller discussion of these clubs, see Metzger, *Das Spiel um Anerkennung*, 43–44, 98–101.

38. Interview with Mehmet Matur, August 4, 2022. Matur's language marks both the old guard and the new sponsor/chairman as men.

39. For more on the club's history, see its website at https://www.bak07.de, accessed September 17, 2022.

40. Norman Börner, "Wie ein integrativer Sportverein über die WM in Katar denkt," *Berliner Morgenpost*, November 20, 2022, accessed June 21, 2023, https://www.morgenpost.de/berlin/article236945885/Wie-ein-integrativer-Sportverein-ueber-die-WM-in-Katar-denkt.html.

41. For more on Hellas-Nordwest and Türkspor, see Michael Nittel, "Hellas kickt nun als Türkspor: Traditionsvereine haben fusioniert," *Berliner Woche*, December 11, 2017, accessed June 22, 2023, https://www.berliner-woche.de/charlottenburg-nord/c-sport/hellas-kickt-nun-als-tuerkspor-traditionsvereine-haben-fusioniert_a138955; Jäger, "Türkeistämmige Fussballvereine in Berlin."

42. For an introduction to the Berlin Football Association's social engagement projects, see https://www.berliner-fussball.de/soziales/kampagnen/ and https://www.berliner-fussball.de/soziales/integration/, accessed September 17, 2022.

43. Interview with Mehmet Matur, August 4, 2022.

44. Mustafa Ekşi, "Berlin'de Yeniden Atatürk Kupası Heyecanı," *Medya Berlin*, June 7, 2022, https://www.medyaberlin.com/berlinde-yeniden-ataturk-kupasi-heyecani, accessed July 29, 2022. Details about the two clubs derive from their respective websites, https://www.brandenburg03.de and https://www.spandauerfcv1996.jimdofree.com, accessed September 15, 2022.

CHAPTER SEVEN

Californization and Sport as Lifestyle

The Development of Skateboarding in West Berlin, 1970–1990

KAI REINHART

Skateboarding is a form of sport, subculture, and lifestyle that developed in the 1960s in California, originating from various sources and inspirations, like scootering, surfing, and skiing.[1] It has so far not been possible to determine exactly when the first skateboard rolled through West Berlin, but it was likely in the first half of the 1970s.[2] Berlin was thus the first German city in which skateboarding was able to establish itself permanently. Some Berliners had contacts in the United States and could get friends or relatives to bring them skateboards. This was how Matthias "Mike" Ernst saw a skateboard for the first time: "A classmate somehow had a skateboard from relatives in the US, and then you rolled around a bit."[3] Martin "Kongo" Böhmfeldt and Hans-Jürgen "Cola" Kuhn had a similar experience in 1976 at the ages of ten and twenty-three, respectively.[4] As in the United States, skateboarding was not just a new sport in Germany but also a new, Californian attitude to life: "I do it to clear my head. Not to go faster, higher, more beautifully, further ... but it has to be fun for me. Whatever fun means to me or to you," explained Jörg Greven, another Berlin skateboarder.[5]

German skateboarding was able to develop particularly early in West Berlin due not least to Berlin's unique situation as an island and outpost of the liberal world within the Eastern Bloc. Its existence depended on Western support. The British and Americans had already proven the reliability of this support in 1948–1949 with the Berlin Airlift. During a 1963 visit to West Berlin after the Berlin Wall was built, American president John F. Kennedy renewed the security guarantee with the famous words, "*Ich bin ein Berliner.*" The city, and especially its youth, opened up to the US, becoming a forerunner of profound social changes throughout Germany—in both the West and, contrary to the will of the socialist regime, in the East. Skateboarding was a publicly visible and prominent part of this development.[6]

Scholarship on skateboarding has expanded in the last twenty years across a variety of disciplines. Iain Borden, in his standard work on the history of US skateboarding, lists approximately 450 related titles, most of which have been published since the early 2000s.[7] The broad spectrum of skateboarding literature ranges from practical sports publications to philosophical reflections and sociological, historiographical, artistic, and architectural theoretical analyses. Frequent topics include tips and tricks for riders, the role and construction of race and gender, skateboarders' use of public spaces, skateboard culture's resistance to the mainstream, the evolution of skate equipment, major events such as the X Games and the Olympics, and (auto)biographies of famous skateboarders.[8] Most studies—even those not by US-based authors—look at skateboarding in the United States, which is considered to be exemplary, or try to analyze skateboarding in general. Despite its international orientation, however, skateboarding has also been shaped locally by the small structures on the ground, demonstrating the need for local historical studies of the sport.[9]

Due to its informal and constantly changing character, the development of skateboarding can only be reconstructed to a limited extent on the basis of written sources, making oral histories indispensable resources for such historical studies.[10] In particular, life history interviews with six contemporary witnesses who were part of the inner core of West Berlin skateboarding from the 1970s until 1990, conducted between 2020 and 2022 as part of a project on the history of West Berlin skateboarding, were critical historical sources.[11] The eyewitnesses also provided numerous photographs for the research project to support and illustrate their statements. A disadvantage of eyewitness interviews is their inaccuracy with respect to dates and figures. An unpublished chronicle by Kuhn, the cofounder and longtime chair, coach, treasurer, and referee of the 1. Berliner Skateboard-Verein (1st Berlin Skateboard Club, BSV), thus provides a reliable resource alongside the interviews.[12] Another important source is a ten-minute report from the children's TV show *Logo* on Sender Freies Berlin (Berlin Public Television, SFB) from 1978, which features various locations and figures of West Berlin skateboarding.[13]

The postwar spread of American culture concerned some Europeans, especially as youth in the 1960s and thereafter adopted music, clothing, and other trends emanating from the United States.[14] For young people around the world, one of the most fascinating regions and cultures in the US was that of California. The spread of skateboarding across the globe can be described as a part of a wider process of Californization—"a particular brand of Americanization" that encompassed other sports such as surfing, BMX riding, and snowboarding.[15] These sports all wanted to distance themselves from (competitive) sports that were too serious and dogged. California stood for "sun, surf and toned bodies," and generally became a symbol for a new attitude in sport in which style and fun were far more important than victories measured in meters and seconds.[16] In this way, California has had a major impact on the development of the sport since the 1960s—even for people who have never been there.[17]

Skateboarding's growth in Germany, and in Berlin in particular, follows this trend. MTV culture and the creation of the X Games in the 1990s accelerated the spread of "lifestyle" or "adventure" sports around the world.[18] Yet, skateboarding's spread to Germany from the United States predated these major entertainment and media forms, arriving in Berlin via magazines and VHS tapes sent through the mail. Berliners actively sought these media sources to incorporate new skateboarding ideas into their own scene. At the same time, West Berlin skateboarders used the urban spaces of the divided city to develop their own skateboarding culture.[19] Skateboarding in West Berlin simultaneously developed as an informal activity, a formal club sport that mirrored traditional German sporting structures, and, ultimately, a lifestyle that transcended its origins as sport.

Deformalization: From the Club to the Street

After their first experiences with skateboards in the neighborhood, the contemporary witnesses report that their desire to meet like-minded people and to skate together grew.[20] In the German tradition, the skateboarders founded a club, the 1. Berliner Skateboard-Verein, with defined rights and duties for its members. In the nineteenth century, the club system had developed into the dominant organizational form of German civil society, which strove for democratic codetermination and national sovereignty. In the tradition established by Friedrich Ludwig Jahn, the father of German gymnastics (*Turnen*), sport clubs provided a school of democracy and national identity and were a central component of this development.[21] With the liberalization and individualization of German society from the late 1960s onward, clubs lost a part of their integrative power, and other more informal and commercial forms of organization gained in importance.[22] This is particularly clear in the history of Berlin skateboarding.

The BSV was not founded out of enthusiasm for a traditional club but primarily to acquire a safe area to skate. Even though there were a number of skateboarders in different neighborhoods of Berlin, meeting each other and finding safe skate spots was not always easy, especially in winter with rain and freezing temperatures. Peter Kramer, who ran the surf and skate store Concrete Wave with his brother, therefore initiated the founding of an official, nonprofit *eingetragener Verein* (e.V., association or club).[23] After securing the necessary seven founding members, Kramer founded the 1. Berliner Skateboard-Verein e.V. on May 17, 1977.[24] Most skateboarders at the time participated in divisions of larger clubs that featured several different sports, such as the Turngemeinde Münster, the Rollsportclub Wiesbaden, or the Turn- und Sportverein Lübeck.[25] The BSV, in contrast, did not officially represent other sports, although some skateboarders experimented now and then with other roller sports such as roller skating or BMXing. Kuhn, one of the founding members of the BSV, became club chair just one year after the club was founded, and his influence shaped the club for decades.[26] The membership fee was initially DM 6 (about $2.70) per month, which was not much. During the warm season, the city authorities allowed the club to use the ice stadium in the district of Wilmersdorf, which had opened only three years earlier. On the very smooth, thawed ice surfaces, it was possible to skate extremely well, and ramps could be set up permanently. The number of members quickly increased to around fifty or sixty skateboarders, but in the cold season the ice stadium was not available to the club, which led some skateboarders to cancel their memberships.[27] Therefore, in the fall and winter the club began to rent factory floors, warehouses, and basement rooms and adapt these facilities for skateboarding. In a factory in Glogauer Straße in Kreuzberg, skateboarding was done up to "just under the ceiling" because of the relatively low ceiling height of 3.5 meters. For safety reasons, the large factory windows were barricaded with mattresses.[28] Despite the cramped conditions and sometimes icy temperatures, these premises seemed very

Windows barricaded with mattresses in a factory in Kreuzberg. *Permission granted by Hans-Jürgen Kuhn.*

attractive to the skateboarders, as Karl Johann "Kalle" Richter remembered: "At that time, they still trained in the winter semester in such a factory hall in Kreuzberg. Then I just went along to the training with a friend and somehow became a member."[29]

In order to gain further support and promotion, to acquire insurance coverage, and to be able to participate in official championships, the BSV joined the Rollsportverband Berlin (Roller Sports Federation of Berlin) in 1978. Two years later, skateboarding was accepted into the national Deutscher Rollsportbund (German Roller Sports Federation, DRB) as the fourth sport alongside roller figure skating, roller field hockey, and speed skating. Furthermore, the BSV received DM 4,000 (about $1,805) in funding from the new Skateboarding Commission of the DRB.[30] The same year, the BSV even organized an exchange program with skateboarders from London with support of the Landessportbund Berlin (Berlin State Sports Association). The Berliners flew to England for a week, where they stayed with host families. This experience allowed them to become familiarized with the skate scene and skate parks, which did not yet exist in Berlin in this form.[31] In return, English skateboarders came to West Berlin. Some skateboarders from the United States also stayed with club members for a while. In later years, bus trips were organized to the European championships in Sweden, France, England, Italy, and the Czech Republic.[32] The club organized the first Berlin championship in 1978, and Berlin television reported on the activities of the busy club in their evening show. Many children and young people became aware of the BSV as a result, and its membership increased to about 150 or 200 people.[33] To further promote both skateboarding and the club, the BSV organized public shows where the skateboarders performed spectacular tricks. The fast-growing company Titus Rollsport (Titus Roller Sports) from Münster, which built a large half-pipe on the Winterfeldtplatz in Berlin-Schöneberg in 1980, also supported the BSV. Public interest in the tricks performed by the participants in this largely unknown sport began to increase, and the anniversary show in 1982, where Titus Rollsport was again present, attracted about three hundred paying spectators to Wilmersdorf.[34]

Despite such support, it became increasingly clear that the cultures of the traditional sport federation and skateboarding did not belong together. At the 1990 German Championships in Rüdesheim, an open confrontation between DRB officials and skateboarders led riders to boycott the rest of the event.[35] As a result, the BSV and many other skateboarders withdrew from the DRB, and on November 11, 1990, the riders founded the National Skateboard Union without the participation of the DRB.[36] Although this incident marked a break with the traditional German sport structure, the creation of a separate skateboarding organization nonetheless perpetuated German sporting traditions.

The Californian character of the skateboarding culture that developed in West Berlin was encouraged by the informal and open skateboarding scene that developed alongside the BSV. Especially in the Märkisches Viertel in the north of West Berlin, "a concrete paradise" with large apartment blocks and 1960s architecture, children and young people discovered the new sport for themselves.[37] The skateboard seemed to appear as the natural means of locomotion in this landscape of smooth surfaces, slopes, stairs, and walls. This community, with about twenty-five riders, was one of the largest groups among West Berlin skateboarders. Other nuclei were Wilmersdorf and Rudow.[38] New friendships developed quickly: "We got along well from the beginning, . . . it's a group of people who meet and it just fits."[39] Skateboard stores played a crucial role in building these communities, as Ernst recalled: "I was actually alone there and just slipped into the scene via this skate shop."[40] They were not only stores but also places to meet people, to watch skateboarding videos, and to hear the latest skateboarding news. "Half a youth club, basically," explained Böhmfeldt.[41] In a time before mobile phones, the skateboarders went to the various skate spots and looked to see who was there.[42] Exploring the city on a skateboard became a part of skateboarding culture, as Arne Krüger recalled: "For me, it was important just to ride around the city and see new things, find new spots."[43]

Skateboarding in the socialist East Berlin remained largely unknown to West Berlin skateboarders. Greven even called skateboarding in East Berlin a "terra incognita."[44] Due to the strict border between East and West Berlin, encounters with East Berlin skateboarders were rare. The informal East Berlin championships were one of the exceptions. There was, however, a special form of "development aid" in which skateboarding equipment was collected in West Berlin and then brought to the GDR by John Haak, an East Berlin skateboarder with a Finnish passport.[45] In 1988, the BSV made Haak its first honorary member for his efforts.

Skateboarders maintained use of their sites for years, some into the early 2000s, returning to these venues without the formalities of prearranged times. An early regular meeting place on weekends was the Teufelsberg, a huge artificial mountain built from World War II debris that was frequently visited by up to two hundred skateboarders for downhill skateboarding. On rainy days and during the winter, West Berlin skateboarders liked to meet at the International Congress Center Berlin where 100–150 skateboarders and in-line skaters could find a dry spot in its distinct, orange-tiled underpass.

BSV membership card for John Haak, an East German skateboarder who received the club's first honorary membership. *Permission granted by John Haak.*

There were also ventilation shafts that could be used as a half-pipe. In the 1980s, the Breitscheidplatz on Kurfürstendamm, called "Schnalle" by the skaters, became another home to the informal scene.[46] A group met there every evening after school or work. "That happened in the summer until late at night. And then we moved on to the surrounding discos and cafés," remembered Richter.[47] In addition to such central spots, skateboarders also found hidden places throughout the city where they used urban space to ride or set up ramps that they built themselves.[48] If the skateboarders were lucky, a ramp could last an entire summer. Skateboarders tested whether a ramp was stable enough to hold up in practice through experimentation: "You nail something together and then there's someone who's particularly crazy, who just rides up there and sees if it holds," said Richter.[49]

Even though many skateboarders were simultaneously members of the BSV and participants in the open scene, there were also skateboarders who exclusively skated on the streets. "They were a different group, compared to those who were also in the club. Maybe they just wanted to ride . . . just hang out and have a smoke and maybe drink a beer or something. That was all a bit more relaxed," explained Richter.[50] In the club, there was a consistent ban on alcohol and tobacco: "Even at club meetings, once a year, we all sat

"Mike" Ernst on a self-constructed ramp. *Permission granted by Matthias Ernst.*

there and drank lemonade," Richter claimed.[51] In contrast to the organized BSV, alcohol and cigarettes were a matter of course in street skateboarding.[52] Nonetheless, even on the street there were unwritten rules, and the community sanctioned anyone who disregarded them, as the young in-line skaters, for example, experienced: "You can't just drop in when someone already has a board on the edge, or things like that. Unwritten rules, they [the in-line skaters] didn't stick to them. Accordingly, they were dissed [criticized]," said Ernst.[53] During conflicts, the community of skaters held together. This was especially evident when provocations arose from outside the community, as, for example, when there was trouble from the police or with football fans from Hertha BSC. "We really stuck together there," said Richter.[54] Looking out for each other was another reason why younger skateboarders were so well integrated into the scene. Even during vacations, skateboarders organized joint activities, such as trips to summer camps in Sweden or Czechoslovakia. Here the skateboarders could train for three weeks with world-class riders and make international contacts.[55]

While some of the older skateboarders in their early twenties made an effort to organize the club activities, most of the younger kids who joined the BSV were merely searching for a surface on which to skate. They also skated outside the club in the streets of West Berlin. The rules and rituals of organized sport ultimately did not conform to the skateboarders' attitudes. Most skateboarders attached importance to individuality and independence; the BSV therefore could never rely on a loyal membership: "It was always just a means to an end."[56] Until the fall of the Berlin Wall in 1989, the BSV mostly had about one hundred to two hundred members. The club nevertheless played a central role in Berlin skateboarding because it offered a secure space for skateboarding, even under adverse conditions such as in winter. It was also able to represent the interests of skateboarders to official bodies of the city and organized sport and provide a formal contact person for anyone wanting to get in touch with the West Berlin skateboarding scene. In this way, the BSV played a significant role in shaping West Berlin skateboarding during this period.

Desportization: From Sport to Lifestyle

When the skateboard came to Germany in the 1970s, it was not yet possible to foresee the potential of these rolling boards. Gradually, skateboarders discovered the possibilities and, with a delay of a few years, followed developments in the United States.[57] Skateboarders replaced the orientation toward established sport with their own, style-defining innovations from the skateboard scene. Associated with this was a rejection of classic modern sport with their specialization, rationalization, bureaucratization, and quantification, and above all with their code of victory and defeat.[58] Instead,

High jump in the Wilmersdorf ice stadium. *Permission granted by Hans-Jürgen Kuhn.*

a culture developed of playful experimentation and friendly competition without clearly defined rules.[59] In this development, skateboarding also absorbed influences from other youth cultures, such as punk and hip-hop. "Skateboarding [is] not only a sport, above all it is also a lifestyle," Münster skateboarder Florian Böhm explained in one of the first widely published articles on the subject, which appeared in the magazine *Der Spiegel* in 1989.[60] The West Berlin skateboarding scene was a particularly good example of this transformation from organized sport to lifestyle.

In the early years of skateboarding, well-known sport disciplines such as high jump, long jump, floor gymnastics, or alpine skiing were often transferred to skateboards. With the improvement of the materials used, skateboarding was able to develop its own forms, such as half-pipe and street skateboarding. The development of the scene's own magazines and skate videos on VHS accelerated this development. Street skateboarding was especially resistant to being squeezed into a grid of sporting norms.[61] Initially, the skateboard was frequently used as an asphalt sled, as Ernst remembered: "In front of our house was a beautiful downhill track. At the end you either crashed into the parked cars, or you managed somehow to ride around the corner."[62] The comparatively simple downhill—lying, sitting, and standing—became one of the first skateboarding disciplines. At the same time, slalom skateboarding, where riders started from a ramp and went through a course in as short a time as possible, was popular in Berlin. Jumping disciplines also emerged early. In the long jump, the rider jumped off the board and landed on a second board. In the high jump, the rider had to clear a bar with a hippie jump (i.e., without the board), and then land on the same board.[63]

Another classic but far more demanding discipline was freestyle. In 1970s Berlin, this was considered the supreme discipline. On a flat surface, the skateboarders each had about two minutes to present a choreography of tricks and figures set to music. The conditions of the Wilmersdorf ice stadium were excellent for this discipline.[64] Since skateboards were expensive and initially hardly available, especially for children and young people, skateboarders developed a pronounced love of experimentation in the early years: "We all made the [boards] ourselves, so there was a lot of tinkering."[65] This also resulted in new creations, such as a skateboard with a sail.[66] Simple "department store boards," which cost about DM 30 to 50 (about $13.50 to $22.60), were often made of plastic and had rigid axles and open ball bearings. In order to afford a decent skateboard, children and young people had to make some sacrifices.[67] Richter took a job during school vacations and tried to sell his Lego bricks and toy cars. "At some point, I simply decided: I don't want any more toys, I'm going to become a skateboarder."[68] When he was in fourth grade, Böhmfeldt also sold all his toys at the flea market in order to afford his first real skateboard, a Calypso, for about DM 130 (about $58.60). Along with protective equipment, the total price to begin skateboarding could quickly exceed DM 250 (about $112.80).[69]

In the second wave of skateboarding in the 1970s, vertical skateboarding emerged in the United States in part because of skateboard improvements, especially wheels made of softer polyurethane instead of metal or clay. Riding on them, skateboarders could feel their way further up sloping walls until the vertical was achieved and topped off with lip tricks or airs.[70] At the end of the 1970s, skateboard development in the United States reached the standard of a "modern global skateboard," which has not fundamentally changed to this day.[71] Relatively early in this period, at the end of the 1970s, vertical skateboarding and high-quality boards also found their way into West Berlin. Making self-built boards became superfluous except for special cases like boards for long and high jump.[72]

Another factor that contributed to changes in the West Berlin skateboard scene was its media development. American and German magazines like *Thrasher* and *Monster Skateboard Magazin*, as well as VHS skate videos, enabled new skateboard tricks to be seen in detailed photo spreads and even in motion, slowed down, stopped, and repeated. This significantly advanced the technical development of skateboarding.[73] These media forms also opened up the wide horizons of skateboard culture to West Berliners, with its own heroes, stories, fashion, music, and habits. In the absence of other sources, skateboarding magazines were extremely valued: "Everybody just memorized them. You could really pray up and down the page, it was the Bible."[74] Acquiring such a "Bible," however, was not easy in West Berlin. At magazine kiosks, such special booklets were hard to find. Many skateboarders therefore subscribed to the American magazines, which arrived up to two months late because of complicated payment and customs regulations. Eventually, skateboard stores began ordering and selling the magazines in larger quantities.[75]

While in California empty pools were used for vertical skateboarding, in West Berlin the vertical was achieved with the help of various ramps, such as mini ramps and quarter-pipes. These smaller ramps were relatively easy to build oneself and could be found all over the city.[76] The pinnacle of skateboarding in the 1980s, however, was the big half-pipe. At first, the BSV had to make do with two quarter-pipes pushed together to form a half-pipe, which required the two ramps to be held in place. From 1979, the club had its own half-pipe in the Wilmersdorf ice stadium. It was built by the company August Schäfer KG and was one of the first half-pipes in Germany. Not everyone dared to ride on this "crap," which was only about two meters wide, four meters high, and did not have a flat section, making it very unforgiving of any errors. In 1988, however, the club could afford the DM 30,000 (about $18,816) needed to buy a large, sophisticated, and even dismountable half-pipe. Working again with August Schäfer, the BSV built the half-pipe in the ice stadium and held ceremonies to mark its opening.[77]

"Mike" Ernst in the first half-pipe of the 1. Berliner Skateboard-Verein. *Permission granted by Matthias Ernst.*

As skateboarding evolved more toward street skateboarding, however, such more or less standardized equipment was no longer needed. Instead, the entire city became the skateboarders' playing field. This also completed skateboarding's desportization, its transformation from a sport into a lifestyle. The ollie, a freehand jump with the board on the feet that is the basis of modern street skateboarding, appeared in Germany and Berlin around 1987. Even before then, however, skateboarders had practiced early forms of street skateboarding. Street skateboarding made skateboarders even more present in public. The tricks were performed on obstacles intrinsic to the urban space, like stairs, railings, or benches. The Breitscheidplatz was particularly well suited for tricks "because there were curbs and some kind of marble benches that went all the way around, on which you could jump up and down really well," noted Richter.[78] Since street skateboarders no longer needed bulky and expensive half-pipes or protected spaces, they were less dependent on the BSV. The informal scene was thus strengthened, and after 1990, skateboarders' willingness to get involved in the club decreased rapidly.[79]

In the club, the logic of traditional competitive sport was largely followed even though many skateboarders did not see themselves as traditional athletes. After the first Berlin championship in 1978, the BSV hosted the 1980 North German Championship and in the following years organized numerous other competitions at local, regional, and national levels. In 1983, the BSV was so well equipped financially and materially that they could host the German Championship in Berlin. With the new, larger half-pipe, the BSV hosted the German Championship again in 1988, and about 2,100 spectators came to the ice stadium to celebrate the skateboarders over the course of the weekend.[80] The BSV not only hosted competitions but also participated at numerous events in and beyond Berlin. For example, about five to ten BSV skateboarders participated regularly in the German championships. Berlin's most successful skateboarders, such as Axel "Starsky" Kleinhans and Markus "Marky" Thummerer, won numerous medals in the high jump and slalom events.[81] This was important for the BSV because "the more successful an association . . . the greater the level of support" that association received.[82] At the ice rink, regular training was offered from 3:00 to 6:00 on Monday, Wednesday, and Friday afternoons.[83] Kuhn, who worked as a teacher and was about ten years older than most of the other members, became a coach and tried to conduct classic practice sessions with warm-up programs and athletic drills. Günter Mokulys, a freestyle world champion from Münster, advised in his book that, "In freestyle, as with all sports, you have to warm up so that your muscles loosen up."[84] BSV skateboarders who wanted to prepare for a competition were given more specialized training and individual advice.[85] The skateboarders were quite ambitious, but the atmosphere at competitions was more like a party, especially in the evenings. According to Greven and Krüger, the focus was on getting together, meeting new people, and having fun.[86] Richter described the atmosphere: "Just imagine a swarm of wasps flying around the honey pot. That's what a skateboarding championship was like."[87] Despite his efforts as a coach, many skateboarders considered

Kuhn more as an older supervisor.[88] Böhmfeldt emphasized that the term *training* "had never crossed his lips."[89] Similarly, Ernst had only done what he enjoyed and was largely self-taught, learning by example, or through tips from other skateboarders, and not from a coach.[90] Richter commented that, "We were more likely to push each other and spur each other on to try new things."[91] Even though they were some of the top skateboarders, they still saw their actions as spontaneous fun rather than the kind of serious, systematic, guided training found in established competitive sports.

Skateboarding's development from sport to lifestyle was also evident in clothing and protective equipment. Skateboarders in the early years of its popularity had mainly focused on functionality. They rode in standard sportswear, and Reaktor sports shorts were particularly popular as their hip pads offered extra protection in the event of a fall. The protective equipment they used consisted of a helmet and elbow and knee pads, which were much narrower and thinner than today's models. Depending on the discipline and rider, the gear could also include gloves, some of which were lined with foam or even had steel inserts.[92] Böhmfeldt did not consider the protective gear to be particularly fashionable but wore it anyway.[93] "Back then, unlike today, it was just standard that we all protected ourselves," Kuhn emphasized.[94] Because of the high cost of specialized equipment, however, club members also wore volleyball pads and hockey helmets. Outside the club, skateboarders usually did not wear any protective gear at all for style reasons.[95] In the 1970s there were only a few special shirts sold by skate brands such as Alva. Surf shirts from Town and Country or Quiksilver were also popular with skateboarders and worn in everyday life. The 1980s saw the arrival of numerous other brands, such as Thrasher, Santa Cruz, and Titus. Having the right footwear was a important from the beginning of the skateboarding scene in Berlin, with American brands such as Vans being particularly popular.[96] "You could say, the people who walked around with Vans always had to be skaters," said Ernst about the recognition value of these shoes.[97] This clothing was not easy to obtain in West Berlin in the 1970s and early 1980s. The main suppliers in the early years were Concrete Wave and Road Runner, two surf and skate stores. Both imported goods from the United States, but the selection remained limited. The stores focused mostly on hardware (i.e., boards, axles, wheels, and helmets), especially in the 1970s, and hardly at all on clothing.[98] "It was like collecting stamps with T-shirts," Kuhn recalled of the scarcity of skateboard clothing.[99] Another option was ordering clothing through contacts in England. There, he says, the skate stores were already bigger. "But you waited three months for a pair of Vans," said Ernst.[100] A third way for individuals to obtain skate fashion in the 1980s was directly from Münster-based Titus Rollsport during skateboard championships.[101]

Over time, the culture of skateboarding combined with other elements of popular youth culture and itself became a highly visible part of that culture. Music played an overriding role in skateboarding, as is evident, for example, in skate videos. Especially in the early years of Berlin skateboarding, punk music from bands like Black Flag or the Suicidal Tendencies was omnipresent.[102] "This punk music and punk culture already had a firm foothold in the skateboard scene," Kuhn recalled.[103] Since the music usually did not match mainstream tastes, sourcing could be a bit more costly. "One really set an alarm clock in the middle of the night and tried to pick up everything new with a cassette recorder," Ernst remembered.[104] Music also came from within the scene itself. In the winter of 1980–81, four Berlin skateboarders from the Märkisches Viertel founded the punk band C&A, or Chaos und Aufruhr (Chaos and Rebellion). Kuhn vividly remembered the BSV's fifth anniversary show in 1982, where the band performed "really heavy punk music" at the ice stadium: "Horrible, today I wouldn't want to listen to that, but back then one thought it was totally okay."[105] In 1984 the band changed its name to Disaster Area in reference to a band of the same name from Douglas Adams's *Hitchhiker's Guide to the Galaxy*, but the musical program remained the same: "Radical rejection to any norms that somehow exist."[106] What may not have pleased the functionary Kuhn, however, was very well received among skateboarders. The band thrilled spectators at the European and world championships held in Münster (Münster Monster Mastership) several times in the 1980s, and in the 1990s they even went on tour with emerging punk rock greats such as the Offspring.[107] Starting in the 1980s, hip-hop and with it breakdancing also enjoyed increasing popularity among skateboarders.[108] At some skate spots, like the Breitscheidplatz, skateboarders and breakdancers watched, cheered, and admired each other, and not infrequently the improvised shows of the skateboarders were enriched by interludes from the breakdancers. Visited both by the people of Berlin and by tourists, the Breitscheidplatz was a perfect place for such shows.[109] Sometimes, crowd of up to five hundred people would gather to watch, which forced the police to intervene "because the people were standing right up to the street and the bus lane was already full of spectators, so they said: 'You can't do that here! You are interfering with the traffic.' Those were real happenings that took place there."[110]

Skateboarder Alex "Starsky" Kleinhans (left) and a visual street artist (right) during a show at the Breitscheidplatz, or "Schnalle," with spectators in the background. *Permission granted by Matthias Ernst.*

Conflicts with the police became an integral component of the street life experience. "We do what we want, you can all go fuck yourselves," was how Böhmfeldt characterized the attitude of many skateboarders.[111] Predefined social rules were rejected.[112] "Skate and destroy" was the motto of the popular magazine *Thrasher*, but Richter emphasized the constructive aspect of this attitude. Skateboarders looted construction sites to build ramps, for example, "but that wasn't the main focus; it was more about just going out, having fun."[113] This fun, however, was reserved primarily for male skateboarders. The hard core of skateboarding comprised of about fifty or sixty boys and men from their teens to their mid-twenties. Girls and women remained more of a rarity in the skateboarding communities of Berlin and Germany more broadly.[114] For example, at the First European Championship in Altenau in 1981, only three of the approximately sixty-five participants were women.[115] Influenced by punk and hip-hop and supported by the skate magazines and the skateboard industry, many skateboarders cultivated a pronounced machismo.[116] Girls and women were welcome as spectators and groupies, but even then they were called the derogatory American term *skate-Betty*. As active skateboarders, women and girls were hardly recognized.[117]

Skateboarding evolved from a sport to a lifestyle. Although there were major competitions in skateboarding, they had more of the character of a big party than a high-stakes athletic championship. For skateboarders, this lifestyle could represent the central purpose of their lives for years. "To school, back home, then skate," is how Böhmfeldt summarized his everyday life.[118] Older skateboarders mostly used skateboarding to switch off after work and to meet up with friends. For some, however, the relationship between work and skateboarding was reversed: they only worked as much as they needed to afford to skateboard.[119] Professional success in middle-class society was not a primary goal for most skateboarders. Punk was not only evident in the music but also in skateboarders' basic attitudes toward themselves, society, and the state. Berlin skateboarding was "not explicitly political, but rather nonconformism."[120] Fun was the focus, not destruction, and not politics.

Conclusion

When skateboarding came to West Berlin, it was initially conceived of within the familiar patterns of organized sport. Athletes established a club, founded a training ground, set training times, and organized competitions and trips. Yet, while the club offered benefits in terms of access to city resources and organized activities, it remained only a means to an end for the majority of skateboarders. Despite the commitment of club leaders, the formal organizational structure of the club ultimately proved to be a product of nineteenth century sports culture that no longer corresponded to the dynamics of skateboarding in Berlin in the late twentieth century; the heart of skateboarding beat more on the street. Skateboarders did not want to be tied down by club membership or a specific training ground but rather wanted to freely and spontaneously explore the possibilities of skateboarding on the streets and squares of the city where the public could watch their feats. Formal club rules were replaced by unwritten laws, rituals, and habits that nevertheless constituted a binding force in the skateboarding community for years. Skate stores served as organizational anchor points, whose function extended far beyond that of offering shopping opportunities. They were places for skateboarders to meet, hang out, network, and inform. As the formal club structure was replaced by the commercial, informal communalization that has characterized skateboarding in Germany since the 1990s at the latest, the BSV has come to represent a certain anachronism in German skateboarding today.

At the beginning of West Berlin's skateboarding history, most disciplines, such as high jump or slalom, imitated established disciplines from other sports. In doing so, they also followed the logic of traditional competitive sports in measuring and defining performance and success. The shift of skateboarding from the club to the street and the development of original forms of skateboarding, such as vertical and street skateboarding, were also accompanied by a cultural shift away from these traditional definitions. Street skateboarding in West Berlin thus developed along a similar trajectory to street skateboarding in the Unites States.

Skateboarding partially broke away from the norms and values of conventional sports and opened up to influences from youth and music culture, especially those of punk and hip-hop. This was evident in the very bold and sometimes truly reckless nature of skateboarding in the half-pipe and on the street. It was also evident in the clothing and protective equipment, which corresponded more to the current fashions and popular styles than to functionality. According to the motto "skate or die," skateboarding became a wild, sometimes provocative, male-oriented, creative, and fun youth and movement culture. With its brazen cheekiness, skateboarding seemed to fit well with the rough and unpredictable culture of West Berlin, the so-called Island of the West fenced in by the Iron Curtain. In 1989 the travel magazine *Merian* put a skateboarder on the cover of its Berlin issue.[121] Through these developments, skateboarding in West Berlin demonstrated the Californization of the sport, with skateboarding emerging as a lifestyle in contrast to the more traditional German trajectory of development through the organized club and association.

Nonetheless, the sporting notion of competing remained a part of the skateboarding subculture, which still leads to debates in the scene today. Most recently, the tension between sporting values and punk values became apparent on the occasion of skateboarding's acceptance as an Olympic sport.[122] Despite its Olympic presence, skateboarding does not fit—or only fits to a limited extent—into the common development scheme of sports from an innovative trend into an established conventional or standard sport.[123] Rather, skateboarding is an extreme and sometimes provocative example of a development that can be observed in more moderate degrees in many German sports, such as in board sports like surfing and snowboarding, in roller sports like BMXing and in-line skating, and in the trend toward informal variants of established sports such as streetball and beach volleyball.

From the mid-1990s, Germans have used the pseudo-Anglicized phrase of *Funsport* to describe many of these developments.[124] If these trends often lack the more punk elements of skateboarding, they nevertheless share its longing for a Californian attitude: an individual, spontaneous, playful, fun-oriented, and style-conscious way of doing sport and living life.

Notes

1. Iain Borden, *Skateboarding and the City: A Complete History* (London: Bloomsbury, 2019), 6–23; Eckehart Velten Schäfer, *Dogtown und X-Games: die wirkliche Geschichte des Skateboardfahrens Körper, Räume und Zeichen einer Bewegungspraktik zwischen Pop- und Sportkultur* (Bielefeld: Transcript, 2020), 58–63.

2. Matthias Ernst, interview by Philip Heitmann, November 17, 2020, 1. Ernst, born 1964, grew up in West Berlin and has been a skateboarder since the mid-1970s. He is a member of the 1st Berlin Skateboard Club, the 1987 world slalom champion, former owner of a skate store, and an employee in the business world.

3. Ernst, interview, 1.

4. Martin Böhmfeldt, interview by Holger Höing-Dresen, June 4, 2020, 1–2; Hans-Jürgen Kuhn, interview by Holger Höing-Dresen, June 5, 2020, 33. Böhmfeldt, born 1966, grew up in West Berlin in the Märkisches Viertel and has been a skateboarder since 1976. He is a slalom, vert, and bowl rider, was for years involved in the 1st Berlin Skateboard Club, and since 2011 is the owner of the Barrio Skateshop Berlin. Kuhn, born 1953, grew up in West Berlin and has been a skateboarder since the mid-1970s. He was a founding member of the 1st Berlin Skateboard Club and has held various club offices over decades, including chairman, coach, treasurer, and referee.

5. Jörg Greven, interview by Lukas Hüging, September 21, 2022, 4. Greven, born 1964, grew up in Berlin and has been a skateboarder since approximately 1976. He is a member of the 1st Berlin Skateboard Club.

6. Kai Reinhart, "Concrete Carving on the Berlin Wall," in *Skateboard Studies*, ed. Konstantin Butz and Christian Peters (London: Koenig Book, 2018), 130–50; Kai Reinhart, "Spiel und Sport: Skateboarden im sozialistischen Dresden," in *Jahrbuch für Historische Kommunismusforschung: Spielen im Staatssozialismus. Zwischen Sozialdisziplinierung und Vergnügen.*, ed. Juliane Brauer, Maren Röger, and Sabine Stach (Berlin: Metropol, 2021), 157–76.

7. Borden, *Skateboarding and the City*, 326–47.

8. Kara-Jane Lombard, ed., *Skateboarding: Subcultures, Sites and Shifts* (Abingdon: Routledge, 2017); Konstantin Butz and Christian Peters, eds., *Skateboard Studies* (London: Koenig Book, 2018); Doug Werner and Steve Badillo, *Skateboarding: New Levels: Tips and Tricks for Serious Riders* (San Diego: Tracks, 2002); John Carr, "Skateboarding in Dude Space: The Roles of Space and Sport in Constructing Gender among Adult Skateboarders," *Sociology of Sport Journal* 34, no. 1 (2016): 25–34; Daniel Turner, "Performing Citizenship: Skateboarding and the Formalisation of Informal Spaces," in *Lifestyle Sports and Public Policy*, ed. Daniel Turner and Sandro Carnicelli (Abingdon: Routledge, 2017), 13–26; Becky Beal, "Disqualifying the Official: An Exploration of Social Resistance through the Subculture of Skateboarding," *Sociology of Sport Journal* 12, no. 3 (1995): 252–67; Rhyn Noll, *Skateboard Retrospective: A Collector's Guide* (Atglen, PA: Schiffer, 2000); Jürgen Schwier

and Veith Kilberth, eds., *Skateboarding between Subculture and the Olympics: A Youth Culture under Pressure from Commercialization and Sportification* (Bielefeld: Transcript, 2019); Tony Hawk with Sean Mortimer, *Hawk: Occupation Skateboarder* (London: ReganBooks, 2000).

9. See, for example, David Snow, "Skateboarders, Streets and Style," in *Australian Youth Subcultures: On the Margins and in the Mainstream*, ed. Rob White (Hobart: Australian Clearinghouse for Youth Studies, 1999), 16–25; Åsa Bäckström and Karen Nairn, "Skateboarding Beyond the Limits of Gender? Strategic Interventions in Sweden," *Leisure Studies* 37, no. 4 (2018): 424–39; Chuang Li, "Cultural Continuities and Skateboarding in Transition: In the Case of China's Skateboarding Culture and Industry," *YOUNG* 30, no. 2 (2022): 183–206.

10. Kai Reinhart, "Oral History in der (Sport-)Geschichte," in *Sport—Geschichte—Pädagogik: Festschrift zum 60. Geburtstag von Michael Krüger*, ed. Emanuel Hübner and Kai Reinhart (Hildesheim: Arete, 2015), 267–85. For oral history's importance in related sports, see Douglas Booth and Holly Thorpe, "Form and Performance in Oral History (Narratives): Historiographical Insights from Surfing and Snowboarding," *The International Journal of the History of Sport* 36, nos. 13–14 (2019): 1136–56.

11. In addition to interviews with Böhmfeldt, Ernst, Greven, and Kuhn, others interviewed were: Arne Krüger, interview by Lukas Hüging, September 7, 2022; Karl Johann "Kalle" Richter, interview by Philip Heitmann, November 22, 2020. Krüger, born 1973, grew up in Berlin-Charlottenburg and has been a skateboarder since 1984. He was a longtime employee and manager of the skateshop Search and Destroy, and since 2003 has been self-employed with the skateboard company Radio Skateboards.. Richter, born 1964, grew up in West Berlin and has been a skateboarder since 1977. He is member of the 1st Berlin Skateboard Club, a semi-professional skateboarder, and self-employed master carpenter.

12. Hans-Jürgen Kuhn, *Geschichte des organisierten Skateboardings im Vereinsbereich* (unpublished chronicle, 2019).

13. Gerhard Widmer, ed., *Logo*, episode 10, first broadcast October 2, 1978, publication ID 19007 and 207100, copyright SFB 1978, found on YouTube, minute 6:40–6:47, accessed July 14, 2023, https://www.youtube.com/watch?v=qpKjo6fOrOI.

14. Richard F. Kuisel, *Seducing the French: The Dilemma of Americanization* (Berkeley: University of California Press, 1993); Richard Pells, *Not Like Us: How Europeans Have Loved, Hated, and Transformed American Culture since World War II* (New York: Basic Books, 1997); Uta G. Poiger, *Cold War Politics and American Culture in a Divided Germany* (Berkeley: University of California Press, 2000); Victoria De Grazia, *Irresistible Empire: America's Advance through Twentieth-Century Europe* (Cambridge, MA: Belknap Press, 2005).

15. Mark Dyreson, "The Republic of Consumption at the Olympic Games: Globalization, Americanization, and Californization," *Journal of Global History* 8, no. 2 (2013): 256–78.

16. Toby C. Rider, Matthew P. Llewellyn, and John T. Gleaves, "Sun, Surf, and Toned Bodies: California's Impact on the History of Sport and Leisure," *Journal of Sport History* 46, no. 1 (2019): 1–4.

17. Anne Barjolin-Smith, "Snowboarding Youth Culture and the Winter Olympics: Co-Evolution in an American-Driven Show," *The International Journal of the History of Sport* 37, no. 13 (2020): 1322–47; Douglas Booth, "Surfing Films and Videos: Adolescent Fun, Alternative Lifestyle, Adventure Industry," *Journal of Sport History* 23, no. 3 (1996): 313–27.

18. Robert E. Rinehart and Synthia Sydnor, eds., *To the Extreme: Alternative Sports, Inside and Out* (Albany: State University of New York Press, 2003); Belinda Wheaton, ed., *Understanding Lifestyle Sports: Consumption, Identity and Difference* (London: Routledge, 2004).

19. The crucial role of subcultural media for alternative sports is analyzed in Becky Beal and Belinda Wheaton, "'Keeping It Real': Subcultural Media and the Discourses of Authenticity in Alternative Sport," *International Review for the Sociology of Sport* 30, no. 2 (2003): 155–76.

20. Ernst, interview, 2.

21. Michael Krüger, ed., *Einführung in die Geschichte der Leibeserziehung und des Sports,* Teil 2, *Leibeserziehung im 19. Jahrhundert: Turnen fürs Vaterland,* rev. ed. (Schorndorf: Hofmann, 2020).

22. Karl-Heinrich Bette, "Sport und Individualisierung," *Spektrum der Sportwissenschaft* 5, no. 1 (1993): 34–55.

23. Kuhn, *Geschichte des organisierten Skateboardings im Vereinsbereich,* 1.

24. *Geltende Satzung: beschlossen in der Mitgliederversammlung vom 26. November 2018,* accessed July 14, 2023, https://www.skateboardverein-berlin.de/dwl/Satzung_BSV -Stand_26-11-2018.pdf.

25. Programs of the German skateboard championship 1979–1981, 1983, 1985–1986; Kuhn, *Geschichte des organisierten Skateboardings im Vereinsbereich,* 1.

26. Kuhn, interview, 5.

27. Widmer, *Logo,* 6:40–6:47, 7:09–7:25; Kuhn, interview, 35.

28. Kuhn, interview, 18.

29. Richter, interview, 2–3; see also Greven, interview, 2.

30. Kuhn, *Geschichte des organisierten Skateboardings im Vereinsbereich,* 1; Kuhn, interview, 4, 48.

31. Greven, interview, 23–24.

32. Kuhn, interview, 37–38.

33. Kuhn, *Geschichte des organisierten Skateboardings im Vereinsbereich,* 1; Kuhn, interview, 35.

34. Kuhn, interview, 19–21.

35. Kuhn, *Geschichte des organisierten Skateboardings im Vereinsbereich,* 2; Kai Reinhart, *"Wir wollten einfach unser Ding machen,"* 198.

36. Kuhn, *Geschichte des organisierten Skateboardings im Vereinsbereich,* 3.

37. Richter, interview, 3.

38. Böhmfeldt, interview, 6.

39. Greven, interview, 2.

40. Ernst, interview, 2.

41. Böhmfeldt, interview, 28.

42. Böhmfeldt, interview, 7–8; Ernst, interview, 2.

43. Krüger, interview, 2.

44. Greven, interview, 22–23.

45. Reinhart, "Concrete Carving on the Berlin Wall."

46. Ernst, interview, 1–2, 8, 18; Richter, interview, 3–5, 8; Widmer, *Logo,* 0:30–1:12; Böhmfeldt, interview, 8, 19; Krüger, interview, 2, 11, 16; Kuhn, interview, 1–2.

47. Richter, interview, 4.

48. Widmer, *Logo,* 1:27–2:13; Ernst, interview, 16; Richter, interview, 6, 9.

49. Richter, interview, 10.

50. Richter, interview, 3–4.

51. Richter, interview, 4.

52. Kuhn, interview, 49; Ernst, interview, 15.

53. Ernst, interview, 20.

54. Richter, interview, 8.

55. Ernst, interview, 23; Böhmfeldt, interview, 24; Richter, interview, 18.

56. Greven, interview, 3; see also Ernst, interview, 8.

57. The United States always remained the Mecca of skateboarding and its skateboard culture set decisive trends worldwide. From here, vert skating and later street skating moved around the world. However, there were always special regional developments, such as the emergence of municipally sponsored skate parks or the world championship (Münster Monster Mastership) in Germany. Kai Reinhart, "Der Münster Monster Mastership und der Skatepark am Berg Fidel," in *Deutsche Sportgeschichte in 100 Objekten,* ed. Michael Krüger (Neulingen: Klotz, 2020), 396–99; Åsa Bäckström and Shane Blackman, "Skateboarding: From Urban Spaces to Subcultural Olympians," *YOUNG* 30, no. 2 (2022): 121–31.

58. Allen Gutmann, *From Ritual to Record: The Nature of Modern Sports* (New York: Columbia University Press, 2004), 15–56; Karl-Heinrich Bette, *Systemtheorie und Sport* (Berlin: Suhrkamp, 2009), 36–40.

59. Veith Kilberth, "The Olympic Skateboarding Terrain between Subculture and Sportisation," in *Skateboarding between Subculture and the Olympics: A Youth Culture under Pressure from Commercialization and Sportification,* ed. Veith Kilberth and Jürgen Schwier (Bielefeld: Transcript, 2019), 53–78.

60. "Wheelies und Ollies," *Der Spiegel,* April 1989, 240.

61. Schäfer, *Dogtown und X-Games,* 59–64.

62. Ernst, interview, 2.

63. Ernst, interview, 18, 7; Widmer, *Logo,* 6:50–7:40, 7:41–7:50; Richter, interview, 13; Kuhn, interview, 18–19.

64. Widmer, *Logo,* 8:10–8:32; Richter, interview, 9, 14. Kuhn, interview, 20.

65. Kuhn, interview, 17.

66. Widmer, *Logo,* 0:00–0:30; Schäfer, *Dogtown und X-Games,* 58–59.

67. Böhmfeldt, interview, 1; Widmer, *Logo,* 2:14–2:45, 5:49–6:00; Greven, interview, 3; Krüger, interview, 1; Richter, interview, 1–2.

68. Richter, interview, 2.

69. Böhmfeldt, interview, 1–2; Widmer, *Logo,* 4:45–5:37.

70. Borden, *Skateboarding and the City,* 98–117.

71. Borden, *Skateboarding and the City,* 14.

72. Ernst, interview, 6; Richter, interview, 11; Titus Dittmann, "Titus Skateboard-Sammlung Historische Boards Teil 2," uploaded April 29, 2020, accessed July 14, 2023, https://fb.watch/39k1xA8dWi/.

73. Böhmfeldt, interview, 22; Ernst, interview, 12; Richter, interview, 17.

74. Ernst, interview, 13.

75. Ernst, interview, 13; Böhmfeldt, interview, 4; Richter, interview, 16–17.

76. Ryan Murtha and Tolga Ozyurtcu, "From Stroke to Stoke: The Multiple Sporting Legacies of the Southern California Home Swimming Pool," *The International Journal of the History of Sport* 39, no. 1 (2022): 92–110; Greven, interview, 9.

77. Widmer, *Logo,* 7:51–8:08; Schäfer, *Dogtown und X-Games,* 146; Kuhn, interview, 17–18, 20; Richter, interview, 20; Ernst, interview, 7; Kuhn, *Geschichte des organisierten Skateboardings im Vereinsbereich,* 3; Kuhn, interview, 23.

78. Richter, interview, 9.

79. Kuhn, interview, 38.

80. Kuhn, *Geschichte des organisierten Skateboardings im Vereinsbereich*, 3; Kuhn, interview, 13.

81. Michael "Scheune" Thummerer, "Disaster Area, the history 1984–2004," 2004, accessed July 14, 2023, http://www.disasterarea.de/press/DisasterAreaBIO.pdf, 1.

82. Richter, interview, 12.

83. Widmer, *Logo*, 6:43–6:47; Kuhn, interview, 4; Ernst, interview, 16.

84. Günter Mokulys, *Freestyle Skateboard Book* (Münster: Monster Verlag, 1990), 22.

85. Kuhn, interview, 5, 22–23, 41.

86. Greven, interview, 3, 5; Krüger, interview, 10–11.

87. Richter, interview, 14.

88. Greven, interview, 5; Richter, interview, 3.

89. Böhmfeldt, interview, 11.

90. Ernst, interview, 16.

91. Richter, interview, 3.

92. Richter, interview, 15; Christian Seewaldt, *Alles über Skateboarding* (Münster: Monster-Verlag, 1990), 25; Kuhn, interview, 45; Böhmfeldt, interview, 19–20; Rector advertisement, *Skateboarder*, July 1977, 41.

93. Böhmfeldt, interview, 22–23.

94. Kuhn, interview, 54; Widmer, *Logo*, 5:09–5:24, 8:32–8:42.

95. Greven, interview, 17; Krüger, interview, 7–8.

96. Richter, interview, 15–16; Kuhn, interview, 45–46; Krüger, interview, 8; Greven, interview, 19.

97. Ernst, interview, 14.

98. Greven, interview, 16–18; Böhmfeldt, interview, 3–4, 15; Ernst, interview, 2–3, 5; Richter, interview, 11–12; Kuhn, interview, 53; Widmer, *Logo*, 2:55–6:50.

99. Kuhn, interview, 52.

100. Ernst, interview, 14.

101. Richter, interview, 12.

102. Krüger, interview, 4–5; Greven, interview, 10; Böhmfeldt, interview, 14; Ernst, interview, 13; Richter, interview, 19.

103. Kuhn, interview, 44.

104. Ernst, interview, 13.

105. Kuhn, interview, 39.

106. Kuhn, interview, 39.

107. Thummerer, "Disaster Area," 3.

108. Richter, interview, 18.

109. Richter, interview, 7; Ernst, interview, 6, 8.

110. Richter, interview, 4.

111. Böhmfeldt, interview, 13.

112. Kuhn, interview, 44–45.

113. Richter, interview, 6.

114. Richter, interview, 5; Ernst, interview, 18–19.

115. Program of the European Championship, 1981, [7–8].

116. Stüssy advertisement, *Thrasher*, November 1987, 37; Photograph and caption, *Monster Skateboard Magazin*, June/July 1987, 30; Kuhn, interview, 50.

117. Richter, interview, 5; Krosigk, *Alles über Skateboarding*, 109.

118. Böhmfeldt, interview, 6.

119. Richter, interview, 5–6.

120. Kuhn, interview, 43.

121. "Berlin," *Merian*, July 1989.

122. Kilberth and Schwier, *Skateboarding between Subculture and the Olympics*; Bäckström and Blackman, "Skateboarding."

123. Markus Lamprecht and Hanspeter Stamm, "Vom avantgardistischen Lebensstil zur Massenfreizeit: Eine Analyse des Entwicklungsmuster von Trendsportarten," *Sportwissenschaft* 28, no. 3/4 (1998): 370–87; Jürgen Schwier, "Soziologie des Trendsports," in *Handbuch Sportsoziologie*, ed. Kurt Weis and Robert Gugutzer (Schorndorf: Hofmann, 2008), 349–57.

124. "Funsport," Duden, accessed July 14, 2023, https://www.duden.de/rechtschreibung /Funsport.

CHAPTER EIGHT

The 2015 European Maccabi Games

The Ambiguities of Historical Reconciliation in Berlin

MOLLY WILKINSON JOHNSON

In early July 2015, a group of motorcyclists wearing T-shirts emblazoned with the slogan "Back to Berlin" set out from Israel and journeyed through Greece, Bulgaria, Romania, Hungary, Poland, and the Czech Republic. They carried with them the Maccabiah torch, customarily displayed at the World Maccabiah Games in Israel, an athletic competition often referred to as the "Jewish Olympics."[1] During their journey, the motorcyclists visited many Holocaust-related sites, where they shared stories of how their own family histories related to the Holocaust. On July 28, they arrived in Berlin, host of the 2015 European Maccabi Games (EMG), a regional competition held every four years in an alternate cycle to the World Maccabiah Games. Over 2,300 Jewish athletes from thirty-eight nations had traveled to Berlin and filled the Waldbühne, an amphitheater built as part of the vast Reichssportfeld from the 1936 Olympic Games, for the 2015 EMG opening ceremony. The motorcyclists with the torch entered the amphitheater, where Nancy Glickman waited. Glickman was the daughter of Jewish American track athlete Marty Glickman who, along with his teammate Sam Stoller, had been removed at the last minute from the United States' gold medal winning 4 × 100 meters relay at the 1936 Olympics, an action subject to some speculation that it reflected an American desire to appease Hitler by excluding Jewish competitors. Wearing her father's uniform from 1936, Nancy Glickman took the Maccabiah torch and lit the cauldron.[2]

The choice of Berlin as the host of the 2015 EMG was highly symbolic, as Berlin had not only been the capital of the Third Reich and the site of much of the Holocaust's planning but also hosted the infamous 1936 Olympic Games, widely known as the "Nazi Olympics," which had excluded Jewish German participants and functioned as propaganda for the Nazi government.[3] For Berlin's municipal leaders, the 2015 EMG were "of immense significance" for the "sports metropolis of Berlin." As Berlin's senator for sport, Frank Henkel, emphasized, the EMG allowed Berlin to "set an example of reconciliation" and to "present itself as a cosmopolitan, peaceful and tolerant metropolis."[4] For Germany's federal leaders (based in the national capital of Berlin), the 2015 EMG, which coincided with the fiftieth anniversary of the opening of bilateral relations between Israel and West Germany in 1965, gave Germany the opportunity to showcase its successful postwar reinvention. At the opening ceremony, German foreign minister Frank-Walter Steinmeier described the event as "only possible because Israel reached us the hand in reconciliation and because Germany accepted responsibility for the Holocaust."[5]

Yet a short scene from *Back to Berlin*, a 2018 documentary on the motorcycle ride from Israel to Berlin, presents a more complex message. In the scene, as the Israeli motorcyclists prepare to cross the Hungary-Serbia border in July 2015, they cross paths with thousands of refugees from the Middle East, guarded by hundreds of border police, armed guards, and military troops, with a police helicopter hovering overhead. The documentary features one refugee—who is not named or identified by state of origin—telling the Israeli bikers that he had been taught that Israel was his "enemy" and should be "destroyed." The Israeli motorcyclists then crossed the heavily guarded border that kept out the refugees and proceeded on their journey to Berlin.[6]

This scene presents dual messages. On the one hand, it shows empathy with the plight of refugees fleeing civil war and political persecution in the Middle East and northern Africa. As motorcyclist Danny Maron states, "a European country, a border like this, sad, sad." Just weeks after the EMG's closing ceremony, Chancellor Angela Merkel in fact opened German borders to what eventually became one million refugees, largely from the Middle East, and seventy-nine thousand of those refugees came to Berlin.[7] On the other hand, however, the documentary's inclusion of the refugee describing his socialization to see Israel as an enemy hints at German discourses that saw such refugees as importing fresh antisemitism into Europe. Merkel's decision ultimately represented a pivotal moment in Germany's political culture while also exposing the contradictions therein, with celebratory messages about Germany's post-Holocaust "welcoming culture" coinciding with a rise in anti-immigrant and anti-Muslim sentiments. The border encounter in *Back to Berlin*, as well as the media coverage of 2015 EMG security measures, reveals that concerns about imported antisemitism were already present in Germany in the months prior to the arrival of new refugees and offered fertile soil in which anti-immigrant sentiment could continue to grow.

Ultimately, the 2015 EMG provides a window onto the successes of historical reconciliation in Berlin, as well as the tensions and ruptures over diversity and multiculturalism that persist within the city. The 2015 EMG allowed German government leaders in Berlin, both national and municipal, as well as the leaders of the organized Jewish German sports community, to celebrate the successes of reconciliation. This process had begun in 1965 with the establishing of bilateral West German-Israeli relations and continued via Germany's process of *Vergangenheitsbewältigung* (coming to terms with the past), particularly prominent through initiatives in Berlin since the 1990s. The 2015 EMG also showcased Berlin as a cosmopolitan and multicultural city. Yet, discourses surrounding the EMG simultaneously questioned the meaning of Berlin's sizable Arab population, particularly those individuals of Palestinian origin, for the city's Jewish communities, thereby displaying ambivalence about the virtues of multiculturalism. The 2015 EMG thus reveal that sport—both as a popular recreational activity and as a vehicle for large events like the EMG—functions as a powerful conduit for Berlin's broader engagements with identity, history, and diversity.

The History of Jewish German Sports in Berlin

In choosing Berlin as the host city for the 2015 EMG, the event's organizers brought the games to a city known not only for its political significance as the capital of both Nazi and present-day Germany but also as the center of Jewish sports in Europe in the pre-Nazi era. EMG planners took steps to showcase this history, both the vibrant Jewish German sports scene in Berlin and the realities of how Nazi persecution of Jewish Germans was manifested in sport. In the process, planners presented the city of Berlin and the country of Germany as entities that had reckoned with their difficult history, thereby enabling the full integration of Jewish Germans into the very center of contemporary German life.

Historian Daniel Wildman describes Berlin as the "organizational and intellectual center of the Jewish gymnastics movement" that emerged in the late nineteenth century in Europe, and Bar Kochba Berlin, founded in

1898, stood at this movement's center.[8] Bar Kochba Berlin reflected Max Nordau's call for the cultivation of what he called "muscular Judaism." He believed that Jews—often stereotyped as "scrawny, and inferior"—should pursue conscious physical training to transform into "muscular Jews." To Nordau, muscular Judaism was not just about the health of the individual Jew, but also about a collective "muscle Jewry."[9] Other Jewish German gymnastics clubs soon emerged, and in 1903, Bar Kochba Berlin joined with these clubs to form the Jüdische Turnerschaft, or Union of Jewish Gymnastics Clubs.[10] Bar Kochba Berlin added its first women's sections by 1900, and by 1912, 80 percent of the associations affiliated with the Jüdische Turnerschaft had female members.[11] Jewish German sports continued to grow after World War I. The Maccabi clubs (which joined the Zionist World Maccabi Union in 1921) existed alongside clubs affiliated with Schild (an association founded after World War I by the patriotic, non-Zionist Reich Association of Jewish Front Soldiers), as well as the smaller and more politically neutral Vintus (Association of West German Neutral Jewish Gymnastics and Sports Clubs).[12] In 1933, there were twenty-five Maccabi clubs with a total of eight thousand members, ninety Schild clubs with a total of seven thousand members, and eighteen Vintus clubs with an unknown number of members.[13] Existing alongside this diverse terrain of Jewish sports clubs were many non-Jewish bourgeois and workers' sports clubs that had Jewish members, including the vast majority of the Jewish athletes who were more serious competitors.[14] As antisemitic rhetoric increased in the early 1930s, Jewish athletic successes became increasingly important to many Jewish Germans, with one newspaper, the *Israelistisches Familienblatt*, moving sports reportage to the more prominent news section of the paper in 1932.[15]

Within months of Hitler's appointment as German chancellor in January 1933, everything changed. As Berlin's sports clubs aryanized and removed Jews from their rosters, Jewish athletes were ghettoized into Jewish clubs, which banded together under the German Committee of Jewish Sports Clubs.[16] Because the highly developed Jewish sports movement in Berlin had supported various Jewish-owned facilities, it was somewhat easier for Berlin's Jewish athletes to continue playing a variety of sports than it was for Jewish residents of other German cities.[17] As late as October 1938, Bar Kochba Hakoah (created through the 1929 merger of Bar Kochba Berlin with Sport-Club Hakoah Berlin) held a fortieth anniversary sports festival and had a table tennis tournament slated for late November. However, regulations following Kristallnacht on November 9 ended organized Jewish sports events and activities both in Berlin and throughout Germany.[18] Discrimination shaped elite sport, too. Only two "half-Jews" competed for Germany in the 1936 Olympics, ice hockey player Rudi Ball in the Winter Olympics in Garmisch-Partenkirchen and fencer Helene Mayer in the Summer Olympics in Berlin. In both cases, the German Olympic Committee only included them to fend off an international boycott of the Games.[19]

The 2015 EMG publicly and visibly celebrated the deep roots of Jewish German sports in Berlin by way of an outdoor historical exhibit, *Zwischen Erfolg und Verfolgung: Jüdische Stars im deutschen Sport bis 1933 und danach* (Between success and persecution: Jewish stars of German sports until 1933 and after), temporarily installed in front of Berlin's central train station. The subtitle, "Jewish stars of German sports," captured the desire of EMG organizers to showcase Jewish athletes as integral to German sport rather than as a separate minority community. The exhibit, prepared by a team of sport historians from Potsdam and Hannover, featured text in both German and English and QR codes that passersby could use to access additional online information. Most prominent among the exhibit's displays were seventeen larger-than-life-sized silhouettes of Jewish German sports stars—described by German Football Federation president Wolfgang Niersbach as the Jewish "Dream team."[20]

The exhibit foregrounds the integral role played by Berlin in the Jewish German sports movement. Representing the early years of Jewish German sports were Berlin gymnasts and cousins Alfred Flatow and Gustav Felix Flatow. Both won team medals in gymnastics at the first modern Olympic Games in 1896, and Alfred also won two individual medals. Both died while imprisoned in the Theresienstadt concentration camp during World War II. Spectators of the exhibit also encountered a giant figure of Lilli Henoch, who won ten German championships in different field events and held world records in discus and shotput in the 1920s. After being forced out of the Berliner Sport-Club in 1933, Henoch became involved in organized Jewish sports, including coaching Jewish children and planning a Jewish school sports festival. Henoch was deported and murdered in 1942. The exhibit also featured Nelly Neppach, Germany's 1925 national tennis champion who was expelled from her Berlin tennis club, Tennis Borussia, in April 1933 and died by suicide on May 8, 1933. A replica of Rudi Ball also greeted pedestrians. Active in the Berlin Schlittschuh-Club, Ball won a bronze medal

Silhouettes of Alfred Flatow and Gustav Felix Flatow in front of Berlin's central train station, with the cupola of the Reichtag building, home of Germany's national parliament, visible in the background. July 26, 2015. *Photo by Soeren Stache/picture-alliance via Getty Images.*

in ice hockey at the 1932 Winter Olympics in Lake Placid, United States, and was then the sole "half-Jew" allowed to compete in the 1936 Winter Olympics. He survived the Holocaust in Berlin, somewhat protected by his half-Jewish status, and emigrated to South Africa shortly thereafter. All of these athletes had competed in well-resourced and competitive non-Jewish Berlin sports clubs before aryanization measures began in 1933. The final featured Berliner was Martha Jacob, the German national javelin champion in 1929 and a member of Bar Kochba as well as non-Jewish Berlin sports clubs. Jacob had also competed for Germany in the second Maccabiah Games in Tel Aviv in 1935, where she had won silver in javelin, discus, and shot put. Her international sport connections enabled her to emigrate to South Africa in 1936.[21]

Organizers and supporters of the 2015 EMG also interwove the complex and tragic Jewish German history into the event's formal ceremonies. The morning of the opening ceremony, twelve buses carried six hundred youth participants to the Sachsenhausen concentration camp outside Berlin, where they met with Holocaust survivors and left wreaths to honor the memory of murdered athletes from their own countries. That afternoon, a ceremony at the Maifeld—the vast demonstration grounds with a capacity of 180,000 adjacent to the Olympic Stadium—commemorated the six million Jews murdered in the Holocaust. At the ceremony, Federal Justice Minister Heiko Maas described Germany's opportunity to host the EMG as an "undeserved gift," noted his "deep shame" at what Germans had done to the Jewish communities of Europe, and pledged continuing vigilance against antisemitism. At the end of the ceremony, ninety-four-year-old Holocaust survivor Margot Friedländer spoke and Rabbi Yitshak Ehrenberg recited the kaddish, the Jewish prayer honoring the dead.[22] The formal opening ceremony at the Waldbühne that evening likewise commemorated Holocaust victims, as well as the Israeli athletes who were murdered during the 1972 Olympic Games.[23] A teammate of the 37-year-old Danish basketball player Dan Uzan spoke the Maccabi oath; Uzan had planned to participate in the games but had been murdered on February 15, 2015, while serving as a security guard outside a bar mitzvah ceremony in Copenhagen.[24]

"Processing history," as Maccabi Germany president Alon Meyer articulated in an interview with Die Zeit, was thus integral to the build-up to the EMG and its opening ceremony. Organizers celebrated Jewish German sport history, acknowledged the German-directed Holocaust, and declared the continued need for vigilance against antisemitism. Yet, Meyer emphasized, the EMG were ultimately "games of the present,"[25] which celebrated German-Jewish reconciliation and offered athletic and social opportunities for Jews from all over the world. As Roy Rajber, from the presidium of Maccabi Germany, stated, "The past will always be with us," but "the time is ripe for a new Jewish life; we can be proud to live in Germany as Jews."[26]

Historical Reconciliation and Jewish Community in Contemporary Berlin

The EMG, with its ceremonial and rhetorical performances of reconciliation, enabled the organized Jewish German community and municipal and federal leaders in Berlin to move forward from the past and to foreground the present and future of Jewish Germans. As cultural theorist Aleida Assmann noted in a conversation with Deutschlandradio Kultur, the EMG did not "forget" or "rewrite" history, but rather "wrote new history."[27] Reflecting this focus on the present and future, EMG planners carefully organized both social activities and athletic competitions to showcase the normalcy and vitality of Jewish life in contemporary Berlin and Germany.

As the exhibit outside Berlin's central train station illustrated, EMG planners wanted the games to make a visual imprint on the city of Berlin. Whereas the train station exhibit focused on Jewish German sports in Berlin's past, a series of 1,500 posters placed throughout the city celebrated thriving Jewish life in Berlin's present. The posters featured Yiddish expressions commonly used in German: "*Ganz Berlin wird meschugge*" (the whole city will get crazy) and "*Die ganze Mischpoke ist am Start*" (the whole family is ready to rumble). In addition, two short films that played off Jewish culture, *Schalömchen* and *Mazel Tov*, were distributed online to promote the EMG. Björn Bremer, chief creative officer and partner at the advertising firm that worked with the EMG, M&C Saatchi Berlin, noted that rather than focusing on history, the firm chose to foreground Jewish life in the present and the "joy of sports" in its design strategy.[28]

EMG organizers hoped that the games would cultivate Jewish identity and community. According to Motti Tichauer from the European Maccabi Confederation, "Maccabi is a large Jewish family, a Jewish microcosm. We pursue Jewish continuity, we work on the future, and we use sports as a means to impart Jewish values and culture."[29] One of the highlights of the event, which underlined the EMG's community-building efforts, was the large Shabbat meal that Maccabi Germany organized at the Estrel Hotel on July 31, 2015. The event, featuring 210 tables and 2,322 official participants, set the Guinness World Record for the world's largest Shabbat dinner, a record that still stood in 2023.[30] The Shabbat meal featured traditional Jewish food like challah and gefilte fish, as well as salmon and chicken. All food served was kosher.[31] Reflecting the diversity of the Jewish participants, three religious services preceded the feast, one orthodox, one liberal, and one specially planned for youth that was described as "lively." Highlighting the community-building goals that organizers brought to EMG planning, Rabbi Yehuda Teichtal and Rabbi Yitshak Ehrenberg praised the "unbelievably positive" atmosphere of the games, declaring that "we see here genuinely vibrant Jewishness."[32]

The opening ceremony, the posters throughout the city, and the Jewish communal events such as the Shabbat meal were only part of the EMG. The heart of the event was athletic competitions involving over 2,300 athletes in nineteen sports. Berlin media interviews with athletes, as well as a series of blog profiles created by Berlin's Jewish Museum, revealed that many participants, echoing the desires of both the city and federal governments and Maccabi Germany leaders, experienced the games as a testament to a new Berlin and a boost to the Jewish community. Twenty-five-year-old field hockey player Sarah Geldmann emphasized the "incredible symbol-ism" of the games and noted that, "we have a Jewish life here and Berlin is now even a hot spot for Israelis." She emphasized that being Jewish, for her, meant "belonging to a community, wherever one finds oneself in the world."[33] Israeli-German football player Li (no first name provided), who had immigrated from Israel to Berlin several years prior to the EMG, shared similar sentiments with the *Jüdische Allgemeine*: "For me, today closes the circle. The Nazis tried to kill my family. Now I am standing . . . at the place that Hitler misused for his propaganda show—that is a victory over history and a testament to how significantly the country has changed."[34] Thirty-two-year-old Berlin field hockey player Rebecca Kowalski likewise championed the EMG as demonstrating that "Jews are no longer excluded." She described Berlin as a "colorful and cosmopolitan city" and hoped that participants would feel so welcome in Berlin that they would carry the message home to their grandparents that, "Berlin is no longer gray and sad, but rather col-orful and livable."[35] These statements demonstrate that EMG participants, as organizers had hoped, recognized and indeed celebrated the powerful historical symbolism conveyed by a Jewish sports festival hosted in the former capital of the Third Reich.

Most remarkable, to many participating athletes, were the social oppor-tunities of the games. At the communal Shabbat feast, the Berlin tabloid *B.Z.* quoted a Dutch football player saying that, "It is like a Jewish Tinder here," referencing the popular dating app, and that she enjoyed hanging out in the lobby to talk about the games and flirt.[36] Well before the EMG, the Jewish matchmaking service Simantov International recruited volunteers by promising them such social opportunities. They noted that volunteers would be able to attend all events for free and, moreover, get "to spend time in Berlin, one of the most vibrant cities in Europe, and to make new Jewish friends. Who knows? You might even meet that special someone you've been looking for!?"[37] During the EMG, an Israel-based dating service hung flyers all over the Estrel Hotel as well as the Waldbühne, the main venue for the opening ceremony.[38] Historian Daniel Wildman emphasized in a media interview that "for the youth participants . . . the Games are above all an inner-Jewish social event."[39] This social aspect persisted all the way through the closing ceremony. The *Jüdische Allgemeine*, noting the "strong sense of community," commented that youth "eagerly took selfies, exchanged cell phone numbers, and again and again struck up spontaneous chants during the speeches."[40]

Ultimately, the EMG, as well as its media coverage in both Jewish and non-Jewish outlets, celebrated the vitality of Jewish life in Germany. Jewish Germans, and Jews from all over Europe, Israel, and the United States, were welcomed in Berlin and celebrated as a vital presence in the city and in contemporary German life. Jewish athletes also formed athletic and social bonds with each other, thereby boosting Jewish community in Berlin, Germany, and abroad. As Meyer, Maccabi Germany president, noted, Jewish Germans had at one time felt ashamed to compete in the Maccabi Games as Germans and wore white and blue jerseys rather than Germany's black, red, and yellow. The 2015 EMG allowed young Jewish Germans to leave behind such feelings of shame and emerge as a "new generation" that "self-consciously identifies with Germany."[41]

EMG Security and the Complexities of Multiculturalism

EMG planners, particularly municipal and federal government leaders, also hoped to use the 2015 EMG as a way to position Berlin, both a major metropolis and Germany's national capital, as a "cosmopolitan city." Constant celebration of Berlin's multiculturalism during EMG festivities, as well as acknowledgment of Berlin's sizable Israeli community, brought this message forward. Yet some aspects of EMG planning and media coverage simultaneously undercut this cosmopolitan message by foregrounding the purported security concerns posed by Berlin's Muslim population. Thus, the EMG fostered very tangible multicultural encounters that brought the two narratives of the games—historical reconciliation and celebration of multicultural cosmopolitanism—into an uneasy relationship in the context of security measures.

Praise of the EMG as evidence of Berlin's multiculturalism was pervasive. Andreas Statzkowsky, sports secretary in Berlin's municipal government, described the 2015 EMG as an "important building block" for "Berlin's image as a tolerant, cosmopolitan city that looks at its past critically."[42] Aleida

Assmann similarly stated that "Berlin is no longer Germania, as Hitler and Speer envisioned it, but a very cosmopolitan city."[43] The immigration of Israelis to Berlin drew particular emphasis. As Michael Roth, Germany's minister for Europe, declared in a ceremony at the Federal Foreign Office, "today Germany is an open-minded and tolerant country, where everybody is welcome." He emphasized the young Israelis who had moved to Berlin "attracted by this city's creativity."[44] *Der Tagesspiegel*, describing the city as "cheap and colorful, exciting and easy going," similarly emphasized the immigration of twenty thousand to thirty thousand Israelis to Berlin.[45] EMG publicity, therefore, framed Israeli visitors to Berlin, and Israeli immigrants more broadly, as a validation of Berlin and of Germany. As sociologist Irit Dekel argues, many Germans interpret the immigration of Israelis to Berlin and other German cities as "proof of Germany's transformation into an open society."[46]

Discourses around immigration were more complex, however, when it came to immigrants of Muslim backgrounds. Some voices were celebratory: *Vorwärts* noted that the TuS Makkabi club, founded in 1970 as a revival of the original Bar Kochba Berlin, had Jewish, Christian, and Muslim members who all played together. "The club is open to all religious orientations," said *Vorwärts*, and all five hundred members shared the goal to "teach and live tolerance."[47] Football player Alec-Ilya Pivalov, a twenty-eight-year-old EMG participant who grew up in Berlin, stated that he understood the Olympic Stadium not only as the site of the 1936 Olympic Games but also as the "location where Hertha BSC plays, which to me is a very multicultural club, in which different religions are represented. It is a stadium which . . . now stands open for multicultural sports events."[48] The EMG opening ceremony celebrated multiculturalism with the joint performance of German Muslim singer Adel Tawil (born in Berlin to an Egyptian father and Tunisian mother) and American Jewish rapper Matisyahu.[49]

Yet EMG security measures created a space for more ambivalent framings of Berlin's multiculturalism to emerge. Especially since the terrorist attacks of September 11, 2001, sport mega-events have functioned as "conspicuous security spectacles," with the Olympic Games constituting the "world's largest security operations outside of war."[50] Considering the specific history of Jews in Germany, the murder of eleven Israeli athletes in a terrorist attack at the 1972 Olympic Games in Munich, and the general appeal of mega-events as sites for terrorist attacks, EMG planners devoted a considerable 25 percent

188 · The 2015 European Maccabi Games

of the event's total budget to security.[51] As Meyer, the president of Maccabi Germany, stated, "Naturally, the question of security stands at the center of this organization of this event. Unfortunately, we must accept this." He continued to say, "I think of 1972 in Munich," and, "nobody wants to experience such a thing."[52] *Der Tagesspiegel* described the security situation in Berlin around the 2015 EMG as "like a state visit." At the Olympic complex there were police "in every corner," and the site was "locked down." At the area around the Estrel Hotel, the main EMG hotel, one street was entirely blocked off, a security measure something no hotels in the area had ever experienced. Police and security were on duty around the clock, guests had to pass through metal detectors, and no automobiles were allowed through without a thorough security check.[53]

Discourses about EMG security were particularly focused on the location of the Estrel Hotel, the only hotel in the city large enough to house all EMG participants together following "the model of an Olympic village."[54] The hotel was located in a neighborhood in the district of Neukölln with a large Muslim population. Berlin is home to the largest Palestinian community in Europe, numbering approximately twenty-five thousand people, although this community receives comparatively little media interest relative to Berlin's Israeli immigrants.[55] *Der Tagesspiegel*, noting the neighborhood's nickname of the "Gaza Strip," emphasized that "every second shop features an Arab sign," and "many Palestinians have taken up residence and fly flags over their shops."[56]

Reflecting common assumptions that Muslims were antisemitic, many media sources presented the Muslim neighborhood of Neukölln as potentially threatening to Jewish EMG participants. The *Berliner Morgenpost* specifically mentioned concerns about "areas in the city that are particularly inhabited by people of Turkish and Arab background."[57] Meyer—who saw the EMG as a new step forward for Jewish Germans—warned athletes not to wear Stars of David or kippahs near the hotel, as did Rabbi Daniel Alter from the Jewish Community of Berlin, who had personally experienced a violent attack in Berlin in 2012 while wearing the kippah.[58]

The corollary to these assumptions of Muslim antisemitism was the belief that Germany had largely abandoned antisemitism, and that the majority of antisemitism that persisted stemmed from "people of migrant background."[59] As Meyer stated, antisemitic and anti-Jewish sentiments from "right-wing extremists" were on the decline, yet "we are experiencing ever stronger hostilities from people with Arab or also Muslim background."[60] Such emphasis on "new anti-Semitism" or "imported anti-Semitism," according to scholars Sa'ed Atshan and Katharina Galor, "relegates German anti-Semitism to a relic of the past while claiming that Germany has dismantled its own anti-Semitic structures."[61] In these discourses, Muslim, Arab, and Palestinian communities become "interchangeable identities" responsible for antisemitism.[62] Moreover, as historian Michael Meng argues, such "alleged Islamification" threatened Germany's "postwar narrative of political redemption."[63] Ensuring the physical safety of EMG participants in Berlin thus became central to successfully using the 2015 EMG to celebrate German-Jewish reconciliation. Emphasizing the German government's special commitment to Jewish safety, federal justice minister Heiko Maas told the *Jüdische Allgemeine*, "We need to do everything we can to ensure that Jews can live safely wherever they wish—in Germany, in Israel, and all over the world."[64]

Not all EMG observers and participants accepted the narrative of an Arab or Muslim threat to Jews. Lukas Hermsmeier of *Der Tagesspiegel* described the area near the Estrel Hotel as "friendly," with "shisha-smoking grandfathers in front of cafés." He stated that "the Muslim community is justified in defending itself against stigmatization," although he acknowledged that "It is precisely the exceptions that more easily remain in our minds" and mentioned a July 2014 video of Abu Bilal Ismail of the Al-Nur-Moschee mosque calling for the destruction of "Zionist Jews." Commenting on the advice for EMG participants not to wear kippahs near their hotel, Hermsmeier asked, "Are such warnings fear mongering?" He noted that some EMG participants ignored the warnings and wore kippahs, including Stéphane Ribette, a tennis player from France, who said he received the email of warning but decided not to abide by it. In contrast, football player and Berliner Ben Lesegeld, who studied at a university in Neukölln, chose not to wear the kippah near the Estrel Hotel. Simultaneously, however, he stated his feelings of safety and belonging in the neighborhood. "I have Arab friends," he told Hermsmeier. "We sometimes disagree over politics, but then we reconcile again." Upon learning that Lesegeld planned to move with his girlfriend to Neukölln, the very neighborhood EMG participants were encouraged to fear, Hermsmeier asked him if Jews were safe there. He describes Lesegeld as "spontaneously and almost defiantly" responding with "Definitely, yes."[65]

As was feared, there were several widely publicized antisemitic acts during the games. Two days after the opening ceremony, two youths insulted six "recognizably Jewish" men between the ages of eighteen and twenty-three with antisemitic phrases near the S-Bahnhof Sonnenallee in Neukölln.[66] The following day, two men were insulted with antisemitic phrases outside the Estrel Hotel. No arrest was made in the first incident, but police arrested a twenty-eight-year-old male in the second incident. Reflecting the rhetorical framing of contemporary antisemitism as imported alongside immigration, the *Jüdische Allgemeine* described the arrested suspect as "stateless," the *Berliner Tagesspiegel* deemed him as stateless but possibly Palestinian, and several days later *Der Tagesspiegel* simply called him "Palestinian."[67] An additional widely publicized antisemitic act, which could not be definitely connected to the EMG, was the painting of antisemitic graffiti over Günter Schäfer's *Vaterland* mural—an image of the German flag with a Star of David on it—at the East Side Gallery of the former Berlin Wall. According to the US-based *Jewish Journal*, "It has not yet been established whether the perpetrator is a neo-Nazi or a religious fundamentalist, but a man of Arabic origin has been questioned over the incident."[68]

At the closing ceremony, Berlin's mayor Michael Müller acknowledged the acts of antisemitism during the EMG, yet emphasized the strong and quick reaction of German authorities as proof that "there is no place in the city for such idiots." He celebrated the power of sports, which "stand for fairness" and are "a symbol that all humans are equal."[69] The EMG were most successful in presenting a public display of historical reconciliation and Jewish belonging in the city and nation. Yet as the concerns about threats to participant safety reveal, the efforts to showcase Berlin's cosmopolitanism and diversity were considerably more complex, with Berlin residents from Muslim backgrounds rhetorically positioned as outsiders who were not entirely compatible with the cosmopolitan ethos of contemporary Berlin.

Conclusion

An evaluation of the 2015 EMG by the *Jüdische Allgemeine* resoundingly celebrated the event's successes. The widespread attention the event garnered in Berlin received particular praise. "Never before was the EMG present in a city to such an extent. The media reported extensively, posters were visible on the streets, the entire political establishment, beginning with the

Federal President, was engaged, the EMG was a subject of conversation." The *Jüdische Allgemeine* deemed the EMG as worthy of "gold," describing it as "a large, colorful, Jewish festival with participants from 38 nations, a demonstration of growing self-assurance."[70] The strong visual imprint of the EMG reflected the mutually beneficial collaboration between the organized Jewish German sports community and Berlin's municipal and federal leaders to use the EMG to celebrate historical reconciliation and to highlight the thriving Jewish communities of contemporary Germany.[71]

The 2015 EMG also had potential implications for a future Berlin Olympic bid. The problematic precedent of the Nazi Olympics and their architectural remnants had influenced some Berlin residents to protest Berlin's early 1990s bid to host the 2000 Olympic Games. Although the bid failed, it did lead to increased engagement with the Nazi history of the Reichssportfeld in the following years.[72] By the time Germany hosted the 2006 FIFA World Cup, the city and federal government had helped fund a historical trail at the Reichssportfeld to present the site's history and display the government's commitment to historical transparency.[73] Yet, the 1936 Olympic Games nonetheless continued to cast shadows over discussions of future Berlin Olympic bids. Within this context, some organizers suggested that the 2015 EMG, with formal events at the Nazi-designed and constructed Waldbühne and Maifeld and with constant celebrations of German-Jewish reconciliation, finally paved the way for Berlin to launch an Olympic bid unencumbered by the 1936 Olympic Games. Maccabi Germany's Meyer described the 2015 EMG as "potentially a precursor for the Olympic Games in 2024 or 2028," and fellow Maccabi Germany leader Oren Osterer celebrated the EMG as having "unparalleled significance" for a future Berlin Olympic bid. "If the Jewish community in Europe supports the [European Maccabi] Games in Berlin," Osterer argued, "that is a symbol, a sign of reconciliation."[74]

The historical reconciliation efforts of the EMG, then, engaged with the central facet of Berlin and Germany's twentieth-century history: its responsibility for the Holocaust. Yet the challenges for future Berlin Olympic bids would involve many more factors than the historical legacies of the 1936 Nazi Olympics. Future bids would likely encounter significant protests from Berlin residents concerned about gentrification and cost of living effects. Berlin would also have to compete with other German cities for the German nomination. In fact, Berlin lost out to Hamburg the last time it submitted an Olympic bid to the German Olympic Committee to compete to host the 2024 Games.[75] Moreover, Berlin remains a highly heterogeneous place with large first- and second-generation immigrant populations, and the history of Berlin and of Germany can be situated within a range of different contexts including not only fascism and the Holocaust but also colonialism and migration. Regardless of whether Berlin ever hosts another Olympics, the city remains a major sports metropolis, where many individuals of all ages and all walks of life enjoy athletic recreation, where major athletic competitions unfold, and where spectacles such as the EMG allow politicians, media, athletes, and sports fans to engage with the past, experience the present, and create the future.

Notes

1. The Maccabiah Games take their name from an ancient Jewish family, the Maccabees, who in the second century BCE rebelled against Seleucid rule, took control of Judea, and reconsecrated the Second Temple. The first Maccabiah Games were held in mandate Palestine in 1932 and 1935. They resumed in 1950, and since 1953 they have been held in a four-year cycle in Israel. Also beginning in 1953, the World Maccabiah Games introduced the lighting of the Maccabiah torch in the city of Modi'in, the birthplace of Judah Maccabee. The Maccabiah flame had featured in prior European Maccabi Games, but 2015 was the first time it was transported to the European host city from Israel via relay. The relay primarily served as an homage to motorcyclists from the 1930s who traveled from mandate Palestine throughout Europe to announce the first and second World Maccabiah Games. The 2015 relay also functioned as a symbolic acknowledgement of and answer to the Nazi origins of the Olympic torch relay during the 1936 Olympic Games. Ron Kaplan, *The Jewish Olympics: The History of the Maccabiah Games* (New York: Skyhorse, 2015); "Jews in Sports: The Maccabiah Games," *Jewish Virtual Library*, accessed September 21, 2022, https://www.jewishvirtuallibrary.org/the-maccabiah-games; Martin Schmidtner, "Trauer, Feier und Symbolik: Die Makkabiade in Berlin, *Vorwärts*, July 31, 2015, accessed September 21, 2022, https://www.vorwaerts.de/artikel/trauer-feier-symbolik-makkabiade-berlin.

2. The motorcycle ride from Israel to Berlin and the opening ceremony of the EMG are featured in the documentary *Back to Berlin*, dir. Catherine Lurie (Harrow, UK: Cat-Mac and Luria Media, 2018).

3. Richard Mandell, *The Nazi Olympics* (Urbana: University of Illinois Press, 1987); Arnd Krüger and William Murray, eds., *The Nazi Olympics: Sport, Politics, and Appeasement in the 1930s* (Urbana: University of Illinois Press, 2003); Barbara J. Keys, *Globalizing Sport: National Rivalry and International Community in the 1930s* (Cambridge, MA: Harvard University Press, 2006), 115–57; Allen Guttmann, "Berlin 1936: The Most Controversial Olympics," in *National Identity and Global Sports Events: Culture, Politics, and Spectacle in the Olympics and the Football World Cup*, ed. Alan Tomlinson and Christopher Young (Albany: State University of New York Press, 2006), 65–81; Christopher Hilton, *Hitler's Olympics: The 1936 Berlin Olympic Games* (Stroud: Sutton, 2008); David Clay Large, *Nazi Games: The Olympics of 1936* (New York: W. W. Norton, 2007).

4. "The European Maccabi Games in Berlin," deutschland.de, published July 22, 2015, accessed July 28, 2023, https://www.deutschland.de/en/topic/politics/germany-europe/the-european-maccabi-games-in-berlin.

5. "Außenminister Steinmeier zum Beginn der European Maccabi Games," Auswärtiges Amt, published July 27, 2015, accessed September 21, 2022, https://www.auswaertiges-amt.de/de/newsroom/150727-maccabi-games/273588.

6. *Back to Berlin*, dir. Catherine Lurie (2018; Harrow, UK: Cat-Mac and Luria Media).

7. Sa'ed Atshan and Katharina Galor, *The Moral Triangle: Germans, Israelis, Palestinians* (Durham, NC: Duke University Press, 2020), 42.

8. Daniel Wildman, "Jewish Gymnastics and Their Corporeal Utopias in Imperial Germany," in *Emancipation through Muscles: Jews and Sports in Europe*, ed. Michael Brenner and Gideon Reuveni (Lincoln: University of Nebraska Press, 2006), 27.

9. Samuel Presner, *Muscular Judaism: The Jewish Body and the Politics of Regeneration* (Abingdon: Routledge, 2007), 2, 4, 107. On the relationship between discourses of degeneration and muscular Judaism, see Moshe Zimmermann, "Muscle Jews versus Nervous Jews," in *Emancipation through Muscles*, 13–26.

10. Wildman, "Jewish Gymnastics," 27.

11. Gertrud Pfister and Toni Niewerth, "Jewish Women in Gymnastics and Sports in Germany, 1898–1938," *Journal of Sport History* 26, no. 2 (Summer 1999): 295–96.

12. Gideon Reuveni, "Sports and the Militarization of Jewish Society," in *Emancipation through Muscles*, 50, 53. See also Berno Bahro, "Lilli Henoch and Martha Jacob: Two Jewish Athletes in Germany before and after 1933," *Sport in History* 30, no. 2 (2010): 273–75.

13. Arnd Krüger, "'Once the Olympics Are Through, We'll Beat Up the Jew': German Jewish Sport 1898–1938 and the Anti-Semitic Discourse," *Journal of Sport History* 26, no. 2 (1999): 355. On Jewish women's athletic participation in the Weimar years, see Pfister and Niewerth, "Jewish Women," 298–303.

14. Krüger, "German Jewish Sport 1898–1938," 364.

15. Jacob Borut, "Jews in German Sports During the Weimar Republic," in *Emancipation through Muscles*, 77–78.

16. Bahro, "Lilli Henoch and Martha Jacob," 279; Krüger, "German Jewish Sport 1898–1938," 356.

17. Hans Joachim Teichler, "Vorwort," in *Forgotten Records—Vergessene Rekorde: Jüdische Leichtathletinnen vor und nach 1933*, ed. Berno Bahro, Jutta Braun, and Hans Joachim Teichler (Berlin: verlag für berlin-brandenburg, 2009), 12–13. Note that this exhibit was presented in conjunction with the Twelfth IAAF World Championships in Athletics, held in Berlin in 2009.

18. Kurt Schilde, "Jüdischer Sport in der Hauptstadt des 'Dritten Reiches'—Zwischen dem Aufblühen ab 1933 und dem Untergang 1938," in *Emancipation through Muscles*, 152–61.

19. Pfister and Niewirth "Jewish Women," 313.

20. "Ausstellung: Zwischen Erfolg und Verfolgung—Skulpturale Ausstellung vorm Berliner Hauptbahnhof des ZdS," Zentrum deutsche Sportgeschichte, accessed January 12, 2023, www.zentrum-deutsche-sportgeschichte.de/zwischen-erfolg-und-verfolgung-skulpturale-ausstellung-vorm-berliner-hauptbahnhof-des-zds; "Sportler zwischen Erfolg und Verfolgung," Die Bundesregierung, July 24, 2015, accessed January 12, 2023, https://www.bundesregierung.de/breg-de/service/archiv/alt-inhalte/sportler-zwischen-erfolg-und-verfolgung-450710. The exhibit was prepared by sport historians Berno Bahro, Hans Joachim Teichler, Lorenz Peiffer, and Henry Wahling.

21. The exhibit, which has been displayed in several cities around Germany since the 2015 EMG, can be viewed online at *Jewish Allstars: Zwischen Erfolg und Verfolgung: Jüdische Stars im deutschen Sport bis 1933 und danach*, accessed January 13, 2023, https://www.jewishallstars .com/. On Henoch and Jacob, see also Bahro, "Lilli Henoch and Martha Jacob," 267–87; Pfister and Niewerth, "Jewish Women," 304–307.

22. Katharina Schmidt-Hirschfelder, "Gedenken auf dem Maifeld," *Jüdische Allgemeine*, July 28, 2015, accessed September 21, 2022, https://www.juedische-allgemeine.de/politik /gedenken-auf-dem-maifeld/.

23. Ayala Goldmann, "Was für ein Symbol," *Jüdische Allgemeine*, July 28, 2015, accessed September 21, 2022, https://www.juedische-allgemeine.de/politik/was-fuer-ein-symbol/.

24. Schmidtner, "Trauer, Feier und Symbolik."

25. Fabian Scheler, "Das deutsche jüdische Sportfest," *Die Zeit*, July 31, 2015, accessed September 21, 2022, https://www.zeit.de/sport/2015-07/maccabi-games-2015-juedische -sportler-berlin-makkabiade.

26. Roy Rajber, "Unser Sommermärchen," *Jüdische Allgemeine*, July 27, 2015, accessed September 21, 2022, https://www.juedische-allgemeine.de/politik/unser-sommermaerchen/.

27. "Makkabi Spiele in Berlin eröffnet: 'Ein wunderbares Geschenk,'" Deutschlandfunk Kultur, July 29, 2015, accessed September 21, 2022, https://www.deutschlandfunkkultur.de /makkabi-spiele-in-berlin-eroeffnet-ein-wunderbares-geschenk-100.html.

28. Eva-Maria Schmidt, "M & C Saatchi macht Berlin meschugge," Horizont, July 15, 2015, accessed September 22, 2022, https://www.horizont.net/agenturen/nachrichten /European-Maccabi-Games-MC-Saatchi-macht-Berlin-meschugge-135380.

29. Ayala Goldmann, "Wie in einem kleinen Olympischen Dorf," *Jüdische Allgemeine*, July 31, 2015, accessed September 21, 2022, https://www.juedische-allgemeine.de/unsere -woche/wie-in-einem-kleinen-olympischen-dorf/.

30. "Largest shabbat dinner," *Guinness World Records*, accessed September 21, 2022, https://www.guinnessworldrecords.com/world-records/largest-shabbat-dinner.

31. Jakob Mühle, "Gefilte Fisch und ein Rekord," *Jüdische Allgemeine*, July 31, 2015, accessed September 21, 2022, https://www.juedische-allgemeine.de/unsere-woche /gefilte-fisch-und-ein-rekord/; Jakob Mühle, "Schabbes der Rekorde," *Jüdische Allgemeine*, August 3, 2015, accessed September 21, 2022, https://www.juedische-allgemeine.de/unsere -woche/schabbes-der-rekorde/.

32. Jakob Mühle, "Größter Schabbat in Neukölln," *Jüdische Allgemeine*, January 8, 2015, accessed February 7, 2024, https://www.juedische-allgemeine.de/unsere-woche/groesster -schabbat-in-neukoelln/.

33. Theresia Ziehe, "Die Makkabiade ist ein starkes Zeichen gegen Antisemitismus," *Blogerim*, August 3, 2015, accessed September 21, 2022, https://www.jmberlin.de/blog /2015/08/sarah/.

34. Philipp Peyman Engel, "Schland, Schland!!," *Jüdische Allgemeine*, July 29, 2015, accessed September 21, 2022, https://www.juedische-allgemeine.de/unsere-woche /schland-schland/.

35. Jan Schapira, "Jung und jüdisch," *Berliner Morgenpost*, July 30, 2015, accessed September 21, 2022, https://www.morgenpost.de/berlin/article205519823/Jung-und -juedisch.html.

36. "Abends machen die Maccabi-Athleten in Neukölln Party," *B.Z. am Mittag*, August 1, 2015, accessed September 21, 2022, https://www.bz-berlin.de/archiv-artikel/abends -machen-die-maccabi-athleten-in-neukoelln-party.

37. "Volunteer at the European Maccabi Games 2015 in Berlin . . . And Meet Your Soulmate?," accessed September 21, 2022, *Simantov International*, http://simantov -international.com/volunteer-at-the-european-maccabi-games-2015-in-berlin-and -meet-your-soulmate/.

38. Schmidtner, "Trauer, Feier und Symbolik."

39. Martin Einsiedler, "Makkabiade in Berlin: Das jüdische Sportfest muss sich neu erfinden," *Der Tagesspiegel*, August 4, 2015, accessed September 21, 2022, https://www .tagesspiegel.de/sport/makkabiade-in-berlin-das-juedische-sportfest-muss-sich-neu -erfinden/12134252.html.

40. Alice Lanzke, "Spiele des jüdischen Stolzes," *Jüdische Allgemeine*, August 5, 2015, accessed September 21, 2022, https://www.juedische-allgemeine.de/unsere-woche /spiele-des-juedischen-stolzes/.

41. Laura Piotrowski, "70 Jahre nach Ende der Shoa ist es Zeit für die European Maccabi Games in Deutschland," Fussball-Gegen-Nazis.de, June 16, 2015, accessed September 21, 2022, http://www.fussball-gegen-nazis.de/beitrag/70-jahre-nach-ende -der-shoa-ist-es-zeit-fuer-die-european-maccabi-games-deutschland-10427.

42. Katharina Schmidt-Hirschfelder, "Bedeutung erkannt," *Jüdische Allgemeine*, April 24, 2015, accessed September 21, 2022, https://www.juedische-allgemeine.de/unsere-woche /bedeutung-erkannt/. Both statements reflect Berlin's urban marketing strategy, begun in the early 2000s, to embrace Berlin's complex history as a strategy to attract international visitors and tourist revenue. See Claire Colomb, *Staging the New Berlin: Place Marketing and the Politics of Urban Reinvention Post-1989* (London: Routledge, 2012), 250–52.

43. "Makkabi Spiele in Berlin eröffnet: 'Ein wunderbares Geschenk,'" Deutschlandfunk Kultur, July 29, 2015, accessed September 21, 2022, https://www.deutschlandfunkkultur .de/makkabi-spiele-in-berlin-eroeffnet-ein-wunderbares-geschenk-100.html.

44. "Rede von Staatsminister für Europa Michael Roth zum Empfang anlässlich der Maccabi Games 2015 im Auswärtigen Amt," Auswärtiges Amt, July 30, 2015, accessed September 22, 2022, https://www.auswaertiges-amt.de/de/newsroom/-/273548.

45. Lukas Hermsmeier, "Jüdisches Sportfest in Berlin: Die Angst spielt mit bei der Makkabiade," *Der Tagesspiegel*, August 2, 2015, accessed September 21, 2022, https://www .tagesspiegel.de/themen/reportage/juedisches-sportfest-in-berlin-die-zahl-antisemitischer -straftaten-hat-zuletzt-zugenommen/12132510-2.html.

46. Irit Dekel, "'You Are My Liberty': On the Negotiation of Holocaust and Other Memories for Israelis in Berlin," in *Rebuilding Jewish Life in Germany*, ed. Jay Howard Geller and Michael Meng (Ithaca, NY: Rutgers University Press, 2020), 224. Dekel notes, however, that many immigrants from Israel identify as Israeli and not Jewish and are not part of the organized German Jewish community in Berlin. See Dekel, "'You Are My Liberty,'" 228, 241. See also Atshan and Galor, *Moral Triangle*, 63–64, 116–24.

47. Schmidtner, "Trauer, Feier und Symbolik."

48. Theresia Ziehe, "Das Olympiastadion ist inzwischen ein Ort für multikulturelle Sportereignisse," Blogerim, July 26, 2015, accessed September 21, 2022, https://www.jmberlin .de/blog/2015/07/alec-ilya/.

49. Schmidtner, "Trauer, Feier und Symbolik."

50. Philip Boyle, "Securing the Olympic Games: Exemplifications of Global Governance," in *The Palgrave Handbook of Olympic Studies*, ed. Helen Jefferson Lenskyj and Stephen Wagg (New York: Palgrave Macmillan, 2012), 393.

51. Ronny Blaschke, "Selbstverständlich in Deutschland," Deutschlandfunk, December 22, 2014, accessed September 21, 2022, https://www.deutschlandfunk.de/european-maccabi -games-selbstverstaendlich-in-deutschland-100.html.

52. "München '72: so etwas will niemand mehr erleben," Berliner Morgenpost, July 27, 2015, accessed September 21, 2022, https://www.morgenpost.de/berlin/article205510131/ Muenchen-72-so-etwas-will-niemand-mehr-erleben.html.

53. Hermsmeier, "Jüdisches Sportfest in Berlin."

54. Hermsmeier, "Jüdisches Sportfest in Berlin."

55. Atshan and Galor, Moral Triangle, 4–5; Matt Unicomb, "Inside Berlin's Famous Palestinian Neighbourhood," Middle East Eye, July 2, 2022, accessed September 21, 2022, https://www.middleeasteye.net/discover/inside-famous-palestinian-berlin-germany -neighbourhood.

56. Hermsmeier, "Jüdisches Sportfest in Berlin."

57. "München '72."

58. Hermsmeier, "Jüdisches Sportfest in Berlin"; Madeline Chambers, "German Jewish College Shuns Skullcaps after Attack on Rabbi," Reuters, August 30, 2012, accessed September 21, 2022, https://www.reuters.com/article/us-germany-rabbi/german-jewish -college-shuns-skullcaps-after-attack-on-rabbi-idUSBRE87T0UZ20120830.

59. As one example, see "Ex-Herthaner kennt Antisemitismus in Berlin," ntv, July 31, 2015, accessed September 21, 2022, https://www.n-tv.de/sport/Ex-Herthaner-kennt-Antisemitismus-in-Berlin-article15630751.html. Atshan and Galor describe the phrase "of migrant background" as an effort to avoid explicit discussions of race, yet note that it has a clear "negative connotation." Atshan and Galor, Moral Triangle, 43–44.

60. Piotrowski, "70 Jahre nach Ende der Shoa."

61. Atshan and Galor, Moral Triangle, 110.

62. Atshan and Galor, Moral Triangle, 97.

63. Michael Meng, "(Trans)National Spaces: Jewish Sites in Contemporary Germany," in Three-Way Street: Jews, Germans, and the Transnational, ed. Jay Howard Gellar and Leslie Morris (Ann Arbor: University of Michigan Press, 2016), 331, 333.

64. Philipp Peyman Engel, "Signal an die Gesellschaft," Jüdische Allgemeine, July 23, 2015, accessed September 21, 2022, https://www.juedische-allgemeine.de/politik/signal-an-die -gesellschaft/.

65. Hermsmeier, "Jüdisches Sportfest in Berlin."

66. Hermsmeier, "Jüdisches Sportfest in Berlin"; "Antisemitische Vorfälle während Maccabi Games," Jüdische Allgemeine, July 31, 2015, accessed September 21, 2022, https:// www.juedische-allgemeine.de/unsere-woche/antisemitische-vorfaelle-waehrend -maccabi-games/.

67. "Antisemitische Vorfälle"; Jana Lotze, "Antisemitismus am Rande der Makkabiade," Der Tagesspiegel, July 31, 2015, accessed September 21, 2022, https://www.tagesspiegel.de /berlin/polizei-justiz/antisemitismus-am-rande-der-makkabiade-beleidigung-gegen-sicherheitsmitarbeiter/12132432.html; Lukas Hermsmeier, "Jüdisches Sportfest in Berlin."

68. "Artist Paints Over Anti-Semitic Graffiti on Berlin Wall Monument," Jewish Journal, August 3, 2015, accessed September 21, 2022, https://jewishjournal.com/news /worldwide/176372/. Schaefer, who noted that his mural had been vandalized fifty-one times, repainted it.

69. Alice Lanzke, "Be Jewish! Be Maccabi! Be Berlin!," Jüdische Allgemeine, August 5, 2015, accessed September 21, 2022, https://www.juedische-allgemeine.de/unsere-woche /be-jewish-be-maccabi-be-berlin/.

70. Detlef David Kauschke and Martin Krauss, "Gold für die Spiele," *Jüdische Allgemeine*, August 3, 2015, accessed September 21, 2022, https://www.juedische-allgemeine.de/politik/gold-fuer-die-spiele/.

71. Building off the successful 2015 EMG in Berlin, the first Maccabi Winter Games since 1936 took place in January 2023 in Ruhpolding, Germany. "Wintergames 2023," *Makkabi Germany*, accessed July 14, 2023, https://makkabi.de/en/wintergames-2023/.

72. Molly Wilkinson Johnson, "The Legacies of 1936: Hitler's Olympic Grounds and Berlin's Bid to Host the 2000 Olympic Games," *German History* 40, no. 2 (2022): 258–77.

73. Clare Copley, *Nazi Buildings, Cold War Traces and Governmentality in Post-Unification Berlin* (London: Bloomsbury, 2020), 86.

74. Alon Meyer, "Ein Vorbote für Olympia," *Jüdische Allgemeine*, March 15, 2015, accessed September 21, 2022, https://www.juedische-allgemeine.de/politik/ein-vorbote-fuer-olympia/; Frank Bachner and Sabine Beikler, "Jüdische Europameisterschaften Maccabi 2015: Der Test für Olympia in Berlin," *Der Tagesspiegel*, March 12, 2015, accessed September 21, 2022, https://www.tagesspiegel.de/berlin/der-test-fur-olympia-in-berlin-5451136.html.

75. "Hamburg Is Preferred Choice for Germany's 2024 Games Bid," Reuters, March 16, 2015, accessed August 1, 2023, https://www.reuters.com/article/olympics-2024-germany-idINL6N0WI4CL20150316.

CONCLUSION

The History of Sports as a History of Berlin

ANNEMARIE SAMMARTINO

Reading this book is a deliberately bewildering experience. While this book does examine some public events such as the 1892 Berlin-Vienna Distance Ride, a horse race that took place between these two Central European capitals, and Berlin's role in hosting the 2015 European Maccabi Games, a quadrennial Jewish sporting competition, many of the familiar landmarks of Berlin's sport history are missing. The city's role hosting the 1936 Olympics is dismissed in the first few pages of the introduction as something that has obscured rather than revealed "the broader history of sport in Berlin."[1] None of Berlin's major professional sports teams are featured in these pages. This book stubbornly refuses to follow the traditional outlines of a history of Germany's capital city. The multiple transformations of Berlin from imperial capital to epicenter of Weimar modernity to divided Cold War city to, once again, capital of a "New Germany," are referred to only obliquely. There is not a single chapter on Nazi Berlin. Mentions of Berlin's mayors and German rulers are few and far between. These pages do not foreground discussions of the outcomes of games, the tactics of sport, or athletic accomplishments.

Instead, this is largely a history from below. The pages of this book are populated by long-forgotten sports writers depicting nascent celebrity athletes, amateur football players repurposing Nazi flags into makeshift uniforms in the rubble of an occupied city, and Turkish immigrants in the late twentieth century simultaneously signaling their belonging to and distance from German culture by forming amateur football clubs. Even those chapters that emphasize larger-scale events focus on the small moments within them. For example, Barnet Hartston's study of the Berlin-Vienna Distance Ride of 1892 discusses the unruly spectators as much as the horsemen they were ostensibly there to celebrate, and Heather Dichter's examination of diplomatic negotiations for the 1964 all-German Olympic team trials discusses the East German regime's fears that East Berliners would celebrate West German athletes as one reason why negotiations over the location of the team trials proved so difficult. In Molly Wilkinson Johnson's contribution, the concerns over the athletes attending the 2015 European Maccabi Games staying in a hotel in a majority Muslim neighborhood of Neukölln (the only hotel in the city large enough for the purpose) is given more attention than the actual competitions. The fact that the essays in this volume only give glancing attention to the familiar periods and waystations of the history of Berlin is a useful reminder that ordinary people's lives are not necessarily defined or demarcated by high politics.

Many of these essays chart how urban identity and urban community were formed through participation in sporting culture as an athlete or as a spectator. For example, in his essay on sports journalism in Weimar Berlin, Erik Jensen discusses the shared language of sport, in which many readers "followed the results of competitions in the pages of the city's proliferating newspapers and magazines, often despite their lack of any genuine interest in doing so."[2] Sports culture was a lingua franca of shared symbols and texts that together formed readers and spectators in Germany's capital city into an imagined community. Benedict Anderson's insight that the distribution of printed texts in vernacular languages was the basis for national consciousness also holds true for urban identity. Berlin's image often takes center stage in the urban history narrated in these pages: Berlin's desire to project its power as the capital of a newly unified state in Hartston's chapter on the Berlin-Vienna Distance Ride, Berlin's insecure status as a cosmopolitan city in Jensen's narrative of sports reporting during the Weimar era, Berlin's attempts to bolster future Olympic bids in Johnson's examination of the 2015 European Maccabi Games. Politicians and others sought to stage and depict sporting events as a means to project the power not only of sports itself but also of the city where the events took place. Furthermore, as Alec Hurley writes in his study of sports commentators in the late nineteenth century, sport was a part of the general *allerlei* of Berlin life—a piece of the "continuous stream of incidents, events, and impressions" that defined the urban experience at the fin de siècle.[3] For sports fans, this was a community that was both horizontal, emphasizing the shared experience of fandom, and vertical, in the veneration of individual athletic achievements.

It is important to note that sport did not function in an identical manner to the other spectacles and texts that saturated urban life in Berlin. Sport allowed for a degree of identification and empathy, as well as degree of uncertainty, that made athletes a different kind of celebrity than actors and football matches a different kind of drama than movies and plays. This identification and empathy may be the reason why the organizers of the 2015 European Maccabi Games, as discussed by Johnson in her concluding essay, believed that the event would allow Berlin to "set an example of reconciliation ... and present itself as a cosmopolitan, peaceful and tolerant metropolis."[4]

This is one example among many in this volume that highlights the importance and complexity of Berliners' multiple levels of identification—from the local to the national to the international—as well as the links between these identities. In the introduction to this volume, the editors note that Berlin has often cultivated "an urban identity that in many ways transcends its Germanness."[5] As Hurley explains, the sports writer Adolf von Guretzki simultaneously described the urban sportscape of Berlin and an imagined sporting competition in distant Egypt. In 1892, authorities sought to use the Berlin-Vienna Distance Ride to both bolster Germany's image on the world stage and also serve nation-building within the still-young Reich. Describing the Berlin of a century later, Jeffrey Jurgens writes that Gençlikspor was one of several Turkish football clubs that functioned as local institutions that allowed Turkish Berliners to create and maintain community where they often felt unwelcome. Sport had the ability not only to bring people together but also to highlight their differences. Johnson shows how the narrative of German-Jewish reconciliation presented during the 2015 European Maccabi Games also posited Berlin's Muslim population as outsiders and potential sources of antisemitic violence. Hartston reveals how the public deaths of several horses involved in the distance ride led many Berliners to castigate the elite cavalrymen whom they saw as responsible for the fate of their steeds.

While some of the essays in this volume stress the role of sports reportage, others make clear that for many sports enthusiasts, the identities and communities forged around sport were based on everyday sporting practices. In Jurgens's essay on Turkish football clubs in late twentieth-century Berlin, he notes that today, exclusively Turkish football clubs have largely receded as players of Turkish descent are integrated into long-standing "German" clubs while "immigrant" clubs that were once overwhelmingly composed of people of Turkish descent now boast a more heterogeneous membership. Rather than the identities of these clubs being forged by the shared connections of players to their country of origin or descent, those identities are now based on the shared experience of practicing and competing together. Given the capacity of sport to forge community, it is not an accident that occupation officials in postwar Berlin sought to use sport as a tool for denazification. As Will Rall demonstrates, sport was so central to Allied plans that in late 1945, the Allied Control Directive on the Limitation and Demilitarization of Sport in Germany sought to create a framework for the regulation of sports to keep them from becoming activities of military training or indoctrination that would hinder the process of demilitarization and denazification. As Rall explains, Allied powers "shared concerns about the potential for sporting clubs and associations to foster nationalist fervor while also recognizing them as an opportunity to promote community-building and democratic values."[6]

The material realities of Berlin are also present throughout this volume. Rall's narrative of everyday life in postwar Berlin describes how weather and ruined infrastructure affected games and transit through the city. In the 1970s, according to Kai Reinhart, the concrete landscapes in West Berlin's modernist Märkisches Viertel made an ideal environment for skateboarders, just as abandoned pools did in Southern California where the sport was born. Skateboarding traditions and communities often developed as a function of the happenstance of where skateboarders could find suitable spaces to skate. Seeing the city from the perspective of a skateboarder meant looking for smooth curves, ramps, and rails where one could ride and practice tricks. In Dichter's narrative of Cold War diplomatic wrangling over the all-German Olympic team, negotiations are made both more urgent and more tangled by West Berlin's location within East Germany. The introduction notes that Berlin's division for forty-five years means that there are no singular professional clubs that claim a monopoly on citizens' loyalties as is the case in many other cities. In all of these cases, the specificity of Berlin's history and landscape are written on its sporting culture.

Materiality is inescapable in this text in other ways as well, not least of which is through the intense physicality of sports. As Kathleen Canning wrote of the rise of histories of the body in the 1990s, "Understanding bodies as another layer of experience, site of subjectivity, or representation of self and social collectivity enriches the history of everyday life."[7] In the case of sport, that physicality is not only present but also on display. It should be no surprise that discussions of this physicality often highlighted the performance of gender roles. Masculinity, in particular, comes up time and time again in these texts. Hartston explains how the Berlin-Vienna Distance Ride was designed as a showcase for martial masculinity, a stage on which elite men could demonstrate their courage, vigor, strength, and endurance. Similar values informed the masculinity on display in the sports reportage analyzed by Hurley and Jensen. Indeed, with the restrictions placed on Germany's military by the Treaty of Versailles, one commentator suggested that track and field could serve as a substitute for military training, noting that British military success could be explained by the fact that it possessed "a youth that had been steeled through sport."[8] These sports commentators were more uneasy about female athletes, fearful both that they would be unable to withstand the rigors of competitive athletics and that they would be masculinized by them. Jensen describes how some athletes and correspondents feared that competitive training would "defame our German girls and make hard, manly bodies out of them."[9] He also notes the droll plea of one female sportswriter who requested that in the future newspapers avoid describing their shock at seeing sweaty, exhausted women after a race. By the postwar period, the unease about the relationship between sport and masculinity became a concern for men as well. Allied authorities worried about the potentially militarizing aspects of competitive sport as they nonetheless authorized football competitions in ruined Berlin. Later, outside observers and participants alike worried about the hyperaggression of Turkish football players. Meanwhile, skateboarders in 1970s West Berlin eschewed traditional masculinity and competition alike as they opted for a more "Californized," relaxed masculinity in a sport that nonetheless continued to be dominated by boys and men.

The embodied experience of sports is also visible in these essays in the ongoing explicit and implicit reckoning with modernity. Modernity is all too often discussed by historians as a kind of abstraction. Perhaps this is due to Georg Simmel's early twentieth century identification of abstraction as key for understanding modern urban life. This book is a helpful reminder that modernity is simultaneously experienced as embodied. Jensen's essay identifies several aspects of modern sports culture in the Weimar period, including its embrace of Taylorist training principles and the focus on athletes as individual celebrities. These two ideas were often in tension: one emphasized the universal benefits of scientific training and the other celebrated

204 · The History of Sports as a History of Berlin

the miracle of unique achievement. Nevertheless, they both were heralded in their time as evidence of sport's modernity. A half century later, modernity took on a different meaning in Berlin's sports culture. In the 1970s, skateboarders eschewed competition to focus on lifestyle and subculture, modeled on a "Californian" ethos of individualism and self-fulfillment. As one skateboarder quoted in Reinhart's piece stated, "I do it to clear my head. Not to go faster, higher, more beautifully, further . . . but it has to be fun for me. Whatever fun means to me or to you."[10] As far apart as Jensen's track athletes and Reinhart's skateboarders might have been in their understanding of what it meant to be modern, they shared the conviction that their athletic achievements were expressions of their modern selves.

The essays in this volume emphasize the ways that sport has served as a kind of invented tradition. In the 1980s, Eric Hobsbawm and Terence Ranger coined the term *invented tradition* to discuss how even traditions of relatively recent vintage can draw upon symbols from the past and use these constructed continuities to foster community cohesion. In these essays, the social power of sport is found not merely in its use of familiar symbols but also in its iterability. For so many of the subjects in this volume, sport provides a sense of routine. The amateur football players in Rall's postwar Berlin used practices and games to organize the rhythms of their days and weeks. As Rall puts it, "Berliners might not have known whether their local store could honor their ration card or where they might find fresh vegetables. Yet, for weeks to come, Berliners knew where they could find competitive football at 2:30 on Sunday afternoons."[11] The same might be said for the new immigrants about whom Jurgens writes who turned to Turkish football clubs for community and structure. For the athletes who took part in the 2015 European Maccabi Games that Johnson chronicles, the importance of the event was such that it organized their training and lives for the preceding months. Fans, too, organize their time around the rhythms of athletic seasons and the predictable routine of sporting events.

Unlike the role that sport has sometimes played in other cities, sport in Berlin does not seem to be the source of urban transformation.[12] It is unclear why that is the case. Nevertheless, it is striking that while Berlin was the stage for urban pageantry and international competition during the Cold War and its aftermath, these events did not lead to the large-scale reimagining or reconstruction of the city. This is particularly surprising as Berlin has repeatedly witnessed large-scale construction and reconstruction projects that have remade its landscape. Yet, in modern Berlin's serial construction and reconstruction projects, sport appears to have largely been an afterthought. Perhaps this is because Berlin was a city defined by so much upheaval in the time span covered in this volume that Berliners looked to sport to provide a sense of continuity amid the tumult.

Sporting events can also be singular events that serve as breaks from routine in more quotidian ways. Whether in a city filled with pomp and circumstance or in the relatively small confines of a stadium, these chapters reveal moments when participants could revel in the extraordinary feats of athletes and the everyday pleasures of community. Mikhail Bakhtin's notion of the carnivalesque has some degree of explanatory power here. As Bakhtin explained it, the medieval carnival was an opportunity for power relations to be stabilized, as laughter and grotesquerie allowed for the suspension of everyday hierarchies and the liberation of behavior from conventional expectations, the "joyful relativity of all structure and order."[13] The end result was an opportunity for participants to attain a degree of human connection, linked by the universality of humor. There are moments of the carnivalesque in this volume. For example, the laughter and community of spectators at the Berlin-Vienna Distance Ride that undermined the goals of its organizers, who had hoped for the event to be "a ritual of unity" and "a showcase for elite values."[14] Yet, the subversion that occurs in these essays is often less one of laughter but one of contingency. From the uncertain outcome of games to the unpredictable events that can affect them, sport of all kinds contains a necessary degree of the unexpected. That plays a role in this book in ways both great and small. Hartston explains that the German rider Clemens von Reitzenstein lost what seemed like his race to win when he took "a last-minute, accidental detour in the fog."[15] The dreary, icy morning of January 6, 1946, at the start of the first postwar Berlin city championship played a role in making the play on the pitch and its role as a symbol of postwar resilience less impressive than it might otherwise have been. In Jurgens's essay on Turkish football clubs, he explains how an incident of conflict forced players and referees to suddenly grapple with the stereotype of "southern" male aggression.

These are all examples of competitions and competitors derailed by contingencies. However, contingency in sport is just as often a source of pleasure and community. I will conclude these reflections with a brief memory of how the success of *Die Mannschaft* during the 2006 FIFA World Cup brought together Berliners in a display of community that shut down the city on game days and filled Berlin's streets with joyous honking after victories. This joy was made all the sweeter because expectations for Germany's national football team had not been particularly great that year, so such moments as the victory over a powerhouse Argentine team in penalty kicks in the second round of the knockout stage were a delightful surprise. A friend who had lived in the city for decades said that the sense of community in the streets of Berlin in the weeks leading up to Germany's third-place finish were the closest that he could recall to the feeling of the city in the delirious summer of 1990.

As anyone who has heard the screams of children on a playground can attest, the joy that playing and watching sports can produce is universal. This book reminds that it is also personal, local, and particular.

Notes

1. Molly Wilkinson Johnson and Heather L. Dichter, "Introduction: Berlin as Germany's Sporting City," 3.

2. Erik Jensen, "Power/Play: Sports, Journalism, and Contested Modernity in Weimar Berlin," 69.

3. Alec Hurley, "Celebrity and Spectacle: Adolf von Guretzki's Influence on Berlin's Early Twentieth-Century Sports Writing," 63.

4. Molly Wilkinson Johnson, "The 2015 European Maccabi Games: The Ambiguities of Historical Reconciliation in Berlin," 178.

5. Dichter and Johnson, "Introduction," 4

6. Will Rall, "Rebuilding the Beautiful Game: Occupation, Football, and Survival in Berlin, 1945–1946," 90.

7. Kathleen Canning, *Gender History in Practice: Historical Perspectives on Bodies, Class, and Citizenship* (Ithaca, NY: Cornell University Press, 2006), 28.

8. Jensen, "Power/Play," 75.

9. Jensen, "Power/Play," 75–76.

10. Kai Reinhart, "Californization and Sport as Lifestyle: The Development of Skateboarding in West Berlin, 1970–1990," 151.

11. Will Rall, "Rebuilding the Beautiful Game," 99.

12. One notable example here is the role of the 1932 Olympics in transforming Los Angeles. See Barry Siegel, *Dreamers and Schemers: How an Improbable Bid for the 1932 Olympics Transformed Los Angeles from Dusty Outpost to Global Metropolis* (Berkeley: University of California Press, 2019) or Wayne Wilson and David Wiggins, eds., *LA Sports: Play, Games, and Community in the City of Angels* (Fayetteville: University of Arkansas Press, 2018), published in the same series as this volume.

13. Mikhail Bakhtin, *Rabalais and His World*, trans. Hélène Iswolsky (Bloomington: Indiana University Press, 1984), 124.

14. Barnet Hartston, "A Failed Showcase: The Great Berlin-Vienna Distance Ride of 1892," 35.

15. Hartston, "A Failed Showcase," 37–38.

Selected Bibliography

Adelman, Melvin. *A Sporting Time: New York City and the Rise of Modern Athletics, 1820–70.* Urbana: University of Illinois Press, 1990.

Alkemeyer, Thomas. *Körperkultur, Kult und Politik: Von der "Muskelreligion" Pierre de Coubertins zur Inszenierung von Macht in den Olympischen Spielen von 1936.* Frankfurt am Main: Campus, 1996.

Atshan, Sa'ed, and Katharina Galor. *The Moral Triangle: Germans, Israelis, Palestinians.* Durham, NC: Duke University Press, 2020.

Bäckström, Åsa, and Shane Blackman. "Skateboarding: From Urban Spaces to Subcultural Olympians." *YOUNG* 30, no. 2 (2022): 121–31.

Bäckström, Åsa, and Karen Nairn. "Skateboarding Beyond the Limits of Gender? Strategic Interventions in Sweden." *Leisure Studies* 37, no. 4 (2018): 424–39.

Bahro, Berno. "Lilli Henoch and Martha Jacob: Two Jewish Athletes in Germany before and after 1933." *Sport in History* 30, no. 2 (2010): 267–87.

Bakhtin, Mikhail. *Rabalais and His World.* Translated by Hélène Iswolsky. Bloomington: Indiana University Press, 1984.

Balbier, Uta A. *Kalter Krieg auf der Aschenbahn: der deutsch-deutsche Sport, 1950–1972: eine politische Geschichte.* Paderborn: Ferdinand Schöningh, 2007

Bale, John. *Sport, Space and the City.* London: Routledge, 1993.

Baranowski, Shelley. *Strength through Joy: Consumerism and Mass Tourism in the Third Reich.* Cambridge: Cambridge University Press, 2007.

Barjolin-Smith, Anne. "Snowboarding Youth Culture and the Winter Olympics: Co-Evolution in an American-Driven Show." *The International Journal of the History of Sport* 37, no. 13 (2020): 1322–47.

Bark, Dennis L., and David R. Gress. *A History of West Germany.* Vol. 1, *From Shadow to Substance, 1945–1963.* Oxford: Basil Blackwell, 1989.

Barth, Fredrick. *Ethnic Groups and Boundaries: The Social Organization of Cultural Difference.* London: Allen & Unwin, 1969.

Beal, Becky. "Disqualifying the Official: An Exploration of Social Resistance through the Subculture of Skateboarding." *Sociology of Sport Journal* 12, no. 3 (1995): 252–67.

Beal, Becky, and Belinda Wheaton. "'Keeping It Real': Subcultural Media and the Discourses of Authenticity in Alternative Sport." *International Review for the Sociology of Sport* 30, no. 2 (2003): 155–76.

Becker, Frank. *Amerikanismus in Weimar: Sportsymbole und politische Kultur 1918–1933.* Wiesbaden: Deutscher Universitäts-Verlag, 1993.

———. "Sportsmen in the Machine World: Models for Modernization in Weimar Germany." *The International Journal of the History of Sport* 12, no. 1 (April 1995): 153–68.

Berkman, Dave. "Long Before Arledge . . . Sport & TV: The Earliest Years: 1933–1947—as Seen by the Contemporary Press." *Journal of Popular Culture* 22, no. 2 (1988): 49–62.

Bernett, Hajo. *Sport und Schulsport in der NS-Diktatur.* Leiden: Brill, 2017.

Bessel, Richard. *Germany 1945: From War to Peace.* New York: Harper Collins, 2009.

Bette, Karl-Heinrich. "Sport und Individualisierung." *Spektrum der Sportwissenschaft* 5, no. 1 (1993): 34–55.

———. *Systemtheorie und Sport*. Berlin: Suhrkamp, 2009.

Black, David. "Dreaming Big: The Pursuit of 'Second Order' Games as a Strategic Response to Globalization." *Sport in Society* 11, no. 4 (2008): 467–80.

Black, Monica. *Death in Berlin: From Weimar to Divided Germany*. Cambridge: Cambridge University Press, 2010.

Blecking, Diethelm, and Gerd Dembowski, eds. *Der Ball ist bunt: Fußball, Migration und die Vielfalt der Identitäten in Deutschland*. Frankfurt am Main: Brandes und Apsel, 2010.

Booth, Douglas. "Escaping the Past? The Cultural Turn and Language in Sport History." *Rethinking History* 8, no. 1 (2004): 103–25.

———. "Surfing Films and Videos: Adolescent Fun, Alternative Lifestyle, Adventure Industry." *Journal of Sport History* 23, no. 3 (1996): 313–27.

Booth, Douglas, and Holly Thorpe. "Form and Performance in Oral History (Narratives): Historiographical Insights from Surfing and Snowboarding." *The International Journal of the History of Sport* 36, nos. 13–14 (2019): 1136–56.

Borden, Iain. *Skateboarding and the City: A Complete History*. London: Bloomsbury, 2019.

———. *Skateboarding, Space and the City: Architecture and the Body*. Oxford: Berg, 2001.

Boyle, Philip. "Securing the Olympic Games: Exemplifications of Global Governance." In *The Palgrave Handbook of Olympic Studies*, edited by Helen Jefferson Lenskyj and Stephen Wagg, 394–409. New York: Palgrave Macmillan, 2012.

Braun, Jutta. "Auf Jahre unschlagbar? Die deutsche Vereinigung als Sportereignis." In *1989–Eine Epochenzäsur?*, edited by Martin Sabrow, Tilmann Siebeneichner, and Peter Ulrich Weiss, 120–43. Göttingen: Wallstein Verlag, 2021.

Braun, Jutta, and Hans Joachim Teichler, eds. *Sportstadt Berlin im Kalten Krieg: Prestigekämpfe und Systemwettstreit*. Berlin: Christoph Links Verlag, 2006.

Brenner, Michael, and Gideon Reuveni, eds. *Emancipation through Muscles: Jews and Sports in Europe*. Lincoln: University of Nebraska Press, 2006.

Breuer, Karin H. "Constructing Germanness: The Student Movement from the *Burschenschaft* to the *Progressbewegung*, 1814–49." PhD diss., University of North Carolina, 2002.

Butz, Konstantin, and Christian Peters, eds. *Skateboard Studies*. London: Koenig Book, 2018.

Canning, Kathleen. *Gender History in Practice: Historical Perspectives on Bodies, Class, and Citizenship*. Ithaca, NY: Cornell University Press, 2006.

Carr, G. A. "The Synchronization of Sport and Physical Education Under National Socialism." *Canadian Journal of History of Sport and Physical Education* 10, no. 2 (1979): 15–35.

Carr, John. "Skateboarding in Dude Space: The Roles of Space and Sport in Constructing Gender among Adult Skateboarders." *Sociology of Sport Journal* 34, no. 1 (2016): 25–34.

Cary, Noel D. "Olympics in Divided Berlin? Popular Culture and Political Imagination at the Cold War Frontier." *Cold War History* 11, no. 3 (2011): 291–316.

Chapman, David. *Sandown the Magnificent: Eugen Sandown and the Beginnings of Bodybuilding*. Urbana: University of Illinois Press, 1994.

Ciesla, Burghard, and Dirk Külow. *Zwischen den Zeilen: Geschichte der Zeitung "Neues Deutschland."* Berlin: Das Neue Berlin, 2009.

Colomb, Claire. *Staging the New Berlin: Place Marketing and the Politics of Urban Reinvention Post-1989*. London: Routledge, 2012.

Copley, Clare. *Nazi Buildings, Cold War Traces and Governmentality in Post-Unification Berlin*. London: Bloomsbury, 2020.

Cullather, Nick. "The Foreign Policy of the Calorie." *American Historical Review* 112, no. 2 (2007): 337–64.

De Grazia, Victoria. *Irresistible Empire: America's Advance through Twentieth-Century Europe*. Cambridge, MA: Belknap Press, 2005.

Dekel, Irit. "'You Are My Liberty': On the Negotiation of Holocaust and Other Memories for Israelis in Berlin." In *Rebuilding Jewish Life in Germany*, edited by Jay Howard Geller and Michael Meng, 223–45. Ithaca, NY: Rutgers University Press, 2020.

Dennis, Mike. *The Rise and Fall of the German Democratic Republic 1945–1990*. Abingdon: Routledge, 2000.

Desbonnet, Edmond. *The Kings of Strength: A History of All Strong Men from Ancient Times to Our Own*. Translated by David Chapman. Jefferson, NC: McFarland, 2022.

Dichter, Heather L. *Bidding for the 1968 Olympic Games: International Sport's Cold War Battle with NATO*. Amherst: University of Massachusetts Press, 2021.

———. "The Diplomatic Maneuvering Against the Short-Lived 1968 Berlin Olympic Bid." *Contemporary European History* 33, no. 2 (2024): 514–28.

———. "Sporting Relations: Diplomacy, Small States, and Germany's Postwar Return to International Sport." *Diplomacy & Statecraft* 27, no. 2 (2016): 340–59.

———. "'Strict Measures Must Be Taken': Wartime Planning and the Allied Control of Sport in Occupied Germany." *Stadion* 34, no. 2 (2008): 193–217.

Dichter, Heather L., Robert J. Lake, and Mark Dyreson. "New Dimensions of Sport in Modern Europe: Perspectives from the 'Long Twentieth Century.'" *The International Journal of the History of Sport* 36, nos. 2–3 (2019): 123–30.

Domeier, Norman. *The Eulenburg Affair: A Cultural History of Politics in Imperial Germany*. Translated by Deborah Lucas Schneider. New York: Camden House, 2015.

Durick, William. "Berlin 1916." In *Encyclopedia of the Modern Olympic Movement*, edited by John E. Findling and Kimberly D. Pelle, 63–69. Westport, CT: Greenwood Press, 2004.

Dyreson, Mark. "The Republic of Consumption at the Olympic Games: Globalization, Americanization, and Californization." *Journal of Global History* 8, no. 2 (2013): 256–78.

Dyreson, Mark, and Matthew Llewellyn. "Los Angeles is the Olympic City: Legacies of the 1932 and 1984 Olympic Games." *The International Journal of the History of Sport* 25, no. 14 (2008): 1991–2018.

Eichel, Wolfgang. *Geschichte der Korperkultur in Deutschland, 1945–1961*. Berlin: Sportverlag, 1965.

Eisenberg, Christiane. "Charismatic National Leader: Turnvater Jahn." *The International Journal of the History of Sport* 13, no. 1 (1996): 14–27.

———. *"English Sports" und deutsche Bürger: Eine Gesellschaftsgeschichte 1800–1939*. Paderborn: Ferdinand Schöningh, 1999.

———. "Football in Germany: Beginnings, 1890–1914." *The International Journal of the History of Sport* 8, no. 2 (1991): 205–20.

———. "Fußball als globales Phänomen: Historische Perspketiven." *Aus Politik und Zeitgeschichte* 26 (June 2004): 7–15.

———. "Massensport in der Weimarer Republik: Ein statistischer Überblick." *Archiv für Sozialgeschichte* 33 (1933): 137–77

———. "The Middle Class and Competition: Some Considerations of the Beginnings of Modern Sport in England and Germany." *The International Journal of the History of Sport* 7, no. 2 (1990): 265–82.

Elzey, Chris, and David K. Wiggins, eds. *DC Sports: The Nation's Capital at Play*. Fayetteville: University of Arkansas Press, 2015.

Ende, Gerd von. *Berliner Hufgeklapper: Pferde als Spiegel der Vergangenheit*. Hamburg: tredition, 2020.

Ewing, Katherine Pratt. *Stolen Honor: Stigmatizing Muslim Men in Berlin*. Stanford: Stanford University Press, 2008.

Frame, Lynne. "Gretchen, Girl, Garçonne? Weimar Science and Popular Culture in Search of the Ideal New Woman." In *Women in the Metropolis: Gender and Modernity in Weimar Culture*, edited by Katharina von Ankum, 12–40. Berkeley: University of California Press, 1997.

Frevert, Ute. *Men of Honour: A Social and Cultural History of the Duel*. Cambridge: Polity Press, 1995.

Fritzsche, Peter. *Reading Berlin 1900*. Cambridge, MA: Harvard University Press, 2009.

Gehrmann, Sigfried. "Symbol of National Resurrection: Max Schmeling, German Sports Idol." *The International Journal of the History of Sport* 13, no. 1 (1996): 101–13.

Goldberg, Ann. *Honor, Politics, and the Law in Imperial Germany, 1871–1914*. Cambridge: Cambridge University Press, 2010.

Gorn, Elliot J., and Warren Goldstein. *A Brief History of American Sports*. Urbana: University of Illinois Press, 1993.

Gray, William Glenn. *Germany's Cold War: The Global Campaign to Isolate East Germany, 1949–1969*. Chapel Hill: University of North Carolina Press, 2003.

Grossmann, Atina. "Grams, Calories, and Food: Languages of Victimization, Entitlement, and Human Rights in Occupied Germany, 1945–1949." *Central European History* 44, no. 1 (2011): 118–48.

Grüne, Hardy. *Von Kronprinz bis zur Bundesliga, 1890 bis 1963*. Kassel: Agon Sportverlag, 1996.

Guttmann, Allen. "Berlin 1936: The Most Controversial Olympics." In *National Identity and Global Sports Events: Culture, Politics, and Spectacle in the Olympics and the Football World Cup*, edited by Alan Tomlinson and Christopher Young, 65–81. Albany: State University of New York Press, 2006.

———. *From Ritual to Record: The Nature of Modern Sports*. New York: Columbia University Press, 2004.

Hake, Sabine. *Topographies of Class: Modern Architecture and Mass Society in Weimar Berlin*. Ann Arbor: University of Michigan Press, 2008.

Hamlin, David. "Water and Empire: Germany, Bavaria and the Danube in World War I." *First World War Studies* 3, no. 1 (2012): 65–85.

Hargreaves, Jennifer. *Sporting Females: Critical Issues in the History and Sociology of Women's Sport*. London: Routledge, 1994.

Harres, Wolfgang. *Sportpolitik an der Saar 1945–1955*. Saarbrücken: Saarbrücker Druckerei und Verlag, 1997.

Hartston, Barnet. *Sensationalizing the Jewish Question: Antisemitic Trials and the Press in the Early German Empire*. Leiden: Brill, 2005.

———. *The Trial of Gustav Graef: Art, Sex, and Scandal in Late Nineteenth-Century Germany*. DeKalb: Northern Illinois University Press, 2017.

Hartwig, Wolfgang, and Gunter Weise. *100 Jahre Fussball in Berlin*. Berlin: Sportverlag Berlin, 1997.

Heck, Sandra, Paul Nierhaus, and Andreas Luh. "Myth or Reality of the Revier Derby? Schalke 04 versus Borussia Dortmund (1947–2007)." *The International Journal of the History of Sport* 29, no. 14 (2012): 2030–49.

Heitmeyer, Wilhelm. "Gesellschaftliche Desintegration und ethnisch-kulturelle Konflikte." In *Ethnisch-kulturelle Konflikte im Sport*, edited by Marie-Luise Klein and Jürgen Kothy, 15–30. Hamburg: Czwalina, 1998.

Hesse-Lichtenberg, Ulrich. *Tor! The Story of German Football*. London: WSC Books, 2002.

Hilton, Christopher. *Hitler's Olympics: The 1936 Berlin Olympic Games*. Stroud: Sutton, 2008.

Hofmann, Annette R. "'Bringing the Alps to the City': Early Indoor Winter Sports Events in the Modern City of the Twentieth Century." *The International Journal of the History of Sport* 29, no. 14 (2012): 2050–66.

Hoffman, Annette R., and Gertrud Pfister. "Turnen—A Forgotten Movement Culture: Its Beginnings in Germany and Diffusion in the United States." In *Turnen and Sport: Transatlantic Transfers*, edited by Annette R. Hoffman, 11–24. Münster: Waxmann, 2004.

Hörstmann, Matthias, ed. *Verlorene Helden*. Berlin: 11Freunde Verlag, 2014.

Hung, Jochen. *Moderate Modernity: The Newspaper Tempo and the Transformation of Weimar Democracy*. Ann Arbor: University of Michigan Press, 2023.

Hurley, Alec S., and Conor Heffernan. "Cartoon as Satire and Source: Jack Nicolle, Physical Culture, and Cartoons in 1920s Britain." *Sport in History* 43, no. 4 (2023): 224–69.

Hutchins, Brett, and David Rowe. *Sport Beyond Television: The Internet, Digital Media and the Rise of Networked Media Sport*. New York: Routledge, 2012.

Huyssen, Andreas. *Present Pasts: Urban Palimpsests and the Politics of Memory*. Stanford: Stanford University Press, 2003.

Imhoof, David. "Sharpshooting in Gottingen: A Case Study of Cultural Integration in Weimar and Nazi Germany." *German History* 23, no. 4 (2005): 460–93.

Irak, Dağhan. *Football Fandom, Protest, and Democracy: Supporter Activism in Turkey*. London: Routledge, 2019.

Jähner, Harald. *Aftermath: Life in the Fallout of the Third Reich, 1945–55*. New York: Knopf, 2021.

Jarausch, Konrad. *After Hitler: Recivilizing Germans, 1945–1955*. Oxford: Oxford University Press, 2006.

Jenkins, Jennifer. "German Orientalism: Introduction." *Comparative Studies of South Asia, Africa, and the Middle East* 24, no. 2 (2004): 97–100.

Jensen, Erik N. *Body by Weimar: Athletes, Gender, and German Modernity*. Oxford: Oxford University Press, 2010.

———. "Crowd Control: Boxing Spectatorship and Social Order in Weimar Germany." In *Histories of Leisure*, edited by Rudy Koshar, 79–101. Oxford: Berg, 2002.

Johnson, Molly Wilkinson. "The Legacies of 1936: Hitler's Olympic Grounds and Berlin's Bid to Host the 2000 Olympic Games." *German History* 40, no. 2 (2022): 258–77.

———. "Mega-Events, Urban Space, and Social Protest: The Olympia 2000 Bid in Reunified Berlin, 1990–1993." *Central European History* 52, no. 4 (2019): 689–712.

———. *Training Socialist Citizens: Sports and the State in East Germany*. Leiden: Brill, 2008.

Judt, Tony. *Postwar: A History of Europe since 1945*. New York: Penguin, 2005.

Kaplan, Ron. *The Jewish Olympics: The History of the Maccabiah Games*. New York: Skyhorse, 2015.

Kalter, Frank. *Chancen, Fouls und Abseitsfallen: Migranten im deutschen Ligenfußball*. Wiesbaden: Westdeutscher Verlag, 2003.

Kater, Michael H. *Hitler Youth*. Cambridge, MA: Harvard University Press, 2004.

Keys, Barbara J. *Globalizing Sport: National Rivalry and International Community in the 1930s*. Cambridge, MA: Harvard University Press, 2006.

Kidd, Bruce. *The Struggle for Canadian Sport*. Toronto: University of Toronto Press, 1996.

Kilberth, Veith. "The Olympic Skateboarding Terrain between Subculture and Sportisation." In *Skateboarding between Subculture and the Olympics. A Youth Culture under Pressure from Commercialization and Sportification*, edited by Veith Kilberth and Jürgen Schwier, 53–78. Bielefeld: Transcript, 2019.

Kiuri, Miranda, and Jacques Teller. "Olympic Stadiums and Cultural Heritage: On the Nature and Status of Heritage Values in Large Sport Facilities." *The International Journal of the History of Sport* 32, no. 5 (2015): 684–707.

Klein, Marie-Luise, and Jürgen Kothy, eds. *Ethnisch-kulturelle Konflikte im Sport*. Hamburg: Czwalina, 1998.

Koerfer, Daniel. *Hertha unter dem Hakenkreuz: Ein Berliner Fußballclub im Dritten Reich*. Gottingen: Verlag Die Werkstatt, 2009.

Koshar, Rudy. *German Travel Cultures*. Oxford: Berg, 2000.

Krüger, Arnd. "Deutschland, Deutschland über alles? National Integration through Turnen and Sport in Germany 1870–1914." *Stadion* 25 (1999): 109–29.

——. "The German Way of Worker Sport." In *The Story of Worker Sport*, edited by Arnd Krüger and James Riordan, 1–26. Champaign, IL: Human Kinetics Press, 1996.

——. "'Once the Olympics Are Through, We'll Beat Up the Jew': German Jewish Sport 1898–1938 and the Anti-Semitic Discourse." *Journal of Sport History* 26, no. 2 (1999): 353–75.

Krüger, Arnd, and William Murray, eds. *The Nazi Olympics: Sport, Politics, and Appeasement in the 1930s*. Urbana: University of Illinois Press, 2003.

Krüger, Michael. *Einführung in die Geschichte der Leibeserziehung und des Sports. Teil 2, Leibeserziehung im 19. Jahrhundert: Turnen fürs Vaterland*, rev. ed. Schorndorf: Hofmann, 2020. First published 1993.

——. "Gymnastics, Physical Education, Sport, and Christianity in Germany." *The International Journal of the History of Sport* 35, no. 1 (2018): 9–26.

——. "Sports in the German University from about 1900 until the Early Years of the Federal Republic of Germany: The Example of Muenster and the 'Westfaelische Wilhelms-University.'" *The International Journal of the History of Sport* 29, no. 14 (2012): 1981–97.

Krüger, Michael Fritz. "Physical Education and Sport between Human Rights, Duties, and Obligations: Observations from Germany." *Societies* 11, no. 4, 127 (2021): 1–12.

Kuisel, Richard F. *Seducing the French: The Dilemma of Americanization*. Berkeley: University of California Press, 1993.

Kuper, Simon. "Cheering the Enemy." *Index on Censorship* 29, no. 4 (2000): 77–83.

Ladd, Brian. *The Ghosts of Berlin: Confronting German History in the Urban Landscape*. Chicago: University of Chicago Press, 1997.

Lamprecht, Markus, and Hanspeter Stamm. "Vom avantgardistischen Lebensstil zur Massenfreizeit: Eine Analyse des Entwicklungsmuster von Trendsportarten." *Sportwissenschaft* 28, no. 3/4 (1998): 370–87.

Large, David Clay. *Berlin*. New York: Basic Books, 2000.

——. *Berlin: A Modern History*. London: Allen Lane, 2001.

——. *Nazi Games: The Olympics of 1936*. New York: W. W. Norton, 2007.

Lempa, Heikki. *Beyond the Gymnasium: Educating the Middle-Class Bodies in Classical Germany*. Washington, DC: Lexington Books, 2007.

Lennartz, Karl. "Die VI. Olympischen Spiele Berlin 1916." *Stadion* 6 (1980): 229–50.

Lewis, Robert A. *The Stadium Century: Sport, Spectatorship and Mass Society in Modern France*. Manchester: Manchester University Press, 2016.

Li, Chuang. "Cultural Continuities and Skateboarding in Transition: In the Case of China's Skateboarding Culture and Industry." *YOUNG* 30, no. 2 (2022): 183–206.

Lippmann, Karsten *". . . und für die Ehre unserer Nation(en)": Olympische Deutschlandpolitik zwischen 1960 und 1968*. Hildesheim: Arete, 2017.

Lombard, Kara-Jane, ed. *Skateboarding: Subcultures, Sites and Shifts*. Abingdon: Routledge, 2017.

Mackenzie, Michael. "From Athens to Berlin: The 1936 Olympics and Leni Riefenstahl's *Olympia*." *Critical Inquiry* 20, no. 2 (Winter 2003): 302–36.

Maginnis, John. *Military Government Journal: Normandy to Berlin*. Amherst: University of Massachusetts Press, 1970.

Major, Patrick. *Behind the Berlin Wall: East Germany and the Frontiers of Power*. Oxford: Oxford University Press, 2010.

Mandell, Richard. *The Nazi Olympics*. Urbana: University of Illinois Press, 1987.

Mason, Tony. "Großbritannien." In *Fußball, soccer, calcio: Ein englischer Sport auf seinem Weg um die Welt*, edited by Christiane Eisenberg, 122–40. Munich: Deutscher Taschenbuch Verlag, 1997.

McAleer, Kevin. *Dueling: The Cult of Honor in Fin-de-Siècle Germany*. Princeton: Princeton University Press, 1994.

McDougall, Alan. *The People's Game: Football, State and Society in East Germany*. Cambridge: Cambridge University Press, 2014.

McFee, Graham, and Alan Tomlinson. "Riefenstahl's *Olympia*: Ideology and Aesthetics in the Shaping of the Aryan Athletic Body." *The International Journal of the History of Sport* 16, no. 2 (1999): 86–106.

Meinhardt, Birk. *Boxen in Deutschland*. Hamburg: Rotbuch, 1996.

Menand, Louis, Paul Reitter, and Chad Wellmon, eds. *The Rise of The Research University: A Sourcebook*. Chicago: University of Chicago Press, 2017.

de Mendelssohn, Peter. *Zeitungsstadt Berlin: Menschen und Mächte in der Geschichte der deutschen Presse*. Frankfurt am Main: Ullstein, 1982.

Meng, Michael. "(Trans)National Spaces: Jewish Sites in Contemporary Germany." In *Three-Way Street: Jews, Germans, and the Transnational*, edited by Jay Howard Gellar and Leslie Morris, 321–40. Ann Arbor: University of Michigan Press, 2016.

Metzger, Stefan. *Das Spiel um Anerkennung: Vereine mit Türkeibezug im Berliner Amateurfußball*. Wiesbaden: Springer, 2018.

Meyer, Monika. "Berlin 1936." In *Olympic Cities: City Agendas, Planning, and the World's Games, 1896–2016*, 2nd ed., edited by John R. Gold and Margaret M. Gold, 215–32. London: Routledge, 2011.

Miller, Jennifer A. *Turkish Guest Workers in Germany: Hidden Lives and Contested Borders, 1960s to 1980s*. Toronto: University of Toronto Press, 2018.

Mitsuda, Tatsuya. "Training Horse and Rider for War? Equine Sport, Military Use, and the Industrialisation of Society: Imperial Germany in Transnational Perspective." *Hiyoshi Review of the Humanities*, no. 34 (2019): 236–38.

Murray, Michelle. *The Struggle for Recognition in International Relations: Status, Revisionism, and Rising Powers*. Oxford: Oxford University Press, 2019.

Murray, Stuart. *Sports Diplomacy: Origins, Theory and Practice*. London: Routledge, 2019.

Murtha, Ryan, and Tolga Ozyurtcu. "From Stroke to Stoke: The Multiple Sporting Legacies of the Southern California Home Swimming Pool." *The International Journal of the History of Sport* 39, no. 1 (2022): 92–110.

Noll, Rhyn. *Skateboard Retrospective: A Collector's Guide*. Atglen, PA: Schiffer, 2000.

Norwood, Stephen H., ed. *New York Sports: Glamour and Grit in the Empire City*. Fayetteville: University of Arkansas Press, 2018.

Partridge, Damani. *Hypersexuality and Headscarves: Race, Sex, and Citizenship in the New Germany*. Bloomington: University of Indiana Press, 2012.

Pells, Richard. *Not Like Us: How Europeans Have Loved, Hated, and Transformed American Culture since World War II*. New York: Basic Books, 1997.

Pfister, Gertrud, and Toni Niewerth. "Jewish Women in Gymnastics and Sports in Germany, 1898–1938." *Journal of Sport History* 26, no. 2 (Summer 1999): 287–325.

Poiger, Uta G. *Cold War Politics and American Culture in a Divided Germany*. Berkeley: University of California Press, 2000.

Poling, Kristin. "Shantytowns and Pioneers beyond the City Wall: Berlin's Urban Frontier in the Nineteenth Century." *Central European History* 47, no. 2 (2014): 245–74.

Presner, Samuel. *Muscular Judaism: The Jewish Body and the Politics of Regeneration*. Abingdon: Routledge, 2007.

Reinhart, Kai. "Der Münster Monster Mastership und der Skatepark am Berg Fidel." In *Deutsche Sportgeschichte in 100 Objekten*, edited by Michael Krüger, 396–99. Neulingen: Klotz, 2020.

———. "Oral History in der (Sport-)Geschichte." In *Sport—Geschichte—Pädagogik: Festschrift zum 60. Geburtstag von Michael Krüger*, edited by Emanuel Hübner and Kai Reinhart, 267–85. Hildesheim: Arete, 2015.

———. "Spiel und Sport: Skateboarden im sozialistischen Dresden." In *Jahrbuch für Historische Kommunismusforschung: Spielen im Staatssozialismus. Zwischen Sozialdisziplinierung und Vergnügen*, edited by Juliane Brauer, Maren Röger, and Sabine Stach, 157–76. Berlin: Metropol, 2021.

Reinisch, Jessica. *The Perils of Peace: The Public Health Crisis in Occupied Germany*. Oxford: Oxford University Press, 2013.

Reusser, Marlen, et al. "Increased Participation and Decreased Performance in Recreational Master Athletes in 'Berlin Marathon' 1974–2019." *Frontiers in Physiology* 12 (2021): 1–10.

Rider, Toby C., Matthew P. Llewellyn, and John T. Gleaves. "Sun, Surf, and Toned Bodies: California's Impact on the History of Sport and Leisure." *Journal of Sport History* 46, no. 1 (2019): 1–4.

Riess, Carl. "Weltbühne Berlin." In *Alltag in der Weimarer Republik: Erinnerungen an eine unruhige Zeit*, edited by Rudolf Pörtner, 32–57. Düsseldorf: Econ, 1990.

Riess, Steven A. *City Games: The Evolution of American Urban Society and the Rise of Sports*. Urbana: University of Illinois Press, 1991.

Rinehart, Robert E., and Synthia Sydnor, eds. *To the Extreme: Alternative Sports, Inside and Out*. Albany: State University of New York Press, 2003.

Rippey, Theodore F. "Athletics, Aesthetics, and Politics in the Weimar Press." *German Studies Review* 28, no. 1 (2005): 85–106.

Riordan, James, and Arnd Krüger. *European Cultures in Sport: Examining the Nations and Regions*. Bristol: Intellect Books, 2003.

Ritchie, Andrew. *Quest For Speed: A History of Early Bicycle Racing 1868–1903*. 2nd ed. Jefferson, NC: McFarland, 2018.

Ritvo, Harriet. *The Animal Estate: The English and Other Creatures in the Victorian Age.* Cambridge, MA: Harvard University Press, 1987.

Roche, Maurice. *Mega-Events and Modernity: Olympics and Expos in the Growth of Global Culture.* London: Routledge, 2000.

———. *Mega-Events and Social Change: Spectacle, Legacy and Public Culture.* Manchester: Manchester University Press, 2017.

Romann-Schüssler, Dieter, and Thomas Schwarz. *Türkische Sportler in Berlin zwischen Integration und Segregation.* Berlin: Der Senator für Gesundheit, Soziales und Familie Ausländerbeauftragter, 1985.

Rosaldo, Renato. *Culture and Truth: The Remaking of Social Analysis.* Boston: Beacon Press, 1989.

Rose, Mathew. *Berlin: Hauptstadt von Filz und Korruption.* Munich: Knaur, 1997.

Rossol, Nadine. *Performing the Nation in Interwar Germany: Sport, Spectacle and Political Symbolism, 1926–36.* Basingstoke: Palgrave Macmillan, 2010.

Rürup, Reinhard, ed. *1936: Die Olympischen Spiele und der Nationalsozialismus.* Translated by Pamela E. Selwyn. Berlin: Arlon Verlag, 1996.

Schäfer, Eckehart Velten. *Dogtown und X-Games: die wirkliche Geschichte des Skateboardfahrens Körper, Räume und Zeichen einer Bewegungspraktik zwischen Pop- und Sportkultur.* Bielefeld: Transcript, 2020.

Scharenberg, Swantje. *Die Konstruktion des öffentlichen Sports und seiner Helden in der Tagespresse der Weimarer Republik.* Paderborn: Ferdinand Schöningh, 2012.

———. "Religion and Sport." In *The International Politics of Sport in the Twentieth Century,* edited by James Riordan and Arnd Krüger, 90–104. London: Routledge, 2007.

Schiller, Kay. "Communism, Youth and Sport: The 1973 World Youth Festival in East Berlin." In *Sport and the Transformation of Modern Europe: States, Media and Markets 1950–2010,* edited by Alan Tomlinson, Christopher Young, and Richard Holt, 50–66. Abingdon: Routledge, 2011.

Schiller, Kay, and Christopher Young. *The 1972 Munich Olympics and the Making of Modern Germany.* Berkeley: University of California Press, 2010.

Schivelbusch, Wolfgang. *In a Cold Crater: Cultural and Intellectual Life in Berlin, 1945–1948.* Translated by Kelly Barry. Berkeley: University of California Press, 1998.

Schwier, Jürgen. "Soziologie des Trendsports." In *Handbuch Sportsoziologie,* edited by Kurt Weis and Robert Gugutzer, 349–57. Schorndorf: Hofmann, 2008.

Schwier, Jürgen, and Veith Kilberth, eds. *Skateboarding between Subculture and the Olympics: A Youth Culture under Pressure from Commercialization and Sportification.* Bielefeld: Transcript, 2019.

Sicks, Kai Marcel. "'Der Querschnitt' oder: Die Kunst des Sporttreibens." In *Leibhaftige Moderne: Körper in Kunst und Massenmedien 1918–1933,* edited by Michael Cown and Kai Marcel Sicks, 33–47. Bielefeld: Transcript, 2005.

Siegel, Barry. *Dreamers and Schemers: How an Improbable Bid for the 1932 Olympics Transformed Los Angeles from Dusty Outpost to Global Metropolis.* Berkeley: University of California Press, 2019.

Smith, Ronald A. "Far More Than Commercialism: Stadium Building from Harvard's Innovations to Stanford's 'Dirt Bowl.'" *The International Journal of the History of Sport* 25, no. 11 (2008): 1453–74.

Smith, Woodruff D. *Politics and the Sciences of Culture in Germany, 1840–1920.* Oxford: Oxford University Press, 1991.

Snow, David. "Skateboarders, Streets and Style." In *Australian Youth Subcultures: On the Margins and in the Mainstream*, edited by Rob White, 16–25. Hobart: Australian Clearinghouse for Youth Studies, 1999.

Stahl, Silvester. *Selbstorganisation von Migranten im deutschen Vereinssport: eine soziologische Annäherung*. Potsdam: Universitätsverlag Potsdam, 2011.

———. *Sportgerichtsurteile im Berliner Fussball-Verband 1999–2009*. Potsdam: Universität Potsdam, 2009.

Steege, Paul. *Black Market, Cold War: Everyday Life in Berlin, 1946–1949*. Cambridge: Cambridge University Press, 2007.

Stokes, Lauren. *Fear of the Family: Guest Workers and Family Migration in the Federal Republic of Germany*. Oxford: Oxford University Press, 2022.

Strom, Elizabeth. "In Search of the Growth Coalition: American Urban Theories and the Redevelopment of Berlin." *Urban Affairs Review* 31, no. 4 (1996): 468–70.

Suri, Jeremi. "The Cultural Contradictions of Cold War Education: The Case of West Berlin." *Cold War History* 4, no. 3 (2004): 1–20.

Sutton, Katie. "The Masculinized Female Athlete in Weimar Germany." *German Politics and Society* 27, no. 3 (2009): 28–49.

Tate, Steve. "Edward Hulton and Sports Journalism in Late-Victorian Manchester." *Manchester Region History Review* 20 (2009): 46–67.

Teichler, Hans Joachim. "Vorwort." In *Forgotten Records—Vergessene Rekorde: Jüdische Leichtathletinnen vor und nach 1933*, edited by Berno Bahro, Jutta Braun, and Hans Joachim Teichler, 10–13. Berlin: Verlag für berlin-brandenburg, 2009.

Teichler, Hans Joachim, and Gerhard Hauk, eds. *Illustrierte Geschichte des Arbeitersports*. Berlin: Dietz, 1987.

Terret, Thierry, and Sandra Heck. "Prologue: Sport and Urban Space in Europe: Facilities, Industries, Identities." *The International Journal of the History of Sport* 29, no. 14 (2012): 1939–41.

Till, Karen E. *The New Berlin: Memory, Politics, Place*. Minneapolis: University of Minnesota Press, 2005.

Tomlinson, Alan, and Christopher Young, eds. *German Football: History, Culture, and Society*. London: Routledge, 2006.

Turner, Daniel. "Performing Citizenship: Skateboarding and the Formalisation of Informal Spaces." In *Lifestyle Sports and Public Policy*, edited by Daniel Turner and Sandro Carnicelli, 13–26. Abingdon: Routledge, 2017.

Ueberhorst, Horst. *Friedrich Ludwig Jahn and His Time, 1778–1852*. Translated by Timothy Nevill. Munich: Heinz Moos Verlag, 1978.

Vamplew, Wray, John McClelland, and Mark Dyreson, eds. *A Cultural History of Sport*. 6 vols. London: Bloomsbury Academic, 2021.

Vermeulen, Floris, and Maria Berger. "Civic Networks and Political Behavior: Turks in Amsterdam and Berlin." In *Civic Hopes and Political Realities: Immigrants, Community Organizations, and Political Engagement*, edited by S. Karthick Ramakrishnan and Irene Bloemraad, 160–92. New York: Russell Sage Foundation, 2008.

Vierra, Sarah Thomsen. *Turkish Germans in the Federal Republic of Germany: Immigration, Space, and Belonging, 1961–1990*. Cambridge: Cambridge University Press, 2018.

Vogel, Jakob. "Military, Folklore, *Eigensinn*: Folkloric Militarism in Germany and France, 1871–1914." *Central European History* 33, no. 4 (2000): 487–504.

Vogt, Timothy. *Denazification in Soviet-Occupied Germany: Brandenburg, 1945–1948.*
    Cambridge, MA: Harvard University Press, 2000.
Volkwein, Karen A., and Herbert R. Haag. "Sport in Unified Germany: The Merging of Two
    Different Sport Systems." *Journal of Sport and Social Issues* 18, no. 2 (1994): 183–93.
Ward, Janet. *Post-Wall Berlin: Borders, Space and Identity.* New York: Palgrave Macmillan, 2011.
Wedemeyer, Bernd. "Theordor Siebert: A Biography." Translated by David Chapman. *Iron
    Game History* 6, no. 3 (2000): 5–13.
Wedemeyer-Kolwe, Bernd. *Der neue Mensch: Körperkultur im Kaiserreich und in der
    Weimar Republik.* Würzburg: Königshausen & Neumann, 2004.
Weinreb, Alice Autumn. "Embodying German Suffering: Rethinking Popular Hunger
    during the Hunger Years (1945–1949)." *Body Politics* 2, no. 4 (2014): 463–88.
Whannel, Garry. "Television and the Transformation of Sport." *Annals of the American
    Academy of Political and Social Science* 625 (September 2009): 205–18.
Wheaton, Belinda, ed. *Understanding Lifestyle Sports: Consumption, Identity and Difference.*
    London: Routledge, 2004.
Wiese, Rene. "Hertha BSC im Kalten Krieg (1945–1961)." In *Sportstadt Berlin im
    Kalten Krieg,* edited by Jutta Braun and Hans Joachim Teichler, 239–84. Berlin:
    Christoph Links Verlag, 2006.
Wilson, Wayne, and David Wiggins, eds. *LA Sports: Play, Games, and Community in the
    City of Angels.* Fayetteville: University of Arkansas Press, 2018.
Wimmer, Andreas. "The Making and Unmaking of Ethnic Boundaries: A Multi-Level
    Process Theory." *American Journal of Sociology* 113, no. 4 (2008): 970–1022.
Young, Christopher. "'Nicht mehr die herrlichste Nebensache der Welt': Sport, West
    Berlin and the Four Powers Agreement 1971." *German Politics and Society* 25, no. 1
    (2007): 28–45.
Young, William Anthony. *German Diplomatic Relations 1871–1945: The Wilhelmstrasse and
    the Formulation of Foreign Policy.* New York: iUniverse, 2009.
Zimmerman, Angela. *Anthropology and Antihumanism in Imperial Germany.* Chicago:
    University of Chicago Press, 2001.

Contributors

Heather L. Dichter is associate professor of sport management and sport history in the International Centre for Sports History and Culture at De Montfort University in Leicester, England. She has published extensively on the Olympics (especially Winter Olympic sports), international sport, and diplomacy, usually with a focus on Germany. Her publications include *Bidding for the 1968 Olympic Games: International Sport's Cold War Battle with NATO* (Amherst: University of Massachusetts Press, 2021), winner of the 2022 Lord Aberdare Literary Prize from the British Society of Sports History, and two edited books: *Soccer Diplomacy: International Relations and Football Since 1914* (Lexington: University Press of Kentucky, 2020) and, with Andrew L. Johns, *Diplomatic Games: Sport, Statecraft, and International Relations Since 1945* (Lexington: University Press of Kentucky, 2014).

Barnet Hartston was raised in Southern California, where his passion for sports was unfortunately not matched by any sort of talent or ability. He is currently professor of history at Eckerd College in St. Petersburg, Florida, and is the author of two monographs: *Sensationalizing the Jewish Question: Anti-Semitic Trials and the Press in Early Modern Germany* (Leiden: Brill, 2005) and *The Trial of Gustav Graef: Art, Sex, and Scandal in Late Nineteenth-Century Germany* (DeKalb: Northern Illinois University Press, 2017). His essay in this volume is related to his first foray into sports-related history: a book project tentatively titled *The Great Berlin-Vienna Horse Race of 1892 and Other Masculine Misadventures.*

Alec Hurley is lecturer in sport management at Cardiff Metropolitan University. His research addresses constructions of immigrant identity through sport, recreation, and leisure in postindustrial urban centers from the early nineteenth to mid-twentieth century. He has published on German sport and identity in *Sport in Society*. In 2022 he won the Gigliola Gori Award from the International Society for the History of Physical Education and Sport.

Erik Jensen is associate professor of history at Miami University in Oxford, Ohio, where he teaches courses on German, European, and world history. His first book, *Body by Weimar: Athletes, Gender, and German Modernity* (Oxford: Oxford University Press, 2010), explores the role of sports in shaping social and cultural ideals after World War I. He has also written on the history of the pink triangle as a symbol of the queer rights movement and on the intersection between athletic practice and sexual behavior. He is currently working on a deep biography of the half-Jewish tennis player and pioneering journalist Paula von Reznicek, whose personal fortunes reflected the political and social fluctuations of twentieth-century Germany.

Molly Wilkinson Johnson is associate professor of history at the University of Alabama in Huntsville, where she teaches German and European history. Her first book, *Training Socialist Citizens: Sports and the State in East Germany* (Leiden: Brill, 2008), explores the political, social, and cultural role of recreational sports and sports spectacles in communist East Germany. She has recently published articles in *Central European History* and *German History* about Berlin's failed bid to host the 2000 Olympic Games, focusing on the bid as a window onto urban planning, protest, and the politics of memory in the reunified city. Her current research explores civic identity, athletic mega-events, and post-socialism in Leipzig's bid for the 2012 Olympic Games.

Jeffrey Jurgens is continuing associate professor of anthropology at Bard College and faculty chair of the bachelor's degree program in the Bard Prison Initiative. He specializes in topics related to migration, citizenship, public memory, urban space, and secularism among Germans of Turkish backgrounds in Berlin. More recently, he has examined the cultural politics of "refugee crisis" discourse in Germany and Europe since 2015, and his current research traces the history of refugee governance in Berlin since the end of World War II. His publications have appeared in journals including *American Ethnologist, Journal of Middle East Women's Studies, Policy and Society, Transit,* and *Turkish-German Studies Yearbook,* as well as the edited volumes *After the Imperialist Imagination* (Oxford: Peter Lang, 2020), *Different Germans, Many Germanies* (New York: Berghahn, 2017) and *Walls, Borders, Boundaries* (New York: Berghahn, 2012).

Will Rall is currently senior academic adviser at the University of Chicago. He earned his PhD in modern German history from the University of Tennessee-Knoxville and wrote his dissertation on the conceptions and practices of charity and welfare during the Third Reich. His previous research has been published as a part of the edited collection *Ruptures in the Everyday: Views of Modern Germany from the Ground* (New York: Berghahn, 2017), and his work has been supported by associations including the German Academic Exchange Service, the German Historical Institute in Washington, DC, and the Central European History Society.

Kai Reinhart is senior lecturer at the Institute of Sport and Exercise Sciences of the University of Münster and visiting professor at the University of Education of Ludwigsburg. He completed his studies in sports science, history, and German philology with a dissertation on official and informal sport in the German Democratic Republic. His scientific interest centers on the history of informal sports (such as skateboarding or mountaineering) and football with a particular focus on communist Germany. His research has been honored with various awards, such as the Science Award of the German Olympic Sports Confederation.

Annemarie Sammartino is professor of history at Oberlin College. She is the author of *The Impossible Border: Germany and the East 1914–1922* (Ithaca, NY: Cornell University Press, 2010), which addresses the political and ideological ramifications of migration during and after World War I, and *Freedomland: Co-op City and the Story of New York* (Ithaca, NY: Cornell University Press, 2022), which examines the history of New York through the lens of a large cooperative development and neighborhood on the margins of New York City. She is currently working on a new project on the meaning and assessment of risk in the modern world.

Index

Images are denoted in italics.